Handbook *for* Successful Inclusion

CAROL A. KOCHHAR, EdD

Associate Professor
Graduate School of Education and Human Development
Department of Teacher Preparation and Special Education
The George Washington University
Washington, D.C.

LYNDA L. WEST, PhD

Professor
Graduate School of Education and Human Development
Department of Teacher Preparation and Special Education
The George Washington University
Washington, D.C.

With Cases by

Juliana M. Taymans, PhD

Associate Professor
Graduate School of Education and Human Development
Department of Teacher Preparation and Special Education
The George Washington University
Washington, D.C.

D1716796

An Aspen Publication®
Aspen Publishers, Inc.
Gaithersburg, Maryland
1996

Library of Congress Cataloging-in-Publication Data

Kochhar, Carol A.
Handbook for successful inclusion / Carol A. Kochhar, Lynda L. West; with case studies by Juliana Taymans.
p.   cm.
Includes bibliographical references and index.
ISBN 0-8342-0709-5
1. Mainstreaming in education—United States—Handbooks, manuals, etc.
2. Handicapped children—Education—United States—Handbooks,
manuals, etc. I. West, Lynda L. II. Taymans, Juliana. III. Title.
LC4031.K63   1996
371.9'046—dc20
95-38588
CIP

Copyright 1996 by Aspen Publishers, Inc.
All rights reserved.

Aspen Publishers, Inc., grants permission for photocopying for limited personal or
internal use. This consent does not extend to other kinds of copying, such as copying
for general distribution, for advertising or promotional purposes, for creating new
collective works, or for resale. For information, address Aspen Publishers, Inc.,
Permissions Department, 200 Orchard Ridge Drive, Suite 200,
Gaithersburg, Maryland 20878.

Editorial Resources: Ruth Bloom

Library of Congress Catalog Card Number: 95-38588
ISBN: 0-8342-0709-5

Printed in the United States of America

1 2 3 4 5

Table of Contents

Preface

in·clude (in klŏŏd)—to have or regard or treat as part of a whole

Inclusion of those who have been left outside is the first step in integration. The word derives from the Latin for shutting the door after someone has come into the house. Some people think that you can speak of integration without inclusion. This seems like nonsense to us. Integration begins only when each child belongs.

—O'Brien and Forest, 1989

There are so many books, pamphlets, reports, and periodicals on inclusion, so why should another book be written and added to the pile? After sifting through a mountain of documents on the subject of inclusion written over the past decade and talking with parents, students, and teachers of special and general education it became apparent that a few striking contradictions exist.

In schools everywhere, students with greater academic and social learning needs are adding to the challenge of teaching. Experts and advocates for inclusion of students with disabilities in the regular classroom *generally* agree that educators must end the dual tracks of special and regular education and create a unified system. Most concur that general education teachers and their attitudes toward inclusion are the "key ingredients" for success in its implementation. Consequently, teachers today are expected to develop educational programs that can serve a diversity of students with "special needs," including students with disabilities, those at risk for failure, former school dropouts, students with limited English proficiency, and teen parents. Today, these "special populations" represent a majority of students in some school systems.

In implementing inclusion, the general education teacher is at center stage. Although there are special education consultants, team teachers, and teacher aides, the main responsibility for creating inclusive classrooms for students with disabilities falls on the general education teacher. At the same time, teachers today are being asked to accept greater responsibility for the performance and achievement of their students. As teachers restructure their classrooms to include a diversity of students, the success of each student depends on what happens there. Teachers are being subject to "pay-for-performance" incentive programs and merit pay plans, yet are uncertain that their hard work in serving students with disabilities in inclusive classes will be considered in the evaluation of their performance. If general education teachers are crucial for the success of students in inclusive classrooms, then their concerns must be addressed.

In inclusion just a fad? It is the 1990s, and the journey toward integration of all children and youths within their community schools has only just begun. The inclusion of children into regular classes has accelerated quickly in the past decade and in many places has occurred too fast and without adequate planning for restructuring. There is a growing concern by teachers, special educators, and administrators that many "bad" inclusion policies are being implemented. Such inclusion efforts are failing to provide the necessary supportive services that students with disabilities need when they are placed into regular classrooms. On the other hand, there are many models of "very good" inclusion. This book focuses on these models of good inclusion. The authors want to provide the reader with an understanding of the possibilities and potential of inclusive philosophy and practices, for the benefit of *all children.*

This handbook is based on the assumption that the goals of public education are most likely to be reached for all children when those children learn, play, and grow together, learning from each other as well as from teachers. The principles of special education—providing individualized instruction, addressing the unique learning styles of students, and adapting materials and curriculum and teaching methods—are important for *all students.* According to recent research, the education of students with disabilities in integrated settings requires, first and foremost, a change in attitude from the view that education of students with disabilities is different or special and the education of nondisabled students is "normal and expected" (Stainback & Stainback, 1992). Students with disabilities can be full and useful members of a community if the community makes an effort to include them.

Inclusion is *not* just a fad. It is *not* a program or a project that has a beginning and an end. It is a vision and a goal that is linked to a greater effort to advance a democratic and civilized society. Like the concept of democracy, it embodies ideals and goals that we continually strive toward, even though we may never reach perfection. We are *never* finished.

Introduction

WHAT MAKES THIS HANDBOOK DIFFERENT?

This handbook is for teachers who want a resource that gets to the point and answers the questions most asked about inclusion of students with disabilities in a regular classroom. It is for teachers who have been searching for a resource balanced enough to address the greatest concerns of teachers about inclusion and its effects on teaching and learning for all students. The authors have assembled in this handbook the information most relevant for teachers. Several books discuss inclusion in 300 to 500 pages, but we have tried to present the information simply and concisely. The purpose of this *Handbook for Successful Inclusion* is to guide regular and special education teachers and related professionals in schools and school-linked agencies in meeting the challenge to better serve special learners in inclusive settings. The book emphasizes inclusion practices that work, practical strategies that can lead to successful inclusion at the classroom level and at the school level, and techniques for overcoming barriers to inclusion.

The handbook is written in a user-friendly, question-and-answer format that is centered on practical inclusion issues. It offers solid, practical help as well as a useful perspective for those challenged to provide educational opportunities for all.

HOW TO USE THE HANDBOOK

School administrators will find this handbook useful as an introduction and overview to the inclusion concept and process for all educators. The content of each part can be divided into material for staff development sessions, in-service themes, and/or workshop sessions. This Trainer's Resource provides a variety of strategies that will be helpful to teachers in understanding and discussing the idea of inclusion.

In order to develop an inclusion initiative in a school, a small group of teachers will need to be selected to spearhead and guide the inclusion process. Consequently, individuals must be carefully selected for their abilities to act as leaders and to exert a positive influence on this important journey. The selection of those individuals is critical to the success of the inclusion process and to the individual success of students who are the beneficiaries.

It is necessary to select teacher leaders who

- are open to learning
- are not afraid of change
- have the interpersonal skills to constructively negotiate change
- can inspire others

- can resolve conflict in a positive manner
- can offer support and praise to teachers in their efforts
- understand the need for reward and renewal.

Once the cadre of teacher-leaders for inclusion has been identified, they should become members of the inclusion planning team.

This handbook provides the necessary tools to help you plan for and implement inclusion.

I

The Challenge of Inclusion

Let no child be demeaned, nor have his wonder diminished, because of our ignorance or inactivity. Let no child be deprived of discovery, because we lack the resources to discover his problem. Let no child ever doubt himself or his mind because we are unsure of our commitment.—Martin, 1993

The ultimate rationale for inclusion is based not on law or regulations or teaching technology, but on values. What kinds of people are we and what kind of society do we wish to develop? What values do we honor?—Gartner and Lipsky, 1992

1. Why Inclusion?

Though perfection may never be reached, this nation remains relentless in its effort to try to achieve two parallel goals in education: (1) excellent teaching, resulting in student achievement, and (2) equal opportunity for all children. These two goals are at the root of fundamental changes occurring in education today.

Age of Anxiety. Today, the education system as a whole in the United States stands at a crossroads—educationally, morally, and socially. Many call this an "age of anxiety" because it is a time of tremendous change and transition. *The transition we are experiencing is not fully understood by those who are involved in the process of* *change in schools, particularly the changes brought about by the inclusion movement.* Special education, specifically its assumptions and practices, is also undergoing great change. Educators are seeking to achieve a new marriage of special and general education in order to move closer to the *goal of achieving equal educational opportunity for all children.*

Failure of Traditional Inclusion Policies. Just as *"all means all"* in regard to who should be served under special education laws, *all also means all in regard to whom is doing the serving.* In other words, the educational community as a whole must prepare all

1

members of the educational enterprise for a new kind of work. This requires all educators to depart from some old values and practices. Teachers and administrators are asking: How can schools improve special education services for students, and how can they develop reasonable policies for inclusion in general education classes? Lessons from past civil rights movements show that *physical access or placement alone* does not achieve integration or inclusion, nor does it guarantee better educational results for students. The practice of inclusion must involve much more than a shifting of physical environments from a segregated class to a mainstream class. Instead, it must address the needs of the student being included, as well as the effects on the learning environment.

A Whole School. There are many reasons for pursuing the goals of inclusion and continuing to improve it. Children with disabilities have received an education that is not equal to that given to other children (Gartner & Lipsky, 1992). Yet the ultimate rationale for inclusion is based not on law or regulations or teaching technology, but on *values*. What kinds of people are we and what kind of society do we wish to develop? What values do we honor (Gartner & Lipsky, 1992)? Fifteen years ago, it was thought that trying to implement inclusion in the schools was "incredibly complex" and ran "counter to the basic structure of the public education system" and that attempting to implement a "concept alien to the school itself was counterproductive" (Turnbull, 1991, p. 50). Much progress and change in attitudes has occurred since then, and the conditions for implementing inclusion in a rational way are beginning to develop. However, many educational organizations believe that inclusion represents a major

revolution in the way schools are organized and administered (National Association of State Boards of Education, 1992). As Lippman said in 1992, "If a child fails in school and then fails in life, the schools cannot sit back and say: 'You see how accurately I predicted this?'" Experts are warning that it is not special education but the total education system that must change.

All Means All. Implementing successful inclusion means that all the people involved in an inclusion placement (student, family, teacher, and principal) are fully informed about the placement. They must all anticipate and understand (a) what is expected for the student with a disability in the new placement and (b) the impact of that placement on the total classroom and the teaching process for all students. Special education laws require that all children must be served in free, appropriate public education programs. The educational community as a whole must prepare all members of the educational enterprise for a new kind of response.

Guiding Beliefs. The assumption upon which this handbook is based is that the goals of public education are not likely to be reached for all children until those children learn, play, and grow together, learning from each other as well as from teachers. The principles upon which special education has been based—individualized instruction, addressing the unique learning styles of students, adapting materials and curriculum and teaching methods—are important for all students. Educators should be guided by the belief that, as a nation, we can develop a policy that echoes in all the states—a policy that prohibits discrimination and promotes equal opportunity and equal access to education.

2. What Is Inclusion?

Disability in Perspective. If students with special educational needs are given the opportunity for small accommodations in the regular classroom, they can thrive in their local community schools. Because of their desire to compensate for their impairments, many of these children are motivated to achieve beyond their peers when given opportunities to learn. *Most of these children are "handicapped" more by the failure of schools and teachers to support them in their forma-* *tive years than they are by their disabilities and disadvantaged lives.* Even children who have severe physical impairments can be expected to achieve as much academically as their nondisabled peers. Because of impairments, some of them may have lower levels of performance and may have more difficulty than other children in applying new information and skills learned in classroom settings. Some may learn more slowly than their peers in all or a few curricular areas and may simply need more time than their peers to complete their work. Others may need to be given directions in very concrete terms or with visual aids such as written notes or pictures. A few may need substantial special educational supports or accommodations to enable them to benefit from regular classes, while others will only require minimal adjustments in the classroom environment to succeed.

Legal Foundation of Inclusion. The 1975 Education for All Handicapped Children Act (P.L. 94-142) and the most recent amendments in 1990, as well as the Individuals with Disabilities Education Act (P.L. 101-476), were enacted to ensure that all students with disabilities under the age of 22 years were guaranteed a free, appropriate public education. Before the law was passed, students with disabilities were either not provided an education at all, were educated in their homes, or were provided an inferior education in a separate setting, apart from their age-mates and peers and separate from their community schools. Through this legislation, Congress declared that every child with a disability had an inalienable right to be educated in the educational setting most appropriate for that child. These laws did *not* contain the word inclusion, but they defined the most appropriate setting as one that was described as the *least restrictive environment*.

What does least restrictive environment mean? Education in the least restrictive environment means that students should, to the extent possible, be educated with their nondisabled peers. The legislation requires schools to ensure that, to the maximum extent possible, children with disabilities in either public or private institutions are educated with children who are not disabled and that special classes, separate schooling, or other removal of children with disabilities from the regular educational environment occurs only when the nature or severity of the disabilities is such that education in regular classes with the use of supplementary aids and services cannot be achieved satisfactorily (Individuals with Disabilities Education Act, P.L. 101-476, 1990).

The term least restrictive environment has raised more questions about integrating students with disabilities into mainstream settings than it has answered.

Early Definitions of Appropriate Placement. In 1975, Congress passed the Education for All Handicapped Children Act (P.L. 94-142) that guaranteed children with disabilities a free and appropriate public education. These children were to be appropriately placed in the least restrictive setting. In 1982, the Supreme Court had the opportunity to interpret the term "appropriate placement" (*Board of Education of Hendrick Hudson Central School District v. Rowley*, 1982).

A Pivotal Case: Supreme Court Interpretation of "Appropriate Placement"

This case involved a deaf student with excellent lip reading skills in the general education classroom. She was able to achieve average grades, but her parents believed she could have attained a higher level of achievement (her maximum potential) if she could have had an interpreter in the classroom. This request was denied and the case made its way to the Supreme Court. Judge Rehnquist, writing the majority opinion stated that "the individualized educational plan. . . . If the child is being educated in the regular classroom of the public education system, it should be reasonably calculated to *enable the child to achieve passing marks and advance from grade to grade*" [emphasis added] (102 S. Ct. 3049). The Court ruled that the sign language interpreter was not needed because the child was performing better than average and was receiving individualized instruction.

This decision was important because it established a requirement that children with disabilities were entitled to a level of services *sufficient for them to benefit from education and also required that special education services be provided in the "least restrictive environment"* (LRE; Osborne, 1992).

A Revolution of Expectation. The Supreme Court's decision on appropriate placement sparked major debate over expectations for students placed into mainstream classrooms—for the student, the academic program, and the teachers. Negative social attitudes about children with disabilities adversely affect expectations about what they can achieve academically. Often, these attitudes cause them to be exempt from standards and tests routinely applied to other students, allowed grades that they have not earned, excused from social and behavioral expectations set for other students, exempt from making personal choices and decisions, and permitted to receive special diplomas (Halloran & Simon, 1995; Gartner & Lipsky, 1992).

These watered-down expectations are thought to be in the best interests of the child (Gartner & Lipsky, 1992). In the future, students with disabilities who are included in general education classrooms can be held to the same standards and assessment measures as their nondisabled peers. They will also be expected to acquire the required Carnegie units needed for regular high school diplomas. The expectations expressed in early interpretations of P.L. 94-142—that the individual educational plan (IEP) should merely enable the child to "achieve passing marks and advance from grade to grade," will not be acceptable for students with mild to moderate disabilities.

Evolution of Inclusion by Court Interpretations. The Rowley ruling by the Supreme Court was criticized by advocates for people with disabilities because it (1) did not provide a clear definition of appropriate placement, (2) was not consistent with what Congress had intended that a school provide, and (3) conveyed a message that students with disabilities should only be expected to receive *minimal or a basic floor of opportunity*, rather than a level of services that allows equal educational opportunity. After Rowley, lower court decisions supported "minimal" education approaches, allowing schools to provide education that was of "some benefit" and provided students access to educational programs. Yet there was a lot of attention to the LRE doctrine. In putting together the "minimal benefit" and LRE principle, some lower courts interpreted "appropriate placement" to mean that students could be placed into mainstream settings for "social benefit," even at the expense of "educational quality" (*Bonadonna v. Cooperman*, 1985). Court cases in the years that followed challenged the idea that IEPs need not provide substantial educational benefits. These cases were successfully argued on the grounds that Congress intended to provide children who have disabilities with an education that would confer *meaningful benefit* (Osborne, 1992). For example,

- North Carolina state standards exceeded Rowley standards, requiring that students with disabilities should be provided an opportunity to achieve their potential in a manner similar to opportunities provided to nondisabled students. Massachusetts state standards required that, in order to be appropriate,

- an IEP should be designed to maximize the potential of a student with a disability (Osborne, 1992).
- Michigan's standards also required IEPs that are designed to develop the maximum potential of the child.

"Maximum potential" did not mean utopian, or the "best" education possible, but education had to be "meaningful." The idea of "meaningful" for students is still unclear and being debated in the states today.

Definitions of Inclusion. Today, inclusion is defined in many ways by many organizations and individuals. Terms such as "full inclusion," "inclusive education," "inclusive classrooms," "progressive inclusion," and "diverse classrooms" have all evolved from the mainstream movement in the 1980s (Stainback & Stainback, 1992). These terms generally all refer to the *maximum integration of students with disabilities into general classrooms or the increase in numbers and proportions of students who receive special services while attending general education classes* (McCoy, 1995; Putnam, 1993; Reynolds, Wang, & Walberg, 1992; Sailor, 1991). The terms have largely replaced the word "mainstreaming" for an important reason. Mainstreaming emerged during the early implementation of special education law and was associated with the placement of children with disabilities into their community schools, but many were still being educated in separate classrooms and even separate buildings or trailers on the school grounds.

Department of Education Definition. According to the U.S. Department of Education, Office of Special Education, the "regular class" includes students who receive the majority of their education program in the regular classroom and receive special education and related services outside the regular classroom for *less than* 21 percent of the school day. It includes children placed in a regular class and receiving special education within the regular class, as well as children placed in a regular class and receiving special education outside the regular class (Sixteenth Annual Report to Congress on the Implementation of the Individuals with Disabilities Education Act, 1994b). The federal definition reflects the recognition that a continuum of services is needed and presumes that some students may not be able to benefit from full inclusion into a general education classroom.

Definition of Inclusion for Students with Severe Disabilities. Inclusion definitions are different for students with severe disabilities (Exhibit I–1).

The rationale for educating students with severe disabilities in integrated settings is to promote a more "normalized" community participation by instructing

Exhibit I–1 Definition of Inclusion for Students with Severe and Multiple Disabilities

Element	Explanation
1. Placement	Classes are placed in the general school building that is the chronologically age-appropriate site for the student.
2. Ratio	Within a single school, students with disabilities represent 5 percent to 20 percent of each class.
3. Interaction	Structured opportunities exist for regular and sustained interactions between severely disabled and nondisabled students.
4. Nonacademic activities	Students with severe disabilities are provided opportunities to participate in all nonacademic activities of the school.
5. Curriculum	A functional life skills curriculum is implemented for students with severe disabilities. The curriculum combines classroom, school, and community-based learning situations (Sailor, Anderson, Halvorsen, Doering, Filler, & Goetz, 1989).

them in the skills that are essential to their success in the social and environmental settings in which they will ultimately use these skills. *"Meaningful educational benefit"* for students with disabilities is being interpreted by many educators as maximum possible social integration with nondisabled peers and the provision of functional life skills. Functional life skills training is best provided in a variety of settings that combine classroom, school, and community-based learning environments. This view and these practices depart greatly from the practice of "dumping" students into general education classes and are profoundly different from the segregated programs of the past (Janney, Snell, Beers, & Raynes, 1995; Hehir & Latus, 1992; Sailor, Anderson, Halvorsen, Doering, Filler, & Goetz, 1989).

How Professional Organizations Define Inclusion. The 16 special education divisions of the International Council for Exceptional Children (CEC) believe in preserving flexibility in educational services for students with disabilities. They support the continuum of services and reject the notion that 100 percent placement into the general education classroom is the universal placement for *all children*. The following display provides examples of how several professional divisions of CEC define inclusion.

Council for Exceptional Children

CEC believes that a continuum of services must be available for all children, youths, and young adults. CEC also believes that the concept of inclusion is a meaningful goal to be pursued in our schools and communities. In addition, CEC believes children, youths, and young adults with disabilities should be served whenever possible in general education classrooms in inclusive neighborhood schools and community settings. Such settings should be strengthened and supported by an infusion of specially trained personnel and other appropriate supportive practices according to the individual needs of the child (Supplement to *Teaching Exceptional Children*, 1993).

Council for Learning Disabilities

The Board of Trustees of the Council for Learning Disabilities (CLD) *supports* school reform efforts that enhance the education of all students, including those with learning disabilities (LD). The council

continues

supports the education of students with LD in general education classrooms when deemed appropriate by the individual education plan (IEP) team. Such inclusion efforts require the provision of needed support services in order to be successful. One policy that the council *cannot support* is the indiscriminate full-time placement of *all* students with LD in the regular education classroom, a policy often referred to as "full inclusion." CLD has grave concerns about any placement policy that ignores a critical component of special education service delivery: Program placement of each student should be based on an evaluation of the student's individual needs. The council *cannot support* any policy that minimizes or eliminates service options designed to enhance the education of students with LD that are guaranteed by the Individuals with Disabilities Education Act (*Learning Disability Quarterly,* 1993).

Council for Children with Behavior Disorders (CCBD; subdivision of the CEC)

Consistent with the Individuals with Disabilities Education Act (IDEA), CCBD supports a full continuum of mental health and special education services for children and youths with emotional and behavioral disorders. Educational decisions depend on individual student needs. Consequently, in contrast to those individuals in groups who advocate for full inclusion, CCBD does not support the notion that all special education students, including those students with emotional and behavioral disorders, are always best served in general education classrooms.

CCBD supports the concept of inclusive schools whereby public schools serve all children and whereby all personnel demonstrate ownership of all children in their school (*CCBD Newsletter,* 1993).

Division for Early Childhood (DEC; subdivision of the CEC)

Inclusion, as a value, supports the right of all children, regardless of the diverse abilities, to participate actively in natural settings within their communities. A natural setting is one in which the child would spend time if he or she did not have a disability. Such settings include but are not limited to home and family, play groups, child care, nursery schools, Head Start programs, kindergartens, and neighborhood school classrooms.

DEC believes in and supports full and successful access to health and social service education and other supports and services for young children and their families that promote full participation in community life. DEC values the diversity of families and supports a family-guided process for determining services that are based on the needs and preferences of individual families and children (Division for Early Childhood, 1993).

Council of Administrators of Special Education, Inc. (CASE; subdivision of the CEC)

CASE believes in and supports the evolving practice of inclusion for all students as an appropriate goal of our educational community. CASE believes that the decisions about an appropriate education for students must be made on an individual student basis. While there are those exceptions [for which] full inclusion is not appropriate, we believe strongly in the goal of including *all* children with disabilities in their own school and community. This necessitates a shift in the focus of IEP terms *from* the place for a student to the intensity and scope of services that a student needs to be appropriately educated (Council of Administrators of Special Education, 1993).

Source: Courtesy of the Council for Exceptional Children, Reston, Virginia.

What Inclusion Is and Is Not

Inclusion Is	Inclusion Is Not
All children learning together in the same schools and the same classrooms with the services and supports necessary so that they can be successful there.	Dumping all children with disabilities into regular classes without the supports and services they need to be successful there.
All children having their unique needs met in the same setting they would attend if they had no disability.	Trading of the quality of a child's education or the intensive support services the child may need for inclusion.
All children participating in all facets of school life.	Doing away with or cutting back on special education service.
Children with and without disabilities having opportunities (and support when needed) to interact and develop friendships with each other.	Ignoring each child's unique needs.
Children who have disabilities attending their neighborhood school (the same school they would attend if they did not have a labeled disability).	All children having to learn the same thing, at the same time, in the same way.
A method of schooling which emphasizes collaboration by melding special and regular education resources (staff, materials, energy, etc.).	Expecting regular education teachers to teach children who have disabilities without the support they need to teach all children effectively.
Supporting regular education teachers who have children with disabilities in their classrooms.	Sacrificing the education of typical children so that children with disabilities can be included.
Children learning side by side though they may have different educational goals.	Serving students with disabilities in separate schools or exclusively in self-contained classes based solely upon their categorical label.
Regular education teachers using innovative strategies for varied learning styles of children in the class.	
Integrating related services (such as speech, physical therapy, occupational therapy, etc.) in the regular classroom.	Scheduling students with disabilities for lunch and other activities at different times than other students are scheduled.
Unconditional acceptance of all children as children.	Placing students with disabilities into regular classes without the planning, supports, and services needed for successful and meaningful participation.
Unconditional commitment to providing as much support as the child needs to be successful in regular education environments.	
A focus on the parents' dreams and goals for their child's future.	Limiting the opportunities for students with disabilities to participate in regular classes by doing all scheduling first for students with disabilities to participate only where space is available.
Educators viewing themselves in new collaborative roles.	
A focus on what the child can do and **not** on what he or she cannot do.	Providing separate staff development for regular teachers and special education teachers, thus reinforcing notions of separate systems.
A team approach which includes parents as equal members and emphasizes creativity and a problem solving attitude.	
An understanding of the fact that students don't need to have the same educational goals in order to learn together in regular classes.	

continues

Inclusion Is	Inclusion Is Not
Strong leadership by school principals and other administrators.	Maintaining separate daily schedules for students with and without disabilities.
Encouraging and implementing activities that promote the development of friendships and relationships between students with and without disabilities.	Serving students with disabilities in age-inappropriate settings by placing older students in primary settings or younger students in secondary settings.
Providing the planning, support, and services necessary for meaningful and successful participation of students with disabilities in regular programs.	Denying students with disabilities services available to regular classrooms because the staff is not willing or hasn't been given direction in how to adapt instruction to meet the needs of diverse learners.
Having a school and district mission that is comprehensive and sets high expectations for all students, including those with disabilities.	
Providing professional development and support for all personnel regarding effective practices for inclusion of students with disabilities.	Referring to special education students in stigmatizing terms such as "the handicapped class" or "the retarded kids."
Scheduling classes for all school activities in a way that maximizes opportunities for participation by students with disabilities.	"Dumping" students with disabilities into regular programs without preparation or support.
Assuring that all schools and grades-level placements are age-appropriate.	Locating special education classes in separate wings at a school.
Having all people on the staff understand and support the notion that students with disabilities can be served appropriately in regular education classes and that this sometimes requires the staff to meet learning needs that differ from those of most students.	Exposing students to unnecessary hazards or risks.

Placing unreasonable demands on teachers and administrators. |
| Using "person first" language ("students with disabilities" instead of "disabled students") and teaching all students to understand and value human differences. | Ignoring parents' concerns.

Placing older students with disabilities at schools for younger children. |
Educating students with disabilities in the same school they would attend if they did not have disabilities.	Maintaining separate schedules for students in special education and regular education.
Providing needs services within regular schools, regardless of the intensity or frequency.	
Encouraging friendships and social relationships between students with disabilities and students without disabilities.	
Allowing students who are not able to fully participate in an activity to partially participate, rather than be excluded entirely.	
Arranging for students with disabilities to receive their job training in regular community environments.	
Teaching all children to understand and accept individual differences.	

Source: Courtesy of the Pisces Full Inclusion Project, Maryland State Deparment of Education.

Beyond Physical Placement

The first goal of early civil rights leaders and special education advocates was the right to basic physical access to all schools and public facilities for minorities and individuals with disabilities. The second goal was that society and the educational system had to change in a much more profound way. A vision of the world was constructed in which integration and acceptance of the individual and his or her differences is comprehensive and infused into all social responses of individuals and institutions. The first goal of physical access was comparatively easy to accomplish. *Achievement of the second goal, however, remains elusive.*

Historically, children with disabilities were educated in separate settings for two reasons: (1) to protect them from the stigma and rejection they would face from nondisabled people and (2) to provide special teaching methods and materials appropriate for the special learning needs of the individual. It was believed that students with disabilities learned differently and that different psychological and educational theories and techniques were needed to educate them (Putnam, 1993). For example, students were thought to need more intensive instruction over longer periods of time regardless of the type and severity of their disabilities. They were also thought to need environments with less stimuli and fewer students. The traditional general classroom was judged not to be appropriate for these students. As early as the 1970s, however, educators argued against the belief that separate theories and psychological principles should be applied generally to students with disabilities (Sarason & Doris, 1978).

Increased Expectations for Teachers

Today, teachers and other school personnel are expected to develop educational programs that serve a diversity of students, including students with disabilities, those at risk for failure, former school dropouts, students with limited English proficiency, and teen parents. Each of these groups may be considered a special population of students possessing unique needs that require *specialized educational services*. In some school systems, these special populations are the majority. Teachers are expected to work to improve the achievement and development of each of these groups of students. Many of the instructional and behavioral approaches once developed for students with disabilities, such as learning strategies, metacognitive strategies, or behavioral strategies (behavior contracts, token economies), are now being applied in the regular classroom because they seem to work with a range of children and youth with special learning needs (Hughes-Booker, 1994; Putnam, 1993).

3. What Are the Major Components of Inclusion?

The term *inclusion* has a relatively long history in this nation. It is rooted in the civil rights movements that arose out of the struggle of people of color for their freedom in America in the 1800s and early 1900s. The following chart depicts the evolution of the term inclusion and of the many terms that have been used to refer to the idea of integration of persons with disabilities into mainstream environments. Each successive term reflects a movement toward closer integration with non-disabled peers in ways that are both qualitative (conditions similar to those of nondisabled peers) and quantitative (amount of time spent and number of settings).

The Many Faces of Civil Rights: Evolution of the Term Inclusion

1900s through 1960s—Normalization. A philosophy imported from Scandinavia, based on the belief that individuals with disabilities should be viewed as being entitled to the same freedoms to choose life circumstances and opportunities as their nondisabled peers.

1950 through 1960s—Deinstitutionalization and community integration. Two principles that gained wide acceptance after the Kennedy administration's leadership in promoting the movement of people with mental retardation out of large institutions and into their families or smaller facilities in their communities.

1970s—Least restrictive environment (LRE). A principle embodied in early special education law (P.L. 94-142), which required that students be educated in settings that were least restrictive of their freedom and most supportive of interaction with nondisabled peers.

1980s—Mainstreaming. A term based on the LRE principle, which represented efforts to restructure school programs to permit students with disabilities to be served to the extent possible in their home schools and in classrooms with their nondisabled peers.

Early 1990s—Inclusion. A term similar to mainstreaming, but which specifically refers to integration of students with disabilities into regular academic classes with nondisabled peers.

Mid-1990s—Full inclusion. A term that refers to the principle and practice of placing any and all students into regular classrooms with nondisabled peers, regardless of the type or severity of their disability, for the social benefits that may be gained.

2000 and beyond—Full participation and meaningful benefit?

Components

Special education and civil rights laws have promoted the practice of educating students who have disabilities with their nondisabled peers, to the extent that this is possible and reasonable. Schools are now required to ensure that special classes, separate schooling, or other removal of a child with disabilities from the regular educational environment occurs only if the student has such a severe disability that his or her education in regular classes cannot be achieved even with the use of supplementary aids and services.

Sailor (1991) proposed six major components for inclusion of students with disabilities in general education classrooms.

Component 1: Home School Placements. Students are educated in their neighborhood schools, which provide opportunities for social inclusion at the school and in the community. No students are educated in separate special schools, magnet schools, or enclaves with high concentrations of students with disabilities.

Component 2: Natural Proportion at Each School.

Each school and each class contain the same proportion of students with disabilities as is found in the general community. For example, in a community in which 10 percent of the population have disabilities, an inclusive classroom would contain no more than 10 percent students with disabilities—2 or 3 in a classroom of 25 to 30 students.

Component 3: A Zero-Reject Philosophy.

Every school serves *all* children within its district; no student is excluded on the basis of type or extent of disability. This philosophy helps to develop a sense of community and fosters a feeling of belonging and interdependence as well as relationships that value diversity (Stainback & Stainback, 1992).

Component 4: Age- and Grade-Appropriate Placements.

Placements in schools and general education classes are age and grade appropriate, so no self-contained special education classes exist. There is no "cascade of services" or continuum of placements for students with differing needs.

Component 5: Cooperative Learning and Peer Instructional Methods.

Cooperative learning and peer instruction are replacing traditional teaching as the preferred methods for inclusive classrooms.

Component 6: Special Education in Integrated Environments.

Special education supports exist within the general education class and in other integrated environments (Sailor, 1991), so that in the inclusive class, special education resources, such as personnel, supplies, and equipment, are redistributed for use by all students in the classroom. Also arrangements for team teaching with general education and special education teachers can be used to individualize instruction for students with disabilities (Sailor, 1991).

There remains a great deal of controversy among inclusion advocates about how to implement these components.

Good inclusion models are effective because they take into consideration (a) the expectations that the student can benefit from the educational program, (b) the conditions and resources needed to attain such benefits, and (c) the actual effects of the placements on the total classroom. It is these models of good inclusion that provide all educators with an understanding of the possibilities and potential of the inclusion movement.

---

4. What Forces Shaped Inclusion?

Many forces have moved policy makers, educators, students, and parents to carefully consider the inclusion concept, although they have often disagreed on how it should be implemented. Overall, these forces have served to strengthen the inclusion movement and to improve current practices.

Changing Definition of Special Needs.

The term special needs populations once meant those who met the legal definition of having a "disability." Now it includes other groups such as at-risk, disadvantaged, incarcerated youths, and teen parents. The sheer number of students who need special educational services has risen sharply over the past decade. About one third of American children are now considered to be at risk for school failure. These children are an average of two years behind their grade level in the 6th grade and four years behind by the 12th grade. Between 1980 and 1990,

the White American population of these children increased by 8 percent, while the African American population grew by 16 percent, the Asian population by 65 percent, and the Hispanic population by 44 percent (Hodgkinson, 1991). The concern for improving education and employment preparation outcomes for children and youths is being extended to include a broader range of individuals with diverse needs who must share the limited resources for special educational services.

Rise in Number of Students with Disabilities.

The second population change affecting inclusion is the increasing number of students with disabilities being served in home schools and general education classrooms. Currently, at least 68 percent of students requiring special education service are attending inclusive classes for at least 40 percent or more of the day or all day (U.S. Department of Education, Fifteenth Annual

Report to Congress, 1993a). This increase in the numbers of students with disabilities served in general education classrooms is likely to continue (Putnam, 1993).

Rise in Dropout Rates. The third population change affecting inclusion is the alarming number of students with disabilities between 15 and 18 years of age who drop out of the school system each year. The school system is failing to meet the needs of students with disabilities in the schools and the regular classroom. As a result of increased requirements for graduation, all students must meet higher standards for graduation from high school. These standards include an increased number of Carnegie units, additional state competency testing, and increased academic requirements for all subjects. Since more emphasis is being placed on academic requirements and improved academic outcomes, students with disabilities, their parents, and their teachers are forced into a dilemma. Given the increased number of academic units required for graduation, these students must enroll primarily in academic courses, which leaves little or no time for vocational education courses, career education, work experience, social skills training, or independent living classes. In all of these areas, there are well-documented needs for students with disabilities (Halloran & Simon, 1995).

Rise in Number of Minority Students. A fourth population change affecting inclusion is the increasing number of students representing minority populations, including immigrants and migrant populations. Educational practitioners and policy makers are coming to believe that educational resources should be directed at producing specific outcomes for students with disabilities in least restrictive environments and that teachers should be explicit about their outcome goals, especially in regard to subpopulation groups that require a special focus (Ysseldyke & Thurlaw, 1993; U.S. Department of Education, Fifteenth Annual Report to Congress, 1993a). An outcome focus on minority populations is viewed as vital to facilitating meaningful improvement in educational services for these groups, since it can provide evidence of improvement and can provide the public with measures of the effectiveness of such change.

Rise in Violent and Aggressive Behavior. A fifth population change affecting inclusion is the rise in violent and aggressive behavior among students with disabilities placed into inclusive classrooms. Researchers have reported that many educators are concerned about the effectiveness of inclusion practices and the quality of services in the regular classroom. For example, Simpson & Sasso (1992) identified three factors that can be correlated with the increasing ag-

gression and violence in our schools: (1) increased societal aggression, (2) increased numbers of students with behavior disorders in public schools, and (3) increased placement of such students in inclusive general education classrooms.

> Public schools are currently serving an ever-increasing number of students who display aggressiveness and violent behaviors, often without the benefit of appropriate human and institutional resources such as community mental health support programs. . . . Accelerating aggression and violence among children and youth may also be a function of increased reliance on general education settings for students with disabilities and those at risk . . . (without) the resources needed to respond to the problem. These resources include management consultants, reduced class size, additional teacher planning time, and inservice training on methods for dealing with aggression and violence. (Simpson & Sasso, 1992, p. 3)

Many students with severe emotional disturbance are being served in general education classrooms without needed supports. Teachers recently surveyed in Washington, D.C., reported that most teachers (72 percent) believed students were becoming more verbally and physically aggressive and that academic achievement was falling (Hughes-Booker, 1994). The rise in violent behaviors among all students is a cause for concern for all teachers. Violent behavior in students with disabilities presents a particular challenge for teachers in general education classrooms and threatens the success of inclusion practices.

Expanding Role of Health and Human Services. Recent research and practice have confirmed the value of early intervention services in preparing infants, toddlers, and young children to benefit from therapeutic and educational services. In response to this new knowledge, legislation has expanded the role of health and human services in providing services to children in the early years and requires preschools to include children with disabilities in mainstream settings. Inclusive early intervention services for young children with disabilities improves the likelihood that children will be successful in inclusive elementary school classes.

National Need To Achieve Better Results. In 1993, the U.S. Department of Education (1993b) established national priorities for outcomes for children with disabilities (National Agenda for Achieving Better Results for Children with Disabilities). These priorities were designed to advance *the goal of inclusive education and options to serve a more diverse population of children within a wider framework of educational services for all.* How schools implement inclusion should not be dominated by interest groups or politicians, but rather by what works and what improves student outcomes.

Economic Forces Impact Inclusion. When P.L. 94-142 was passed, the federal government promised to reimburse states at a rate of 40 percent of the expenditure per pupil for each student with a disability served. The actual funding appropriated by Congress for special education never reached more than 12 percent and is now at about 9 percent. States have had to make up the difference in order to serve an increasing number of students in a growing number of disability categories. Inclusion decisions, such as the number of placement options, class sizes, the number of trained personnel, and the amount of available support services, are dependent on available funds. Some districts have found that mainstreaming is consistent with cost-saving solutions, yet others recognize that good inclusion practices require more favorable student-teacher ratios, additional support staff, and a continuum of placement options (Singer & Butler, 1987).

Budget reductions and changes in priorities in the states are likely to affect the quality of inclusive practices over the next decade. In search for cost savings, local administrators often turn to cutting the major cost item in their control—personnel. Local educational agencies often respond to cost issues first by narrowing the eligible population, then reducing the amount of service, and also the professional qualifications needed for providing it (Singer & Butler, 1987). Particularly vulnerable are personnel who provide support services that are not specifically mandated by law. Reductions in personnel for special education, vocational support teams, and related services are occurring throughout the states today. In addition, severe cuts in career-vocational education programs and services in local educational agencies and school districts greatly limit opportunities for students to gain work-related skills. These cuts are occurring despite evidence that vocational-technical education courses are effective in preparing many high school students with disabilities for gainful employment (U.S. Office of Vocational and Adult Education, 1994).

In the future, innovative combinations of funding sources will be required to preserve the range of supportive services needed by students in general education classes.

5. What Is the Shared Responsibility for Inclusion?

Another major force that has accelerated the inclusion movement is the drifting together of general and special education over the past 12 years. Since the *Nation at Risk* report was released in 1983, the educational system in the United States has been criticized for its inability to prepare all learners for an increasingly complex society. It has also been criticized for jeopardizing its leadership role in the global economic political arena. The federal government responded by establishing an ambitious set of national education goals. It also set in motion unprecedented attempts to restructure and improve the public education system and to improve both academic and social outcomes for all children at all grade levels.

Special Education under Fire. Special education, as a component of general education, has also been under fire for many years. After 20 years of implementation the Education of All Handicapped Children Act

(P.L. 94-142) was amended in 1990, and the Individuals with Disabilities Education Act (IDEA; P.L. 101-476) was enacted. Subsequently, parents, educators, and policy makers have begun to demand sweeping reforms in the service delivery system and in the way special education has been organized and administered at the federal, state, and local levels. As special education restructuring and reorganization efforts advance, educators have called for less emphasis on strict "procedural compliance" and more on improving the quality of the special education services and the outcomes for students. Educators have begun to believe that improvement in outcomes for all children requires a "shared responsibility" for educating all children. An initiative known as the *regular education initiative* was developed by the U.S. Office of Special Education to convey the importance of the idea of inclusion as the nation began to craft massive education reforms (Will, 1983).

Lack of Information about What Works. Many researchers have been trying to discover whether separate education and classes for students with disabilities help or hinder their progress. In general, over the last decade, researchers have not been able to clearly demonstrate that separate, special education "pull out" programs have had significant benefits for students (Hehir & Latus, 1992; Skrtic, 1988, 1993; Lipsky & Gartner, 1989). The cumulative effects of these changes, however, have divided educators into at least two camps: (1) those who advocate increased academic expectations, higher standards, and more standardized educational offerings, and (2) those who advocate increased options in accommodating diverse student abilities, interests, and aspirations (Kochhar & West, 1995).

A fundamental mission of all educators is to define a system that blends both approaches. This mission requires a continued blending, not only of general and special education, but also of many disciplines and service sectors.

A broader, shared effort to improve outcomes for all school children means that disciplines and agencies must work together in a different way. It means that schools and school-linked agencies must address the needs of children in an integrated manner.

Teachers Feeling Unprepared. Many general education teachers are fearful and feel unprepared to work in the regular classroom with students who have disabilities. Teachers feel they have not had adequate training in how to adapt instruction, facilitate socialization, manage a diverse class, and adapt technology to accommodate special learners, nor do they receive technical help when they need it (Putnam, 1993). *The traditional practice of viewing special education teachers as those who teach special learners and general education teachers as those who teach "regular" children is being seriously questioned.* Colleges and universities are also questioning the separate degree programs for special and regular educators and are experimenting with combined and integrated teacher training programs. Such a broader, shared effort can help support teachers in achieving national education goals for all children.

Collaboration with School-Linked Human Service Agencies. Human service agencies, however, respond to human needs in different ways. Traditionally, needs such as health, education, and employment have been addressed by separate agencies that work in isolation. For example, if an individual has multiple needs for health, remedial education, job training, and family counseling, he or she goes to the public health clinic, adult education center, employment services center, and the mental health center to obtain the different services needed. Each agency may "serve" the individual without communicating with the other agencies providing services to that same individual. Schools and school-linked agencies must collaborate more closely.

Teaching the Whole Person. Educators and human service personnel are now realizing that it is much more effective to serve the individual as a *whole person* and to address his or her needs in a way that coordinates services. Schools and community service systems are finding that "shared" approaches to addressing student needs bring the combined thinking, planning, and resources of many agencies to bear on the problems of the individual student in a way that is not only more efficient, but also works to improve the life of the child (Schalock, 1983).

Sharing the Responsibility. Teachers who have conducted research in inclusive classrooms recommend that six conditions should exist if the inclusive experience is to be a success:

1. Two or more teachers with subject knowledge must share responsibility for planning and teaching.
2. Team teaching requires a relationship of trust between the teachers.
3. Teachers must have previously agreed on goals for the students.
4. Team teachers must have a common planning time each day.
5. Students placed in the class from the pool of students with disabilities must be screened to determine the probability of success in the large class.
6. Teachers must share responsibility for the success of all students in the class.

Many teachers claim that they do not get a common planning time each day and often have to plan over lunch for the following day. The availability of classroom aides for planning time is becoming more limited. In the next century and beyond, educators will come to realize that successful inclusion of all children requires more than general-special education collaboration. Rather, it requires a profound and fundamental rethinking of how educational programs for children and youths are organized and how they can respond to their varying capacities and needs.

6. What Are the Major Controversies surrounding Inclusion?

Wide Range of Beliefs about Best Practice.
There are a wide range of beliefs about best practice in inclusion. Some educators believe that all children, including students with severe disabilities, should be included in general education classrooms, regardless of their ability to benefit from the mainstream curriculum. This is termed *"full inclusion,"* and means excluding no student from general education classes. For example, a 14-year-old student with severe cognitive disabilities would be placed in a general ninth grade class but would be provided with an individual educational program at a first grade level. This inclusion placement achieves *social* inclusion, but not *academic* inclusion.

Other inclusion experts believe that the full inclusion model is not successful and is promoting failure and backlash among students, teachers, and parents. They believe that the question of benefit should be considered and that there should be varying levels of inclusion according to a set of conditions for "successful" and meaningful placement (Putnam, 1993).

Application of Least Restrictive Environment.
Just how should the principle of least restrictive environment be applied? Is there no longer a need for separate classes or schools? What does "restrictive" mean, and what is "most" or "least"? Of whom and how? In 1981, a task force on least restriction was convened by the American Association on Mental Deficiency to study and help to clarify the principle so that it might be better understood and applied by professionals and other policy makers (Turnbull, 1991). In the late 1970s and early 1980s, students of this principle were more concerned with how it applied to individuals in institutions who might be better served in their communities. Today, the application is more complex. Students with disabilities are largely being served in their community schools to varying degrees of integration. It is useful to compare the problems with applying the principle of least restrictive environment 20 years ago and today (Exhibit I–2).

Reasons for Mandating Least Restrictive Environment. There are many reasons why the principle of least restrictive environment was written into special education law. These reasons include the following:

- The Supreme Court created the principle as a matter of constitutional (fundamental) law.
- There is a long history of segregating students with disabilities from nondisabled students.
- There is ample evidence that many students with disabilities can be educated effectively in programs for students without disabilities.
- Students with disabilities should have the opportunity to associate with and to learn from nondisabled students.
- A separate special education system is unjustifiable if it does not benefit students.
- It is expensive to operate two education systems—one for special education and one for general education.
- Any kind of segregation in education violates the U.S. Constitution, which seeks to treat all people equally (Turnbull, 1994).

The Individuals with Disabilities Act (IDEA; P.L. 101-476, 1990) contains a *presumption in favor of educating students who have disabilities with nondisabled students.* Furthermore, a school may not remove the student from general education unless he or she cannot be educated there successfully (with educational benefit), even after the school provides supplementary aids and support services for the student. Recently, the courts have taken into account *social inclusion as well as physical and academic inclusion* (Turnbull, Turnbull, Shank, & Leal, 1995).

The Core of the Controversy: Age- and Grade-Appropriate Placement. Age- and grade-appropriate placement is the most controversial component of inclusion because it is based on ideals, values, and goals that are not congruent with the realities of today's classrooms. During the 1980s, major studies of long-term integration of students with severe and multiple disabilities were carried out by the California Research Institute. Researchers studied over 200 classes serving more that 2,000 students with severe disabilities in 20 schools. They found fixed outcomes. Students' progress and achievements differed depending on the amount of in-class support they received from teachers, aides, and consultants. The National Education Association (NEA) also reviewed the direct experiences of many teachers in inclusive classrooms across the United States. Teachers saw significant progress with special learners as long as they had the resources, administrative support, and adequate times for instructional planning and consultation (Dalheim, 1994). In the NEA's report, *Toward Inclusive Classrooms* (Dalheim, 1994, p. 7), teachers who shared their experiences concluded that the task of "turning the wheel in the direction of equality was worth it. . . . Toward schools—schools where all students, regardless of their physical, mental, or emotional challenges can learn with their peers." Exhibit I–3 presents several issues at the core of the controversy, a description of each controversy, and a summary of opinion in the field.

One Key Problem Unresolved. The age- and grade-appropriate component of inclusion is most controversial and divisive because it is based on ideals, values, and goals that are not congruent with the reali-

ties of today's classrooms. Proponents of full inclusion assume that the general education classroom can and will be able to accommodate all students with disabilities, even those with severe and multiple disabilities. They assume that such students can obtain educational and social benefits from the placement. Those who oppose full inclusion argue that, although methods of collaborative learning and group instruction are the preferred methods, the traditional classroom size and resources are often inadequate for the management and accommodation of many students with disabilities without producing adverse effects on the classroom as a whole. Some special education experts, however, believe that some students are unlikely to receive appropriate education without placement into alternative instructional groups or alternative learning environments, such as part-time or full-time special classes or alternative day schools (Kauffman & Hallahan, 1993; Lieberman, 1988).

Exhibit I–2 Important Issues Regarding Least Restrictive Environment: Yesterday and Today

1970s	1990s and beyond
1. Centered on people and conditions in individuals or in separate schools	1. Movement of elementary students from a general education class into a special education class once they are assessed to have a disability
2. Commitment to institutions	2. Placement of severely disabled students into general education classes
3. Determination of appropriate length of time of placement in the institution	3. Determination of the amount of time appropriate in general classrooms
4. Right to refuse treatment	4. Determination of the amount of individualization appropriate for the student and possible within the resources of the general classroom
5. Amount of supervision received and needed	5. Degree to which students with disabilities can be accommodated in the use of new technologies
6. Sterilization of female adolescents with severe disabilities	6. Assessment of range and types of educational alternatives possible within schools and communities
7. Approaches for care of individuals with self-injurious behavior	

Exhibit I-3 Summary of Controversial Issues and Options on Inclusion

Issue	Controversy	Opinion in the Field
Issue 1: Should the continuum of placements be eliminated?	The continuum makes more restrictive placements legitimate and infringes on students' rights, is based on a readiness model, supports the dominance of professional decision making, and rejects the idea that specialized services can only be provided in separate settings (Taylor, 1988). There is an expectation that general education classrooms have the capacity to accommodate any and all students with disabilities.	There is little consensus and much diversity in opinion about eliminating the continuum of placements. It is not a federal requirement to reduce or eliminate the continuum of services. Rational assessment of students' needs should guide placements and flexibility in providing placements is implied in the law.
Issue 2: What is the appropriate amount of time for students with disabilities to spend in the general classroom?	The expectation of inclusion is that spending all day in the general education classroom is appropriate for all students.	In general, inclusion advocates do not insist on 100% placement into the general academic classroom for all students.
Issue 3: What extent or severity of disability *should be* accommodated in the general classroom in order to yield an educational benefit for the student?	The expectation is that placement into the general classroom will yield academic and social benefits for all students with disabilities.	Inclusion advocates do not uniformly insist that all students with all levels of disability should be placed into the regular academic classroom.
Issue 4: What extent or severity of disability can be accommodated in the general classroom without producing a negative impact on the majority of students in the classroom?	The expectation is that the placement would not have a negative impact on the total classroom.	Inclusion advocates do not uniformly insist that all students with all levels of disability should be placed into the regular academic classroom.
Issue 5: What extent or severity of disability *can be* accommodated in the general classroom without producing a negative budgetary impact?	The expectation is that the accommodations required in the general class will be reasonable and affordable.	There is general agreement that the student should not be placed in the general classroom if such placement would result in "harm" to the student (e.g., inadequate support or no capacity to accommodate the student).
Issue 6: What is the appropriate rate at which children with disabilities should be transferred from more restrictive settings and placed into general classrooms?	The expectation is that the process of transferring students is not harmful to the individual student being transferred or to the students in the receiving classroom.	There is a consensus among experts that the process of integrating students with disabilities into general education classes should not be harmful to the individual student being transferred.

7. What Is the Conclusion about Inclusion?

There is no general consensus about inclusion. The various positions and disagreements educators have about inclusion can be summarized as follows:

1. We need to know more. There is a lot we need to know about the effectiveness of inclusion and "meaningful benefit" of educational placements, and the field is in active dialogue about the meaning of the term.

2. No operational definition of full inclusion has been agreed upon in the field.

3. The benefits of inclusion outweigh the costs for students with or without disabilities.

4. Most advocates of inclusion do not require full inclusion—100% placement of students with disabilities in the regular classroom.

5. Appropriate placement must show benefit. The courts agree that for students who are educated in general education classes, "appropriate educational placement" means receiving passing grades and advancing from grade to grade. For students with severe disabilities, progress toward greater self-sufficiency and functional skills would be more reasonable (Osborne, 1992).

6. Individualization is a hallmark of special education, and no single educational placement is always appropriate for meeting every student's academic, social, or career-vocational goals. There are no universal solutions for all or absolute answers.

7. Do no harm. There is general agreement that placement should not "harm" the student. Thus, students should not be placed into a regular classroom if there is inadequate support or capacity to accommodate the student. Also, extremely rapid transition and integration of students with disabilities into general education classes should not take place if the students are unprepared and these processes would be harmful to the student being transferred.

8. Overall improvement in the educational system is needed. There is general agreement that the effort to improve education for students with disabilities must be accomplished within a broader effort to improve education for all students. Advancing inclusive placements alone without restructuring the classroom, curriculum, and instruction will lead to the failure of inclusion and, ultimately, to the increasing failure of "regular" students (McCoy, 1995; Janney et al., 1995; Turnbull et al., 1995; Dalheim, 1994; Fuchs & Fuchs, 1994; Kauffman & Hallahan, 1993; Salisbury, Palombaro, & Hollowood, 1993; Lieberman, 1988; Reynolds, Wang, & Walberg, 1992; Sailor, 1991; Taylor, 1988; Osborne, 1988).

The central theme of the IDEA is that all placement and programming decisions must be made on an *INDIVIDUALIZED* basis.

Perspective: Unfortunately, there is no single answer to the question "what works?" because of the tremendous and growing diversity of students attending schools today. Cultural and language diversity in the classroom, for example, means that no single mode of teacher-student relating and no single pedagogical (teaching) style is likely to be effective for all children in that classroom. Among students with disabilities, too, the great variation in their abilities and disabilities underscores the critical importance of the individualized programs that are one of the hallmarks of special education, as required by law. (U.S. Department of Education, 1992a, p. 102)

8. How Do We Develop a Rational Approach to Inclusion?

Need for Balance in Defining Inclusion and the Least Restrictive Environment. Special education law was passed in order to establish a right for all children and youths to benefit from an education that is appropriate to their needs. It was also passed to ensure that individuals are not subject to excessive restrictions and to protect their right to live lives as close as possible to the normal lives of nondisabled peers. The concepts of benefit, individual liberty, and freedom from restriction are central to the principle of the least restrictive environment—a pivotal concept in the law. This principle is linked to the democratic principles of freedom and individual liberty. Yet none of us are entirely free, we are constrained in our behavior socially, legally, economically, morally, and ethically (Turnbull, 1991). Freedom is relative and the freedoms of the individual must be balanced against the freedoms of others in society.

Perspective on Individual Freedom and Responsibility. In education, individual freedom is restricted for social and moral reasons. For example, children are required by law to go to school. Students are not permitted to carry radios, beepers, or weapons to school. They are not allowed to keep medicines in their possession or in lockers, and they are restricted to some extent in their dress. These restrictions are considered to be imposed because of their benefits to students and individuals and groups. Students are protected from inappropriate use of medicines, violent and dangerous behaviors, potential injuries from weapons, and distractions of radios and beepers.

Behavior and choices of students and parents are also limited by costs, since schools cannot afford to make all possible options available to everyone. Choices are also limited by the decisions of governments. Governments and courts can set forth two kinds of "rules" to govern human behavior and to mediate among competing individual rights. They can establish firm or absolute rules on behalf of whole groups of individuals or broad guidelines or "preferred" choices. This second category of rules has a great deal of flexibility and is highly subject to interpretation.

Firm Rules. Firm rules often are established for children as a special group. For example, no minor is permitted to purchase alcohol or to smoke tobacco. Firm rules exist for minors because parents, educators, and society in general are responsible for the health, development, and welfare of children at a vulnerable age. More flexible guidelines exist which can be "bent" if adequate circumstances exist.

The principle of least restrictive environment is a technique for making *decisions* about students with disabilities that falls into the category of broad guideline or preferred choice, for which there is flexibility and room for interpretation. The practice of inclusion has evolved from this principle to include an accepted array of placements depending on the needs of the individual (e.g., general education class, resource room, or separate special education class). The least restrictive or more inclusive setting is the preferred choice because it favors the student's greater liberty. Leaning in favor of a student's greater liberty is, therefore, the preferred choice in general, unless there is a need to accomplish a greater purpose or a valid reason for not granting the more inclusive choice. The greater purpose may be to protect the safety and well-being of other students. For example, if the student is self-destructive or violent, has a highly communicable disease, or has uncontrollable behavior, then the general classroom as the least restrictive environment would not be appropriate.

Suppose the greater purpose is not for safety, but to meet the educational needs of the student. *The preferred choice of placement, then, may not always be the least restrictive placement.* The least restrictive placement of the fully inclusive classroom may not be appropriate to benefit the student.

Toward a Sensible Framework for Inclusion. Many inclusion advocates highlight the difference between inclusion and the principle of the least restrictive environment. They argue that this principle as expressed in the U.S. Department of Education's Regular Education Initiative (Will, 1983) sought to restructure general education so that it could improve access to and better accommodate the needs of students with disabilities in general education classrooms (Turnbull et al., 1995). Inclusion, on the other hand, is a

value that is expressed in the way we plan, promote and conceptualize the development of children. In inclusive programs, the diverse needs of all children are accommodated to the maximum extent possible within the general education curriculum. . . . Driven by a vision of schools as a place where all children learn well what we want them to learn, schools become creative and successful environments for adults and the children they serve. (Salisbury et al., 1993)

Framework for Rational Inclusion. Based on this discussion, inclusion, according to contemporary educators, differs from the principle of the least restrictive environment because it is a *broader and more comprehensive reform effort*. Yet this principle and the concept of inclusion share the common assumption that all children should "learn well." Rational inclusion, therefore, is defined as inclusive practices that are consistent with five principles of inclusion.

Inclusive Principles for Rational Inclusion

Principle 1: Special education law was passed in order to establish a right for all children and youths to benefit from an *education* that is beneficial and appropriate to their needs. In a democracy, ensuring that all children have access to appropriate educational opportunities is a social responsibility. The 1975 Education for All Handicapped Children Act (P.L. 94-142) required that placements be "based on the child's individualized education program in which appropriate services are described. To the maximum extent appropriate, children with disabilities must be educated with children who are not disabled and special classes, separate schooling, or other removal of children with disabilities from regular educational environments occurs only when the nature or severity of the disability is such that education in regular classes with the use of supplementary aids and services cannot be achieved satisfactorily."

Principle 2: The restrictiveness of the placement is integrally linked to the potential of the placement to benefit or provide appropriate education. These two factors cannot be separated.

Principle 3: Less restrictive placements, to be in accordance with the intent of the law, cannot be made without regard to educational benefit, and determinations about educational benefit should not be made without regard to placement.

Principle 4: A placement should not be any more restrictive than is necessary to achieve educational benefit. In implementing the doctrine of the least restrictive environment, the focus should remain on the creation of less restrictive alternatives, rather than only on the reduction of overly restrictive choice (Turnbull, 1991). The experience of freedom and greater control over one's life is a prerequisite for growth and development.

Principle 5: Social benefits are related to but *are not synonymous* with educational benefit, and the least restrictive environment for some students may not be the general education classroom. Yet some children who differ greatly from the norm (e.g., the 12-year-old with a genius IQ who is ready for college material) would find the general seventh grade class very restrictive. Similarly, children with severe cognitive, behavioral, and emotional disabilities need curriculum modification and differentiated educational services, goals, and standards. Some children with more severe disabilities may need differentiated services delivered in settings that provide a reduced teacher-student ratio and other modifications to the environment that cannot be provided in a general education classroom. These decisions must be driven by assessed individual student needs.

Balanced Decision Making for Inclusion.
Many factors must be considered before decisions are made about an appropriate match between the student's needs and the capacity of the classroom to accommodate the student. Integration of the principles for rational inclusion permits a balanced approach to implementing inclusion that integrates the ideas and

requirements of educational benefit, individual liberty, and least restrictive environment. Each of these factors is an important element in defining the success of inclusion.

Two implementation principles can be set forth. The first addresses the placement decision; the second addresses the effects of the decision on the classroom.

Implementation principle 1 is that placement is based on student need and expectation of benefit. The first and primary principle on which the placement decision is based is the need of the student and an expectation of benefit for that student (*appropriate placement first*). The questions related to the first principle are:

- With reasonable accommodation, can the student be expected to participate in and benefit from the curriculum being delivered in the regular classroom?
- With reasonable accommodation, can the student benefit from the support of the teacher or cooperative team of teachers during class or in an afternoon or after-school help session?
- With reasonable accommodation, can the student maintain a level of achievement comparable to the level in the self-contained class or in a previous placement?
- With reasonable accommodation, can the student be expected to display social behavior that is appropriate for the grade level and to interact positively with others?
- With reasonable accommodation, can the student be assessed by using the assessment methods being used for all other children in the classroom?

Implementation principle 2 is that the classroom accommodates the student. If the condition in principle 1 is met, then the second decision relates to the response on the part of the teacher and the student's peers to the new student's placement. This principle requires that the teacher assess the impact that placement is likely to have on the learning environment for other students. The teacher does not assess impact in order to argue against the placement, since the condition in principle 1 has been met. Rather, the teacher does so in order to determine how the class and program can best accommodate the student and prepare peers for the changes that need to occur in the classroom.

The questions related to the second principle are:

- How can the classroom and curriculum be reasonably modified to accommodate the student and ensure that he or she can attain levels of achievement similar to those of others?
- How can the student's peers be best prepared for the participation of the new student?
- How can the assessment process be reasonably modified to ensure accurate assessment of the student at the level of his or her peers?

- How can the student with a disability receive academic support from students in the general education class?
- How can the student with a disability be helped to feel comfortable as a participating member of the class?

Once the condition in principle 1 has been met, principle 2 requires that the responsibility for making an accommodation for the student lies with the parent or guardian, the school principal, and the teacher. Part III of this handbook provides illustrations of how these principles are applied in real classroom situations.

General Educators Are Essential to the Process. General educators have recently indicated that they feel left out of the process of planning for and implementing inclusion in their schools and have not had a strong voice in shaping the debate about inclusion (Putnam, 1993). The concerns of general education teachers, therefore, should be squarely and honestly addressed if they are required to manage and teach in inclusive classrooms. General educators need answers to the following questions:

- Do inclusion programs really work, and how is success defined?
- How are the programs implemented?
- Will I need more training?
- Will I have adequate help to teach these students?
- Must I have different expectations for these students?
- Will my other students need training or special preparation?
- How can I enlist the expertise and help of the special educator?
- What kinds of adaptations can I make?

In addition, general education teachers also want answers to more difficult questions:

- How do I teach children with diverse abilities when my education program did not prepare me to teach them?
- What is "appropriate placement"?
- How many students with disabilities should be placed into a regular class?
- Will my school still provide a continuum of services for more needy students?
- Will there be negative effects on my other students, and will they be short-changed?

- Where will the money come from for extra materials, equipment, technology, or support staff?
- Will my class composition or class size change if I take students with disabilities?
- Do the benefits outweigh the costs?

As Putnam (1993) concluded, it only seems fair that teachers who are asked to educate students with differing abilities receive adequate preparation, special supports and services, the commitment of administration, and opportunities to engage in positive team approaches.

The Inclusion Bill of Rights (Part III, Exhibits III–3, III–4, and III–5) views the set of implementation principles previously described as necessary for the success of inclusion. Considering the rights and needs of one group responsible for implementing inclusion at the expense of another's is to jeopardize the inclusion process and its quality.

All professionals involved in the education process must have a voice in the planning and implementation of inclusion.

Teachers: The Key to Successful Inclusion.
Experts and advocates for inclusion generally agree that we need to end the dual tracks of special and regular education and create a unified system. Most concur that general education teachers and their attitudes toward inclusion are the "key ingredients" to success in its implementation. In implementing inclusion, the general education teacher is at center stage, though there are special education consultants, team teachers, and teacher aides. A major responsibility for creating an inclusive environment for students with disabilities falls on the general education teacher.

Perspective: Attempts to reform education will make little difference until reformers understand that schools must exist as much for teachers as for students. Schools will be successful in nurturing the intellectual, social, and moral development of children only to the extent that they also nurture such development of teachers. Special educators will approach problems successfully only if they use the same problem-solving strategies that they recommend for students. (Kauffman, 1993; Sarason & Doris, 1978)

A Whole School. Some inclusion books say special educators are the most important professionals involved in inclusion. Others will say the general education teachers are most important. Actually, it takes a whole school to work toward successful inclusion. Everyone involved in the education of students within a school needs to participate in the inclusion process.

Importance of Related Interagency Personnel to Implementation of Inclusion. Many agencies and organizations are essential to comprehensive planning for inclusion.

The role of students, parents, and parent leaders should be considered as educators engage the school and community in the inclusion initiative, and parents and parent leaders should be enlisted as advisors and planners. Parents should be included in planning activities. They are often opinion leaders in a school

Inclusion: A Role for Everyone		
Educational Needs	**Support Services Needs**	**Social, Physical, and Recreational Needs**
<ul><li>Student</li><li>General education teacher</li><li>Special education teacher</li><li>Parent or guardian</li></ul>	<ul><li>Social and family service personnel</li><li>Rehabilitation therapist</li><li>Counselor and case manager</li><li>Job coach</li><li>Job placement specialist</li><li>Work adjustment specialist</li><li>Occupational therapist</li><li>Physical therapist</li><li>Reading specialist</li><li>Speech/language therapist</li></ul>	<ul><li>Classmates</li><li>Physical education teachers</li><li>Sports coaches</li><li>Personal assistant</li><li>Extracurricular, activity, and school club leaders</li><li>Theater, chorus, and music program teachers</li></ul>

Other Community Members Who Are Needed To Support the Inclusion Initiative	
<ul><li>Parents and advocates</li><li>Educators and administrators</li><li>Related and support services personnel</li><li>Rehabilitation personnel</li><li>Adult and community-based services personnel</li><li>Public and private health services personnel</li><li>Post–secondary institution personnel</li><li>Employers, employment services, and private nonprofit agency personnel</li><li>Job training program personnel</li></ul>	<ul><li>Business-education liaisons</li><li>School board members and other community decision makers</li><li>Probation and parole workers</li><li>Police</li><li>Advocacy agency leaders</li><li>Recreation and leisure service providers</li><li>College and university personnel</li><li>Civic and religious group leaders</li><li>Local and state politicians</li><li>Social services personnel</li><li>Business-industry personnel</li></ul>

and community and sometimes the best "champions" for change or new initiatives—if they support the effort. Parent and advocacy organizations are an essential link between educational agencies and the community. They need to understand how the new initiative will benefit their children, the school, and future opportunities for their children. Parent groups may include school alumni, parent association leaders, par-

ent school board members, Parent-Teacher Association leaders, parent volunteers, and advocates.

The strongest champions for inclusion can emerge from any sector of the community, once the value and benefits of the initiative are communicated. It takes the whole school working together—believing in inclusion, working through inclusion decisions, and resolving inclusion problems—to create a successful process.

9. What Are the Benefits and Outcomes of Inclusion?

The benefits of inclusion far outweigh the difficulties for students with and without disabilities, for families, and for the community. The following chart summarizes the many benefits of inclusive classrooms for students, teachers, parents, and the wider community.

Benefits of Inclusion	
Benefits to Students with Disabilities	• Facilitates more appropriate social behavior because of higher expectations in the general education class • Fosters higher self-esteem as a result of direct and frequent interaction with nondisabled peers • Promotes higher sense of personal success from inclusion in the general education classroom • Improves ability to keep up with the everyday pace of instruction • Creates enjoyment of working with learning teams and being viewed as contributing members of the class • Improves ability to adapt to different teaching and learning styles • Provides opportunity to be evaluated according to the same criteria applied to all students • Promotes achievement at levels higher or at least as high as levels achieved in the self-contained classes • Heightens enjoyment of the social interaction in the larger classes • Provides for the development of an individualized education plan • Increases opportunity for personal decision making and setting of personal goals and plans that are realistic • Provides opportunities to participate in career/vocational and school-to-work transition activities with nondisabled peers • Offers a wider "circle of support" and social support system that includes nondisabled classmates • Provides opportunities to take risks and learn from successes and mistakes along with classmates • Improves quality of life through more satisfying and meaningful experiences • Offers a greater opportunity to complete Carnegie units required to receive a regular high school diploma • Provides opportunities to receive specialized support in the general education environment • Increases skills in self-determination and self-advocacy for youth with disabilities, through peer teams and learning groups

continues

Benefits to Nondisabled Peers	• Facilitates greater acceptance of students with disabilities in the classroom and learning teams • Promotes better understanding of the similarities and differences between students with or without disabilities • Facilitates learning that it is not always easy to identify classmates who have disabilities • Provides opportunities to be group team leaders • Offers the advantage of having an extra teacher or aide available to help them with the development of their own skills • Provides opportunities to tutor or guide a classmate who has a disability • Increases learning about the range of different types of disabilities and the abilities of such students to adapt and cope with general education classes and class work
Benefits to Schools and Teachers	• Improves school atmosphere supportive of diversity • Provides greater student awareness of each other and are less self-centered • Provides greater teacher awareness of the needs of students with disabilities • Provides teachers who are knowledgeable about individualization of education • Provides teachers who are able to apply specialized educational strategies to students who are not disabled but need extra help • Provides teachers who are learning more about support services available in the community for students and families
Benefits to Parents or Guardians of Students with Disabilities	• Provides parents with a broader support network through linkages with parents of nondisabled students • Involves parents as equal partners in the educational planning process • Links parents with teachers, counselors, and administrators • Includes parents in student exhibitions and demonstrations of student performance • Includes parents in the school-to-work transition planning process • Better prepares professionals to help parents strengthen personal decision making, goal setting, and self-advocacy in their children
Benefits to At-Risk and Dropout Youths with Disabilities	• Creates strategies to locate and motivate dropout students who have disabilities to return to school to complete their degrees and learn skills they need to live and work in their communities • Develops strategies to identify, recruit, train, and place youths with disabilities who have dropped out of school • Provides services to diverse students by development of integrated academic vocational-technical education that meets industry-based performance standards • Provides intensive support to students who return to school to complete their education • Creates innovative alternative performance assessments (exhibitions and demonstrations) of achievement and outcomes in vocational-technical areas • Promotes sharing of resources between inclusive schools and other community agencies for career-vocational education and work experiences for all students • Promotes development of business-education partnerships to enable educators to expand the learning environment to include both the school and community; to increase the relevance of education to adult life; and to establish bridges between schools and community resources to facilitate transition • Provides methods for early identification and assessment of at-risk youths and dropouts, in order to provide earlier intervention

continues

Impact on Teacher Knowledge and Local Knowledge Sharing	• Encourages teachers to demonstrate methods and strategies that promote cooperative learning among students with or without disabilities
	• Helps teachers understand the support needs of students in various transitions between classroom settings
	• Introduces general education teachers to the individual education planning process and the role of the student in that process
	• Helps teachers understand that the individual planning process requires that *learning* not be separated from ***deciding to learn*** and the expectation that students can and should envision and direct the planning for their own future
	• Produces products that can be shared with other local schools, such as:
	  1. teacher strategy manuals describing the implementation process
	  2. principal's records describing the planning process, problems, and solutions worked out
	  3. in-service training and orientation manuals that prepare new teachers and staff
	  4. handbooks for parent involvement in full inclusion
	  5. curriculum manuals describing adaptations and team collaboration
	  6. inclusion evaluation reports
	• Provides a "living laboratory" in which to experiment with and evaluate new assessment approaches and the IEP decision-making process and its impacts on students
	• Helps teachers learn and integrate strategies into their teaching that could be beneficial for all students, such as:
	  1. assessment methods and strategies, including student-developed portfolios and exhibitions
	  2. performance-based vocational assessment, including situational, center-based, community-training-based, and employment-based assessment strategies
	  3. a student-centered and student-directed educational planning process that promotes self-determination and decision making
	  4. implementation of the interdisciplinary team process
	  5. development of an ongoing assessment process
	  6. integration of technology into instruction
	  7. involvement of families as integral partners in the student's decision-making process

Benefits for the Marriage of Special and Regular Education	• Increases the number of students with disabilities who are appropriately placed into general education classes and can benefit from the regular curriculum • Includes students with disabilities and their needs in annual school goals and assessments of resource needs • Provides joint orientation and training to general and special educators • Promotes partnerships among schools and rehabilitation agencies • Increases the number of teachers in a district who are skilled in interdisciplinary planning, curriculum adaptations, and team consultation
Benefits for Student Assessment and Empowerment in the Learning Process	• Promotes student goal setting and cooperative learning • Encourages students to engage in self-evaluation of their own performance and progress • Promotes more alternative assessment strategies and more authentic assessment of student performance • Develops strategies that engage the student in self-assessment of his or her own performance and products • Encourages students and teachers to keep portfolios of student work and to use multiple forms of assessment • Builds on youths' natural attraction to applied work experiences and use of innovative technology

Benefits for Creating a Positive Climate for Learning	• Reinforces a holistic (whole-child) view of the student learner and his or her needs • Reinforces the holistic (whole-classroom) view of the teaching and learning environment in which student diversity is celebrated and built on to enrich the educational process • Creates an atmosphere conducive to successful curriculum integration across subject areas • Creates multimedia environments through use of hands-on activities, computers, and a variety of teaching strategies • Promotes cooperative learning in student teams • Shifts the role of teacher as isolated subject matter specialist to that of collaborator and promotes the formation of subject matter teams • Promotes regular (e.g., monthly) teacher in-service training and learning sessions • Allows for orientation of students to "the rules of engagement," such as making responsible choices, working cooperatively, seeking and giving help, setting goals, using computers and equipment correctly, and keeping records • Promotes advanced training for peers in team building and conflict resolution
Benefits for Cost Sharing among Schools and Community Agencies	• Promotes interagency collaboration for support services to children and youths • Stimulates sharing of resources among schools and support service agencies • Promotes collaboration among schools and social service agencies
Benefits to Businesses and Community Agencies	• Promotes innovative linkages with the business community to provide career-vocational and school-to-work transition services • Shifts the locus of vocational support services to real-world work environments • Transforms the role of the business and community agency partners from that of donors and philanthropists to active partner in the school restructuring and career-vocational education development process • Combines the resources of employers and community agencies in improving student outcomes through interagency linkages • Promotes teacher opportunities to update, upgrade, or maintain their skills or acquire more in-depth knowledge about the labor market, community industries and businesses, and community service agencies, as well as the needs and opportunities of the workplace • Provides educators with firsthand knowledge and experience of the expectations of the business community, with knowledge of effective curricula and methods of instruction based on workplace needs and experience, and with resources that better prepare them to guide students regarding their options and opportunities

continues

Benefits to Schools in Partnership with Local Colleges or Universities	• Promotes long-term partnerships among schools and universities that prepare general and special educators for area schools • Promotes long-term partnerships for in-service training between general and special education personnel • Provides resources for in-service training in the integration of academic and vocational-technical education and school restructuring • Promotes use of skilled student interns in inclusion efforts and goals • Provides teacher trainees with internship experiences directly related to the inclusion efforts of area schools and teachers • Promotes opportunities for teachers in training to participate in the development and evaluation of school inclusion initiatives • Improves the rate of employment for teachers in training in area schools • Strengthens the focus of university teacher training programs to respond to the needs of area schools

Note: This table was developed with material synthesized from the works of Janney et al., 1995; McCoy, 1995; Turnbull et al., 1995; Cornett, 1995; Kochhar, 1995; Dalheim, 1994; U.S. Office of Vocational and Adult Education, 1994; Bruno, Johnson, & Gillilard, 1994; Sherer, 1994; Turnbull, 1994; Fuchs & Fuchs, 1994; Leconte, 1994; Ysseldyke & Thurlaw, 1993; National Council on Disability, 1993; Council for Exceptional Children, 1993a, b; U.S. Department of Education, 1993a; Putnam, 1993; Evans, 1993; National Information Center for Children and Youth with Disabilities, 1993; Rusch, Destafano, Chadsey-Rusch, Phelps, & Szymanski, 1992; Sitlington, 1992; McLaughlin & Warren, 1992; Sailor, 1991; MacMillan, 1991; Wagner et al., 1991; West, 1991; Lipsky & Gardner, 1989; National Alliance of Business, 1987; Biklen, 1985.

II

Strategies for Implementing Inclusion

Part II is designed to help general and special education teachers and related professionals in their challenge to better serve special learners in inclusive settings. It emphasizes inclusion practices that work, practical strategies that can lead to successful inclusion at the classroom and school levels, and techniques for overcoming barriers to the process. This part also emphasizes teamwork and shared effort among all professionals concerned about the educational success of all students.

10. What Are the Major Strategies for Overcoming Barriers to Inclusion?

Implementing special education laws to serve students with disabilities has required schools to undergo rapid and complex change. Educators and policy makers agree that, since the passage of P.L. 94-142 in 1975, great gains have been made for students with disabilities in two areas: enrollment in home schools and access to mainstream classrooms. Nevertheless, much work remains to be done to improve the acceptance of students with disabilities in inclusive settings and to improve the overall quality of education provided.

Barriers to Inclusion. It is helpful to teachers who manage inclusive classrooms to understand that the success of inclusion can be affected by a variety of barriers related to the organizational structure and management of schools and classrooms and to the attitudes and knowledge of educators. This section presents some of the common problems and barriers to building inclusive education and ways to overcome them. Barriers to implementing inclusion can be clustered into three categories: *organizational, attitudinal, and knowledge barriers* (Kochhar & Erickson, 1993).

- **Organizational barriers:** barriers related to the differences in the way schools and classrooms are structured and managed, how they define their goals, and how they design instruction
- **Attitudinal barriers:** barriers related to the beliefs, motivations, and attitudes that different teachers

have about educating children and youths, accommodating students with special needs in general education classrooms, communicating with parents, and the community participation of students

• **Knowledge barriers:** barriers related to the differences in the knowledge and skills of various teachers about instructing students with special needs, providing support services, adapting curriculum and instruction, and structuring the classroom for optimal inclusion

These barriers have been determined on the basis of questions most often asked by teachers about including students in general education classrooms. Several strategies have been found to be effective in overcoming such barriers (Exhibit II–1).

Searching for children's strengths. Instead of concentrating on students' weaknesses, teachers need to identify the strengths that many low-achieving children possess and that many have used to compensate for their difficulties. Thus, instruction and curriculum modifications can be built around the existing strengths

and special skills of these children. For example, many children have well-developed kinesthetic abilities and may learn rapidly by doing, provided that they are taught through concrete learning experiences. Many may benefit from having information introduced through a variety of teaching media including oral, visual, and tactile methods. For this reason, teachers and educational administrators need to be able to determine the strengths and weaknesses of the children and to devise appropriate instructional strategies and modifications. Assessment information can then be used to determine appropriate instructional levels and to modify instruction. With relatively modest accommodations, many children with special educational needs can lead fully normal lives and, in some cases, surpass their peers (Lynch, 1995).

All students benefit when teachers work to improve the full participation for all children with potential to succeed in general education classrooms. As individual schools and as a nation, we can achieve equal opportunity in education and end discrimination in school programs and related activities. The barriers to inclusion discussed here can be overcome with careful planning.

Exhibit II–1 Barriers to Inclusion: Organizational Structure and Management, Attitudes, and Knowledge

Barrier 1: Lack of administrative commitment and support to implement inclusion—Many inclusion initiatives fail because there is a lack of strong commitment from administrators to provide teachers with the freedom and resources they need to revise their teaching strategies, modify curriculum and classroom organization, or form collaborative teams.	**Strategy to overcome barrier:** Educators should add the goal of inclusion in the general school goals related to improving the teaching and learning environment for all students. Most importantly, the goals should include the *outcomes* expected from the teachers and students as a result of the inclusion effort. Teachers should examine other schools' or teachers' goals and policies on inclusion to learn what degree of freedom teachers have to implement inclusion, what resources are being provided, and what goals are being expressed.
Barrier 2: Budget tightening threat to continuation of inclusion efforts—What help will teachers get for including very diverse students in their classrooms? Where will the money for extra technology or teacher assistants come from? As education and social services budgets tighten, the pressure can lead to disputes about the amount and kinds of resources that should be committed to achieve inclusive schools.	**Strategy to overcome barrier:** Efforts should be made to ensure that inclusion goals are built into the school's budget and planning process. Educators should serve on committees for planning and evaluating the success of inclusion. They should keep records on the resources (e.g., time and staff) needed to serve students with disabilities in the classroom, so that additional costs can be anticipated and requested for future years. Teachers should share resources through teacher teams and interdisciplinary collaboration.

continues

Exhibit II–1 continued

Barrier 3: Time and incentives for inclusion— Will teachers get extra pay for serving students with disabilities in general education classrooms, or will they have fewer students? Many teachers claim that they do not get a common planning time each day and often have to plan over lunch for the following day. The availability of classroom aides for planning time is becoming more limited. Without a common planning time, teachers spend many hours outside of contract time planning for and reflecting on the progress of the children in their classroom.	**Strategy to overcome barrier:** Many schools are experimenting with ways of building in more planning time for collaborating teacher teams, particularly for general education teachers serving students with disabilities. Substitute teachers or student interns are being relied on to help provide such planning time. Other strategies include using the shortened school day one day a week for teacher planning, providing early morning sessions, or using teacher in-service days. Schools are also experimenting with ways to provide incentives for teachers serving students with disabilities, including smaller class sizes, targeted resources, support for team teaching, and extra planning time.
Barrier 4: Classroom management concerns— Increased class size and teacher workloads have been found to be major concerns of teachers who teach students with disabilities in regular classes (National Education Association, 1994). The common objections to inclusion are lack of teachers' time, impact on other students, diminishing resources, inadequate support for teachers and students, lack of teacher training, and mixed administrative support. Other concerns are how inclusion is affecting learning environments and which children are being moved from segregated schools and classrooms into more integrated settings.	**Strategy to overcome barrier:** A thorough assessment of the school's readiness to implement inclusion should be conducted. Factors to be considered are interdisciplinary planning, physical environment, support services, educational accommodations, student assessment, administrative planning, commitment, teacher training, technical assistance, and parent involvement. In-service training in classroom management and use of resources, including generating new resources, is essential.
Barrier 5: Time-consuming requirements for developing the IEP, as well as for reporting and data collection— There has been a long-standing concern of teachers and administrators that the instructional time of teachers and the resources of the school are sacrificed in order to comply with heavy data collection and reporting requirements for students with disabilities.	**Strategy to overcome barrier:** Computer-based IEP software now enables teachers to develop individualized instructional programs easily and swiftly. Such software programs also make the review and revision process much easier. Team teaching involves at least two teachers in the process of creating IEPs, thus reducing the load for the individual teacher.

continues

Exhibit II–1 continued

Barrier 6: Funding and resource barriers—In the past, formulas for special education funding provided incentives for placing students into separate, more restrictive placements and therefore rewarded segregated services. Use of these funds to help students who are considered at risk of needing special education (prereferral interventions) has not been permitted. Thus, teachers who have special education aides or consulting teachers in a class have been unable to use these additional resources to help other students in the class who could benefit from the knowledge and strategies of the consulting teacher.

Strategy to overcome barrier: Special education law is now undergoing change to allow the use of special education resources and equipment to benefit all students in a classroom, not just the student(s) with disabilities. Revisions to the IDEA include more discretion on the part of schools and teachers to experiment with ways to improve the teaching and learning environments for individuals with disabilities in inclusive classrooms. Special education funds can be used to benefit students with disabilities through whole-school improvement efforts, which include reducing barriers to inclusion and to team teacher coordination. Teacher teams should agree early in a semester on the goals they are working toward for the students with disabilities and on how resources will be shared. Regular meetings of teachers to discuss the coordination effort usually leads to continuous and constructive troubleshooting of most problems that arise.

Barrier 7: Legislative shifts, complex regulations, and organization priorities—For years, many local school districts have had problems complying with complex special education requirements, particularly the requirement for due process, ensuring least restrictive environment, and developing students' IEPs. Now, school reform and improvement initiatives are changing the way teachers' and students' performance is measured and what is expected from them. Yet, in many of these initiatives, it remains unclear how students with disabilities are expected to be included.

Strategy to overcome barrier: Teachers should learn and help to educate others about changes in special education and elementary and secondary education laws and what these changes mean for teachers' roles and expectations. They should ask the principal or coordinating teacher to gather resources about changes in laws and state and local policies. Teachers should invite speakers for in-service days to discuss these changes and what they mean for teachers' roles and responsibilities.

Barrier 8: Confusion about the relationship between section 504* and the IDEA—The relationship between section 504 requirements and IDEA requirements remains confusing to most teachers and administrators. The section 504 standard of "appropriate education" requires that schools meet the educational needs of students with disabilities *as adequately* as they meet the needs of nondisabled students (comparability test) and that all procedural requirements be met. However, most educational agencies do not have a clear standard of what constitutes an appropriate education for students without disabilities.

Strategy to overcome barrier: The relationship between section 504 and the IDEA is linked to address two central issues related to disability and protection against discrimination.
1. There is a population of persons with disabilities who are not eligible for special education under IDEA but who still require protection against discrimination because of a disability as defined under section 504.
2. There is an obligation to provide services (special education, evaluation, regular education, and related services) regardless of eligibility for special education under the IDEA.

continues

Exhibit II–1 continued

	The 1995 amendments to the IDEA address the following questions: • Does FAPE and access to a comparable education (education reasonably designed to confer benefit) mean the same thing under the IDEA as it does under section 504? • Should special education and related services be provided for students with disabilities who are not eligible under the IDEA? • Will discipline practices change if a different or heightened standard for equal treatment is applied? Policy decisions on the relationship between section 504 and the IDEA could be supported by a synthesis of studies related to judicial decisions on court cases and to their implications.
Barrier 9: Problems with mediation and due process provisions in the IDEA—Until recently, there has been little attention paid to improving due process procedures for resolving disputes related to special education placement. The adversarial relationships among parents, teachers, and school officials are often made worse because there are few alternatives to due process court proceedings. Educators are asking whether some form of mediation should be available to parents and teachers.	**Strategy to overcome barrier:** Amendments to the IDEA (1995) are likely to cross-reference a section of the ADA: "Where appropriate and to the extent authorized by law, the use of alternative means of disputes resolution, including settlement negotiations, conciliation, facilitation, mediation, fact-finding, minitrials, and arbitration, is encouraged to resolve disputes arising under this Act."
Barrier 10: Need to clarify the shared responsibility for inclusion by other community agencies—In many school districts, there are strong interagency agreements among schools and community agencies for sharing the responsibility and resources to support students with disabilities in inclusive schools. When interagency agreements are weak or nonexistent, the schools assume the primary responsibility for the cost of related and transition services.	**Strategy to overcome barrier:** Teachers should find out whether their school or district has a formal interagency agreement with outside agencies to provide services such as rehabilitation, social services and mental health, juvenile justice, family, legal, public health, employment, and speech and hearing services to students with disabilities and their families. In-service days could be used to bring local teachers together with professionals from other agencies to discuss linkages and relationships and strategies for sharing resources.

continues

Exhibit II–1 continued

Barrier 11: Barriers to participation in inclusive schools and classes (lack of transportation, child care, and service coordination)—There are often many barriers for students who are placed into some schools or general education classrooms, particularly for those who have been in special schools or classes. These barriers can include lack of transportation, before and after school care, assistance with accessing counseling and support services, and family linkages and support.	**Strategy to overcome barrier:** Many schools are retrofitting more school buses so that students with physical disabilities have greater access. Schools are also adapting arrangements for care before and after school care to include students with disabilities. Some schools are restructuring teacher roles so that each student with a disability is assigned a teacher-advocate who is responsible for knowing the student and his or her needs and for determining additional service needs. Teacher-advocates often work closely with school social workers and psychologists to identify and link the student and/or family with needed services in the community.
Barrier 12: Problems in linking assessments to educational services—There are concerns that special education law has resulted in (1) an emphasis on assessing students in order to label them with specific disabilities, (2) use of assessments that may not be reliable or that may be culturally biased, and (3) assessment practices that fail to assist teachers to determine appropriate instruction and support services in the classroom. Labels only serve to stigmatize students. There is a need to strengthen the definition of assessment and its purposes, as well as the range of assessment alternatives permitted in schools.	**Strategy to overcome barrier:** Schools that use assessment effectively use it not only to establish the existence of a disability or condition, but also in very useful and functional ways: • to understand the specific nature of the condition and how it affects the individual's development and physical condition • to understand how the disability affects the learning process and potential of the individual • to identify the specific educational or support services that are needed Labeling has been criticized by teachers as stigmatizing, but there are many ways that the use of labeling can be modified so that its benefits are preserved and its negative effects minimized.
Barrier 13: Dual system of general and special education—In the 1970s, the development of specialized educational services for children with disabilities created two systems of education that have been largely disconnected from each other. This dual system continues to create organizational problems and to provide barriers to the integration of special educational services within the general education framework. Special and general education have traditionally had different student target groups and different instructional purposes; this has made collaboration and shared goal setting for inclusion more difficult.	**Strategy to overcome barrier:** Educators should become involved in promoting additional training for all teachers, in blending special education services in general education classrooms, in developing team teaching strategies, and in establishing teacher-advocate and peer-advocate arrangements to support students with disabilities. They should be supported in learning all they can about instructional strategies such as student cooperative learning and team approaches.

continues

Exhibit II–1 continued

Barrier 14: Attitudes and misconceptions about students with disabilities—Many teachers harbor attitudes about students with disabilities that prevent their commitment to inclusion. Examples of these beliefs are

- Students with disabilities always become distracted in a class with so many other students.
- When completing tests and assignments, these students always need additional time.
- Such students have difficulty remembering to complete homework assignments.
- Such students always need more help in taking notes and maintaining notebooks.

Strategy to overcome barrier: These attitudes may be partially true, but they are also partially true for other students in most general education classrooms. Teachers who share their success stories about serving students with disabilities say that the strategies they work out for special students usually benefit other students. For example, teachers help some students to reduce distraction by changing physical location in the class. They offer more time to complete tests and assignments and provide extra structure and reminders to help students complete homework assignments and longer-term projects. They also provide extra help or team students to facilitate note taking and maintaining notebooks.

Barrier 15: Staff turnover and reorganization—Among the most severe barriers to inclusion are turnover among classroom teachers and aides and changes in school leadership. Inclusion efforts are most successful when there are school and community "champions" to lead the effort and promote collaboration and new ideas. For example, the loss of a respected teacher champion for inclusion, who has fought to strengthen the effort in a time of economic constraint, can result in the loss of progress.

Strategy to overcome barrier: Administrators should examine the staff recruitment, orientation, and training efforts. Do they include team-building strategies, development of cooperative attitudes, and communication among teachers and administrators? Administrators should examine how well teachers document their strategies and approaches for assisting and supporting incoming staff. Incentives should be provided to keep teachers motivated and appreciated; small expressions of support make a significant difference.

Barrier 16: Uncertainty about the effects of inclusion on students without disabilities—Many teachers are concerned about whether there will be negative effects of inclusion on regular students. Teachers want to know how they can change the attitudes of nondisabled peers and change their acceptance of classmates with disabilities. Some have had bad experiences in the past in other schools in which inclusion was poorly implemented.

Strategy to overcome barrier: Research on inclusion has found that students who are appropriately placed into inclusive classrooms are more successful when their nondisabled peers are accepting and supportive. Many schools are establishing peer-mentor relationships to educate nondisabled peers and to help build relationships that provide emotional and social support. The peer-mentor provides support and encouragement and "enables" the student with a disability to solve problems, make decisions, and adjust to the classroom and new expectations. Peer-mentors can also help students with disabilities prepare for tests and project demonstrations and in some schools they are provided with special training to prepare them to understand the needs of students with disabilities.

continues

Exhibit II–1 continued

Barrier 17: Parent orientation, participation, and support—Teachers are often concerned about whether parents will be involved with and supportive of their child's education in a way that is supportive of the placement. They are unclear about the rules regarding parental access to student records and the tape recording of IEP meetings. There are additional concerns about the requirements for parent notification of meetings and of changes in the student's curriculum or IEP.

Strategy to overcome barrier: Parents and guardians play a crucial role in the success of inclusion. Each parent is responsible for the educational progress of the child and for protecting rights to education and support services under the IDEA. By diminishing parental access to information, we diminish the power of parents to support their child's educational programs and the goals of inclusion. Teachers in inclusive schools should communicate regularly with parents, not only about placement, but also about specific curriculum requirements and activities. In many schools, parents are invited to orientation sessions to introduce the goals and objectives of the school and the inclusive class. Parents are invited to attend portfolio reviews and demonstration and exhibition sessions during the year to observe the skills gained by the students. Parents may be honored at these events for their participation and support of their sons or daughters and of the school as a whole.

Barrier 18: Political pressures from the community—As economic pressures force schools to economize, inclusion efforts can be vulnerable to political pressure inside and outside the school. They can be torn by competing pressures of school personnel and community leaders to change directions and to reduce the commitment to inclusion. These forces can cause great conflicts among teachers and school officials, parents, and students.

Strategy to overcome barrier: Teachers can work with the PTA and school officials to demonstrate to the parents and to the wider community how inclusion is working and producing results. Clear communication with the community about the school's goals for inclusion is helpful in battling detractors and naysayers.

Barrier 19: Territorialism—Teachers sometimes feel threatened that their "territory" is being encroached upon and that they will be asked to change the traditional ways of doing things in their classes. Most teachers know that inclusion requires new teaching techniques, new team teacher relationships, and new attitudes.

Strategy to overcome barrier: Veteran teachers can informally help to orient new teachers and aides about the school's commitment to inclusion. They can challenge new teachers and staff to accept change in their roles, in traditional teaching practices, and in attitudes.

Barrier 20: Lack of understanding between special education and general education teachers about their goals and missions—Inclusion is not likely to be successful if special education and general education teachers do not understand each other and the differences in their traditional missions and if they fail to recognize each others' complementary strengths.

Strategy to overcome barrier: As a first step toward collaboration, teachers who are forming teams should share their perceptions and understanding of each other's roles. Teacher orientation and inservice sessions can also be devoted to promoting better understanding among general education teachers, special education teachers, and support service personnel.

continues

Exhibit II–1 continued

Barrier 21: Lack of knowledge about whether and how inclusion programs work—Teachers often have little access to information about the benefits, successful strategies, and results of inclusion. They are often unclear about whether they will need to vary their expectations for students with disabilities or assess them differently.

Strategy to overcome barrier: Teacher in-service days can be used to share and learn new information about inclusive classrooms, strategies, and information about what has been learned in other local areas and states. Local college and university personnel can help to provide such information. Teacher seminars have been effective in many schools to bring together teachers of inclusive classrooms within a school or among several schools to share, discuss, and demonstrate methods and techniques that can be used in their classrooms.

Barrier 22: Lack of knowledge about the continuum of placements—Teachers are often unclear about the reasons for placement of certain students into their classrooms. They are often not told in advance, nor given much information about the students before they arrive. They are often unaware about special requirements such as medical attention or assistive devices or about behavioral problems. This lack of information and preparation by the teacher contributes to poor outcomes of inclusion.

Strategy to overcome barrier: Teachers should be provided with in-service training on the continuum of placements and on the decision-making process for placing students into general education classes. They should also work to establish specific school policies that ensure adequate information about new students and the special educational accommodations they might need. School policies should also have procedures for troubleshooting or constructively solving problems with placements that require additional support or intervention. Teachers should also be alert to the kinds of "problem placements" that require special preparation or reconsideration, such as students with severe emotional or behavioral problems who are a danger to themselves or others, or those with complex medical needs who do not have adequate personal assistance or expert care.

Barrier 23: Lack of knowledge about teaching strategies for inclusive classrooms—Teachers often ask: How do I teach these students when my teacher education program did not prepare me to teach children with diverse abilities? Will I have to short-change my other students? Are there reasonable adaptations I can make? Will I need more training?

Strategy to overcome barrier: General education teachers should be provided with in-service training in new teaching strategies for inclusion into general education classes. Teacher in-service days and teacher seminars are proving to be effective in many schools to bring together inclusive teachers from several schools to share, discuss, and demonstrate innovative methods and techniques they use in their classrooms. Again, local college and university personnel can be useful in teaching and providing demonstrations of such strategies.

continues

Exhibit II–1 continued

Barrier 24: Lack of knowledge about individualized educational programming—General education teachers often have not been provided with training in individualized educational programming. They may view it as too cumbersome and difficult, or they may not understand its essential purpose for students with disabilities.

Strategy to overcome barrier: General education teachers should be provided with orientation and inservice training in developing and evaluating for students in inclusive classes. Teacher planning time is essential for developing IEP programs that are understood by all teachers involved with the special student. For team teachers, it is very important that each teacher agrees on the educational goals and expectations. Again, local college and university personnel can be helpful in teaching and providing information about IEP planning and collaborative development.

Note: IEP, individual education plan
Section 504, IDEA, Individuals with Disabilities Education Act
FAPE, Free and Appropriate Education
ADA, Americans with Disabilities Act
PTA, Parent-Teacher Association

Source: Synthesized from materials from McCoy, 1995; Turnbull et al., 1995; National Education Association, 1994; National Council on Disability, 1994; U.S. Department of Education, 1993; U.S. General Accounting Office, 1994a; National Center on Education Outcomes, 1993; Putnam, 1993; Searle, Ferguson, & Biklen, 1985.

*Section 504 of the Rehabilitation Act: "No otherwise qualified individual with disabilities . . . shall solely by reason of his disability, be excluded from the participation in, be denied the benefits of, or be subjected to discrimination under any program or activity receiving Federal financial assistance."

11. What Is the Continuum of Placement Options?

Placement of Students in Segregated Settings. Several special education studies reveal a large variation among states in the number of students with disabilities who are educated in separate classes or in separate facilities. For example, one state educates about 90 percent of its students who have mental retardation in separate classes, while another state educates only 27 percent in separate classes. One state places over 49 percent of its students with mental retardation in separate public schools, while at least three states place no students with mental retardation into separate public schools (Sawyer, McLaughlin, & Winglee, 1992).

More Than Physical Placement. Inclusion has come to be synonymous with a change in physical placement of a student with a disability from one environment to another that is less restrictive and allows closer integration with nondisabled peers. But the concept of inclusion involves an idea with much greater

breadth than that of shifting physical environments. Inclusion is founded on two broad beliefs:

1. All children have a right to basic physical access to community schools and public facilities.
2. For inclusion to succeed, society and the educational system must undergo comprehensive change.

The second belief expresses a vision of a world in which integration and acceptance of the student and his or her differences is broadly accepted and infused into all school programs and activities. The first goal, physical access, has been much more easily accomplished. *The second goal remains elusive.*

A Continuum of Inclusion Models. Inclusion can take many forms and can be achieved in a variety of ways. There is no one specific way to implement inclusion. Inclusive schools are encouraged to build programs around individual student needs, rather than try to force-fit students into existing programs (Dover, 1994). Dover described several models that represent a continuum of placement options available to schools.

- **Self-contained model**—The student stays in a special education classroom or resource room for 100 percent of the school day.
- **Mainstreaming model**—The student takes part in activities in the regular class as long as he or she demonstrates an acceptable level of performance and behavior.
- **Nonacademic model**—The student participates in regular class activities in the areas of art, music, and physical education.
- **Pull out (resource) model**—Special education staff provide instruction and support to the student on a one-to-one basis outside the regular classroom, as needed.
- **Home class model**—The student participates in regular classroom opening and closing activities.
- **Social mainstreaming model**—The student is included during regular classroom instruction to provide him or her with appropriate exposure to nondisabled peers. The student is not required to complete instructional assignments.
- **Supported instruction model**—Special education staff provide support services within the regular classroom instruction.
- **Collaborative model**—Special education and general education staff work together and problem solve to meet the student's needs.
- **Full-inclusion model**—The student is placed in a regular classroom 100 percent of the day. The special education staff provide consultative support to the teacher.

No Uniform Solutions. Most school districts use a variety of the models like the ones described by Dover. Several of these models can be implemented within a single school district. There is no one "right model," because each school has its own unique needs and student populations. There is, however, one common principle that inclusion implementors do need to share—the imperative *to keep the focus on the student's individual needs, not on the convenience of the model. It is essential that inclusion decisions are made on the basis of what is most appropriate for ensuring the educational success of the student.* This principle assumes that there must be choices and options, rather than uniform "solutions," for the students, as appropriate placement decisions are made.

U.S. Department of Education Definition. The U.S. Department of Education collects data from the states on the types of placements provided to students with disabilities in public and private schools. The Department of Education *does not provide rules or prescriptions* for which placement options are appropriate for students with different disabilities. These decisions are left to the discretion of the state and local educational agencies. The U.S. Department of Education (1993), therefore, has permitted wide experimentation and demonstration of the following options in the field.*

- *Regular class*—includes students who receive the majority of their education program in the general education classroom and receive special education and related services outside the regular classroom for *less than* 21 percent of the school day. This option includes children placed in a regular class and receiving special education within the regular class, as well as children placed in a regular class and receiving special education outside the regular class. (Of all students with disabilities in the United States, 33.7 percent were served in this type of class.)
- *Resource room*—includes students who receive special education and related services *outside* the regular classroom for at least 21 percent but not more that 60 percent of the school day. This placement option may include students placed in resource rooms, with part-time instruction in the regular class. According to the U.S. Department of Education Office of Special Education Programs (1993), 34.6 percent of students with disabilities in the United States are served in this placement option.
- *Separate class*—includes students who receive special education and related services outside the regular classroom for more than 60 percent of the school day. Students may be placed in self-contained special classrooms full time or with part-time instruction in regular classes. These students are on the regular school campus. Of all students with disabilities in the United States, 25.2 percent are served in this option.
- *Separate school*—includes students who receive special education and related services for more than 50 percent of the school day in separate day schools for students with disabilities. Of all students with disabilities in the United States, 4.9 percent are served in this option.

---

*Fifteenth Annual Report to Congress on the Implementation of the Individuals with Disabilities Education Act, 1993a, pp. 15–16.

- *Residential facility*—includes students who receive education in a public or private residential facility at public expense for more than 50 percent of the school day. Of all students with disabilities in the United States, .08 percent are served in this option.
- *Homebound/hospital environment*—includes students receiving special education in hospital or homebound programs. Of all students with disabilities in the United States, .07 percent are served in this option.

The number of students with disabilities being placed into regular classrooms is increasing, according to U.S. Department of Education data. The following illustration provides some facts about placement patterns across the United States.

Facts about Placement of Students with Disabilities in the United States

1. Younger elementary age students with disabilities are more likely to be placed into the least restrictive settings because they are more easily accommodated. The elementary school curriculum may pose fewer significant challenges to these children than does the junior high or high school curriculum to youths with disabilities.

2. Students with less severe disabilities, such as learning disabilities or speech and language impairments, are served in less restrictive settings (e.g., regular class or resource room).

3. Students with more severe disabilities, such as multiple disabilities, deafness and blindness, or severe mental retardation, are served in more restrictive settings.

4. Eighty-four percent of students with orthopedic impairments and other health impairments receive their education in a regular class, resource room, or separate class. They are also more likely to receive services in homebound and hospital settings.

Source: Fifteenth Annual Report to Congress on the Implementation of the Individuals with Disabilities Education Act, 1993, p. 18.

Assessment procedures to determine if a student is eligible for special education services are specified in the Individuals with Disabilities Education Act (IDEA; P.L. 101-476). However, *the legislation does not define a specific continuum of placements. Instead, it provides the guiding principle of least restrictive environment and conveys a clear preference that **all** students should be included in general education classes and activities to the **maximum extent possible** while still obtaining an educational benefit for the student.*

Student Needs Central to Placement. The individual needs of each student should take center stage in each placement decision. No single and uniform test or procedure can determine placement for all students. Evaluation and placement decisions are made by a multidisciplinary team who seriously contemplate the strengths and individual needs of each student. The placement of a child must be reviewed at least annually to determine if the placement has been successful and is meeting the educational and developmental needs of the student. Determining the needs of the student should lead a multidisciplinary team to a placement decision that is strictly *student centered*. Student-centered decisions are based on:

- informal and formal assessments
- understanding of the student's disability in the educational environment
- effect of the disability on learning
- curriculum and instructional modifications that result in the student's progress and continued benefits from the placement.

12. How Are Student Needs for Instruction in the Inclusive Classroom Assessed?

Individuals needs assessment is defined as the process of gathering and interpreting information about the education, health, or human service needs of individuals in the school and using this information to establish priorities for support services, the appropriate placement option, and individual goals and objectives. The student's needs are documented in the individual educational plan (IEP).

Diagnosis is a more specific term that refers to the process of identifying the presence of an illness, disease, impairment, or condition by using examinations, tests, and assessment instruments. One purpose of a diagnosis is to classify the condition or place it into a specific category, such as learning disability, developmental disability, visual disability, cognitive disability, neurological disorder, hearing impairment, or traumatic brain injury. The diagnosis also serves other functions, such as establishing eligibility for particular types of service, such as early intervention, special education, or health or mental health services.

Definition of Assessment. In the regulations for the Individuals with Disabilities Education Act (IDEA), assessment is defined under Section 300.16, Related Services. These services include supportive services required to assist a child with a disability to benefit from special education, including early assessment of disabilities in children, and medical and psychological services for diagnostic or evaluation purposes, such as

- medical services provided by a licensed physician to determine a child's medically-related disability that results in the child's need for special education and related services
- psychological services including psychological and educational testing
- other assessment procedures including interpreting information about child behavior and conditions related to learning and classroom participation
- consultation with other staff members in planning school programs to meet the special needs of children as indicated by psychological tests, interviews, and behavior evaluations

- planning and managing a program of psychological services including psychological counseling for children and parents
- diagnosing and appraising hearing loss and implications for learning
- diagnosing and appraising specific speech and language impairments and implications for learning
- assessment of vocational educational needs, employment preparation, and school-to-work transition service needs
- assessing the child's need for counseling, social work services, and school and community resources to enable the child to learn as effectively as possible in his or her educational program.

The School-To-Work Opportunities Act (P.L. 103-239, 1993) also defines student assessment for educational purposes. It requires regularly scheduled assessments and evaluations that involve ongoing consultations, interpretation, and problem solving with students to identify academic strengths, weaknesses, and progress. It also requires workplace knowledge and skills, goals, and needs for additional learning opportunities to master core academic and vocational skills. The act requires each state and local school district to:

- describe the performance standards that it intends to meet
- describe the manner in which the state or local district will specify measures of learning and competency gains in both academic achievement and vocational skills that are unbiased to special populations
- describe the manner in which the state or local district will assess the needs of students
- develop an adequate plan to provide supplementary or support services to enable all students to participate in school-to-work transition programs.

Source: Data Research Inc. 1994. Statutes, Regulations and Case Law Protecting Individuals with Disabilities, Rosemont, MT; 34 CFR Part 300, Section 300.16.

Factors Affecting Student Performance and Assessment. It is also important to be aware of the many other factors in the student's environment that can affect general performance and level of functioning. Exhibit II–2 provides some examples of these needs of children and youth that can interact with each other to create greater challenges to learning and growth.

Needs assessment at any level should not be a one-time event for the student; it should be an ongoing process that extends throughout the student's tenure in school.

Interaction of Factors Affecting Individual Achievement. It is also important to understand the interaction among the many factors in the student's environment that can affect developmental or educational progress. For example, a student who needs academic tutoring but who is also troubled by alcohol abuse may not necessarily improve when given academic help. He or she may also need other support services such as counseling and substance abuse treatment. Many other social, environmental, and developmental factors interact with academic needs to produce a child who is at risk for failing in the regular educational environment.

Changing Needs of Students. The needs of students change over time, so needs assessments must be conducted periodically. (The IDEA requires reassessment of the disability every three years.) As students' needs change, so must the goals and priorities of the classroom support services and the goals in the IEP. Ongoing needs assessments can help the teachers to remain alert to the adjustments they need to make for the student.

Assessing Needs at the Individual Level. Each teacher who enters a collaborative relationship might define student educational priorities differently. So how does an interdisciplinary team of professionals reconcile their different viewpoints and determine a "common mission" or set of goals for the student and for the classroom environment into which he or she is placed? What strategies are needed to form an effective working relationship that can assist the student to make genuine progress?

The Interdisciplinary Team. The interdisciplinary team is defined as a group of professionals, including a special education teacher working in collaboration with general education teachers, counselors, and sup-

Exhibit II–2 Needs of Students in Inclusive Classrooms and Education and Support To Meet Needs

Need	Education and Support
Developmental and Functional	Functional training and training in independent living skills; training for travel; leisure skills training; training in sexuality and family life skills, survival skills, money management skills, and family relationships
Physical, Health, and Nutritional	Medical services; drug treatments; physician care; surgical procedures; training in hygiene and nutrition; personal attendant services; assistive technology, medical devices, and prosthetics; special diets; family nutrition education; neurological, medical, and health assessments
Cognitive and Educational	Special education; remedial education; assistive technology including speech and hearing aids; training in a second language; enrichment services; in-home teaching; educational consultation; guidance services; school-to-work transition support services; academic and vocational assessments
Social, Psychological, and Mental Health	Mental health services; psychological services; behavior management services; crisis management and support; psychological assessments; individual and family counseling
Social Services	Social services; juvenile and parole services; correctional education; legal services; advocacy services; residential planning services; assistance in decisions regarding guardianship and health insurance

port services personnel in designing IEPs for students with special needs. The interdisciplinary team would perform the following assessment functions:

- Review school records, medical records, vocational evaluation and rehabilitation information, social and behavioral information, and other information that would be pertinent to a placement decision.
- Make referrals for additional assessments if necessary.
- Consider the placement options within the schools, and make appropriate recommendations for placement.

Negotiation is sometimes required among the professionals and parents as they discuss the appropriate placement. In some instances, a trial period in the classroom may be needed to allow the interdisciplinary team to observe the student in the less restrictive setting. The duration of this trial period must be adequate (at least one month) in order to permit a full range of observations. During this critical period, the interdisciplinary team must be as supportive as possible to the student and the teacher or teacher team, in order to provide every opportunity to adjust to and benefit from the inclusive classroom environment. Technical assistance to the general education teacher or team may be required during this period.

Deciding on Priorities. In thinking about *what* needs should be addressed by an interdisciplinary team, two assumptions may be helpful.

- **Assumption 1**—The primary focus for an interdisciplinary team should be on addressing the priority needs of students so that they can achieve greater levels of functioning or achievement in the range of functional domains (e.g., physical health, academic and vocational achievement, or social competence).
- **Assumption 2**—The interdisciplinary team should focus on *how* it can better coordinate the supportive and school-linked services to children, youths, and families so that they can achieve greater goals or so that their lives can be improved.

Defining Individual Goals. An important step for the interdisciplinary team is to determine *the appropriate new levels of achievement for students placed in general education classrooms.* Once new goals are established, the student's current level of performance can be compared with the future target goals. The gap between what the student can do now and what he or she is expected to be able to do in the new classroom is the basis for determining the priority needs of the student. The "gap" is the difference between the current conditions and the future goal for the individual. For example, Johnny is a sixth grader who reads at a fifth grade level but needs to achieve a seventh grade level to enter the mathematics-science program at the middle school. Once this gap is determined, the interdisciplinary team can decide what classroom accommodations and support services will be needed. Thus, the four questions to ask in planning a student needs assessment are:

1. What new goals will be set in the functional domains, such as academic, vocational, social, and physical areas?
2. What is the current level of performance for the student? What are the gaps between present functioning and future target goals?
3. What are the needs of the student and the family, in order to close the performance gaps?
4. How can the interdisciplinary team be supportive of the student and family and help to close these performance gaps?

Assessment Activities To Support Placement Decisions. A student needs assessment should focus on *the student's current level of skills, functioning, or condition, as well as his or her highest level of functioning before a more inclusive placement was sought.* The appropriate placement, classroom accommodations, and support services can be established for the student on the basis of an assessment of individual needs. Assessment activities for the *individual student for purposes of placement decisions* include:

- conducting comprehensive assessments of the strengths and the development needs of the student in a variety of functional domains
- reviewing assessments and renewing them on a periodic basis
- communicating and interpreting assessment information in terms of what the diagnostic information means to the teachers who will teach the student
- adapting assessment tools for individuals with disabilities and eliminating cultural bias*

*According to special education law (IDEA, 1990), testing and evaluation materials and procedures used for the purposes of evaluation and placement of children with disabilities must be selected and administered in a manner that is not racially or culturally discriminatory. Such materials or procedures must be provided and administered in the child's native language or mode of communication.

- documenting assessment and diagnostic information in the individualized educational plan
- making specific recommendations for educational placement, additional assessment and diagnostic needs, curriculum modifications, classroom adaptations, social skills training, supportive services, or vocational-technical skills training, based on assessment information in the relevant functional domains.

Establishing New Goals and Expectations. An important step for inclusion planners and teachers is to determine *the new goals or expectations for students being transferred into more inclusive settings.* What is the status of factors such as disabling conditions, health status, level of functioning, and skill levels at the time the student enters the school or new class? What changes or outcomes can be reasonably expected within one year or less if the support services, accommodations, and adaptations are provided? Once the goals are established, the gaps in performance can be determined by comparing the student's present level of functioning with a level expected in the future.

Goal Posts and Performance Gaps. Once an accurate assessment of priority student needs has been conducted, the interdisciplinary team can consider more specific target goals for the student. Goals for students must be expressed in terms of specific outcomes for academic performance, social and behavioral skills, or physical status. Only then can it be determined what "distance" students have to go to achieve increased levels of education, functioning, or health. That distance (gap) helps to define the needs of the student and the appropriate strategies for assisting the student to achieve greater achievement or progress. Assessment of the current status of students requires two additional pieces of information:

1. baseline information on students (status at the time of placement into the new classroom or school) against which to compare the current status
2. clearly defined "goal posts" for an expected level of progress or achievement in the future.

The IEP team establishes performance standards or target goals (goal posts) for student progress and achievement. The gap between current status and future target goals can be measured once there is reliable information on the levels of skills and functioning at the time he or she enters the classroom (Kochhar & Erickson, 1993). The elements of a comprehensive student assessment are described in Exhibit II–3.

Assessment To Promote Self-Determination. In the responsive classroom and school, educators hold as a highest principle the belief in options and choices for students and the freedom to consider the life paths that they will take. Students are encouraged to be engaged in the process of *self-determination*, a personal decision-making process that helps them to connect present educational experiences with future visions and goals. As part of the developmental process, these decisions must be guided by accurate and comprehensive assessment information about the student. Such assessment should encompass three domains: individual attributes, current and potential environments, and the comparability or interaction between the two (Leconte, 1994). Therefore, in order to provide appropriate education, comprehensive assessments of the educational needs of students being placed into general education classrooms must consider the strengths and needs of the student, as well as the needs of the teacher and classroom environment.

Prioritizing Student Needs at the School Level. Many other social, environmental, and developmental factors interact with academic needs to place a child at risk for failing in the regular educational environment. When there are several groups of students competing for additional resources and support services in the educational environment, how does a school establish priorities for addressing these needs? Here are a few principles that can help to guide the inclusion planning team's decision about students' needs that should take top priority for inclusion.

Exhibit II–3 Elements of a Comprehensive Student Assessment

Type of Disability	• Assessment and diagnosis of the specific disability for the purposes of determining (1) the student's needs for special education and related services and (2) his or her ability to benefit from general educational programming, adapted educational programming, and supportive services
Ability to Perform Independent Living Activities	• Self-help skills (e.g., dressing, bathing, and cleaning) • Maintenance of home or personal space • Basic safety and self-protective skills (e.g., locking doors, turning off stove, and knowledge of emergency numbers) • Meal preparation
Management of Personal Health	• Personal hygiene, nutrition, and eating habits • Appropriate use of medications • Routine visits for health, vision, and dental care • Cooperation with ongoing medical treatment • Contact of physician in emergency
Social Supports and Social Functioning	• Relationships with family, siblings, and others • Marital status and number of children • Presence of other children in the home who are also in need of services • Presence of other adults who are cared for in the home • Social skills and peer relationships • Sexual behavior and functioning • Record of antisocial activities or problems (e.g., criminal record) • Leisure and recreational activities
Financial Resources and Management	• Personal income and additional sources • Eligibility for public support (e.g., SSI/SSDI, food stamps, subsidized housing, and/or Medicaid) • Personal financial management skills • Financial health
Educational Placement and Academic Skills	• Current school placement and grade level • Academic level and deficits • School attendance patterns and record • Extracurricular activities • School performance and grades • Diplomas or certificates
Vocational and Technical Skills	• Employment history and patterns of performance • Vocational education or job training program participation • Vocational/technical skills gained • Job skill certificates or occupational licenses obtained • Work behaviors and readiness
History and Current Services	• Previous services • Experience with previous services • Services in use currently

Note: SSI, Social Security Income; SSDI, Social Security Disability Income

---

Determining Priority Needs for Additional Resources and Support Services at the School Level

The following principles may be useful in setting priorities for addressing student needs:

1. **Priority based on individual student needs**—Consider the assessment and diagnostic information on each student in order to determine what specific educational strategies are needed in the general education classroom.

2. **Priority based on the size of the student population in need**—Consider the largest at-risk group or groups in the school (e.g., individuals with limited English proficiency, individuals with emotional disabilities, learning disabilities, physical disabilities, or communication disorders).

3. **Priority based on past resources**—Consider the relative help given to at-risk students with disabilities in the past. For example, perhaps a lot of resources have already been provided to help students with mental retardation, and now there is a need to begin to help children with learning disabilities who have not received adequate assistance.

4. **Priority based on seriousness of the need**—Consider the relative seriousness of the problems of different student groups. Some problems may be more serious than others or may represent threats to other children (e.g., violent behavior, substance abuse, conduct disorders).

5. **Priority based on past exclusion of students**—Consider the special needs of individuals who have been excluded in the past from school classrooms and related activities. (For example, until recently, students with disabilities were excluded from regular vocational and technical education classes because they were considered at risk of being hurt.)

School needs assessments should be adapted to reflect variation among schools and communities and changing conditions.

Considering Functional Domains. The placement decision for the student is not simply a question of whether he or she can keep up with a general academic program. Placement decisions should take into consideration the *full range of domains of functioning* that the individual student may need help in developing. These domains include all of the skill areas that students are expected to develop as they mature and move into adult roles.

Functional Domains

- Physical development and health needs
- Independent functioning
- Social functioning
- Behavioral functioning
- Academic functioning
- Vocational development
- Employment skills
- Recreational and leisure functioning
- Psychological functioning
- Family relationships

Inclusion placement may refer to integration with nondisabled peers in all activities except academic instruction, inclusion with nondisabled peers for academic and nonacademic activities, or inclusion with nondisabled peers for recreational and leisure activities only. For example, the student with mild to moderate mental retardation may need an adapted curriculum in order to gain academic skills, but could benefit from inclusion in nonacademic activities for development of recreation and leisure skills and social skills. Such a student could also benefit from additional training in functional skills, as well as inclusion in general vocational classes and community-based work experiences that are available to all students. The student may also need additional assistance to help the family understand and reinforce learning in the home.

Unfortunate Realities of Inclusion Initiatives. In reality, student placement decisions are often determined by factors such as administrative convenience, availability of classroom space, teacher willingness and effort, fear of external legal pressures, parent attitudes, or political pressure. When decisions are made on the basis of *reasons that are not student centered*, serious consequences often result for the student, teacher, peers, and for the classroom as a whole. While these decision factors alone can lead to unsuccessful inclusion practices, students often benefit from placement in the general education classroom despite a poorly designed initiative. These successes in the context of poor inclu-

sion policies usually attributed to the commitment and creativity of individual classroom teachers who make it work. The failures of inclusion policies in many schools can often be attributed to precipitous transitions to inclusion, failure to prepare administrators and teachers for the change, and lack of knowledge about effective inclusion strategies.

13. What Does Inclusion Mean for Teaching and Learning?

After a student is placed into the general education classroom, the teacher must make many decisions in order to prepare to accommodate the student.

Establishing Clear Expectations. Clear expectations for the student's behavior, attendance, and achievement are required. These expectations are essential to successful inclusion so that

- the teachers involved understand their role and responsibilities
- the student understands what is expected and that a change is taking place in the classroom for his or her benefit
- the student's peers understand the purposes of the changes in the classroom
- the parent(s) understands the implications of the modifications in the physical classroom, curriculum, or instruction.

Relationship of Inclusion to Functional Domains. The accommodations for the student must also take into account the many functional domains. The student, teacher, and parents must understand the domains in which the student is expected to be integrated or included with nondisabled peers. For example, it is important that the student and parents understand why an inclusion decision involves all school activities except academic activities and why the student will be receiving academic instruction in a resource classroom. Or, in the case of a physical disability, the student may be included in all school activities with nondisabled peers, except for physical education.

Planning Time—An Essential Element. Teacher planning time is an essential element in the implementation of successful inclusion, especially early in the

inclusion process, when the student is new to the classroom. Administrators must allow for such planning and facilitate the planning process. Teachers can use a variety of methods for instructional planning in order to prepare to accommodate the special needs of students with disabilities in the general education classroom. For example, teachers may be provided with additional planning time, parent volunteers, paraprofessionals or aides, interns from local universities, and other supports. Here are some examples:

- Teachers hold a special meeting after the initial or annual IEP meeting to discuss new implications for curriculum or instruction.
- Teachers have daily meeting times in the morning to plan instruction for the day.
- Teachers use part of their regular in-service days for semester planning or reviews of student progress.
- Teachers have an established afternoon with an extended planning period to prepare for the following week; substitute teachers or parent volunteers are enlisted to cover for the period.
- Teachers use after-school hours to prepare for the following day.

Teachers often struggle to find adequate time for planning, but *regular meetings of general education, special education, and consulting teachers are essential to the success of inclusion.* Many teachers cite lack of planning time as the critical barrier to providing adequate supports to students with disabilities in the general education classroom.

Social Relationships and Inclusion. The success of inclusion is also determined by the degree to which the student with a disability feels that he or she belongs in the general education classroom. The feeling of belonging positively affects the student's self-image and self-esteem, motivation to achieve, adjustment to the larger classroom and new demands, behavior, and general level of achievement. The impact of the new student on the general classroom is a major consideration for inclusion planners. Fostering positive social relationships among students with disabilities and their peers requires the preparation of nondisabled peers in the classroom so that they understand the needs of their new classmate(s). A positive classroom environment can only enhance the mutual benefit an inclusive classroom can provide. Teachers use many strategies to help the student feel that he or she belongs in the class and school. These strategies include the following:

• Discuss expectations with the student's peers and encourage interaction. The school counselor, social worker, or psychologist can be helpful in preparing classes for a new student with a disability and in discussing the benefits of positive peer relationships.

• Use cooperative group learning in which students are teamed for activities or projects and must cooperate, share ideas and materials, and share in the development of project products. Learning teams are also effective when students are required to prepare for classroom demonstrations and exhibitions.

• Assign peer-advocates, a peer-mentor, or a "buddy" who is responsible for interacting and helping the student in classroom activities and social situations. The peer-advocate provides support and encouragement and enables the student with a disability to solve problems with class activities and generally adjust to the new classroom environment.

• Assign a teacher-advocate to the student, whom the student can consult for guidance, general support, or crisis assistance.

• Include the new student in the class pictures and place the student's work on bulletin boards.

• Establish a lunch-buddy system (particularly helpful for young students in the first weeks of class).

• Include students in the daily roll call.

Teacher Modeling of Acceptance. Probably the most important influence on positive classroom relationships and social attitudes is the attitude of the teacher and the degree to which the teacher models acceptance of students with special needs. Research on inclusion has found that students who are appropriately placed in inclusive classrooms are more successful when their nondisabled peers are accepting and supportive. Many schools are establishing peer-mentor relationships to educate nondisabled peers and to help build relationships for emotional and social support.

Development of Social-Cognitive Skills. Social relationships become an important aspect of the learning process and the classroom environment. Research has clearly demonstrated that a significant proportion of students who fail to adjust socially to the classroom environment lack effective skills in solving social problems. These problems include poor ability to be empathetic and take the perspective of others, poor impulse control, and inability to generate effective solutions to problems in the classroom. *Deficiencies in skills for solving cognitive problems often lead to emotional and behavioral disorders requiring treatment.* The teacher in the inclusive classroom needs to address the social-behavioral domain as well as the academic domain. Research on teaching indicates that, when youths who are at risk of failure in general education classrooms are trained in both social and cognitive skills, the results can be improvement in social effectiveness, and reduction of problem behaviors.

Modifying the Physical Classroom. The arrangement of the classroom must also be considered when preparing for a new student with a physical disability. For example, the teacher needs to consider the existing arrangement of the classroom (e.g., traditional individual seating or group table seating)? Is the classroom crowded and does it have space adequate for a wheelchair? Can a student in a wheelchair maneuver adequately to get to the work stations or computer stations available to all students? Teachers use many considerations and strategies to modify the physical environment, including the following:

• Assign buddies to assist students by transmitting assignments and materials.

• Secure papers to the desk by using tape.

• Use common nonskid devices such as Velcro.

• Create opportunities outside the school for community-based instruction.

• Develop learning centers in the classroom for optimum use of classroom space.

Enriching Classroom Resources. Classroom resources may be required to assist the student who has a disability. Such resources include adaptations to computers and classroom materials and special instructional supplies. Business organizations also offer a wide variety of useful instructional materials for the creative classroom teacher. Such materials are excellent for promoting development of functional skills and for making curriculum more applicable to real life.

14. How Can Readiness for Inclusion Be Assessed?

As a school prepares for inclusion or prepares to expand the inclusive practices it has already begun, it is helpful to have some tools for assessing "readiness" for inclusion. Due to the emotional impact that often accompanies the inclusion process, it is important to determine if, in fact, the school environment is conducive to successful inclusion. Frequently, schools move to adopt inclusive practices with little understanding of the demands and effects of inclusion on the whole school. Administrators may fail to engage in "strategic planning." Part III of this handbook contains a tool for assessing the readiness for implementation of inclusion in the classroom and the school (Exhibit III–2).

15. What Are the Ten Steps to Inclusion?

Part IV of this handbook discusses ten steps that are useful in planning for the development and implementation of inclusive practices in the classroom and the school (see also Exhibit II–1). These steps:

- can be initiated by a single teacher or jointly by several teachers
- are relevant for schools that have not initiated inclusive practices and that have underdeveloped collaborative practices
- are relevant for schools that have already begun to implement inclusive practices and have developed more advanced collaborative relationships
- can form the basis for the design of evaluation of inclusion initiatives, relationships, and outcomes.

The steps are designed to provide a path of activities and strategies for those who are beginning the process of developing inclusive practices. They can help inclusion planning teams develop initiatives and processes that are uniquely suited to the local school, service system, or community.

These steps are offered as guideposts for developing school-based and classroom-based inclusion action plans and they are based on the experiences of inclusive schools around the nation. Rather than setting a single model, these steps provide a *menu of options for inclusion planning*. The process must remain flexible!

Part I of this handbook also contains a planning and readiness checklist for inclusion planners.

Step 1—Conduct a Needs Assessment and Scan the Environment

Performance of a needs assessment is essential for schools which are reorganizing for inclusion. Assessment activities involve (1) developing methods for collecting important data needed for planning inclusion activities and (2) planning focus groups for parents, teachers, and support personnel to discuss the services available for students with disabilities. Assessment can also involve asking an independent, objective, external professional to conduct the focus groups and an assessment and report to the planning team. Pre-planning assessment is defined as follows.

Ten Steps in Assessing Readiness for Implementation of Inclusion

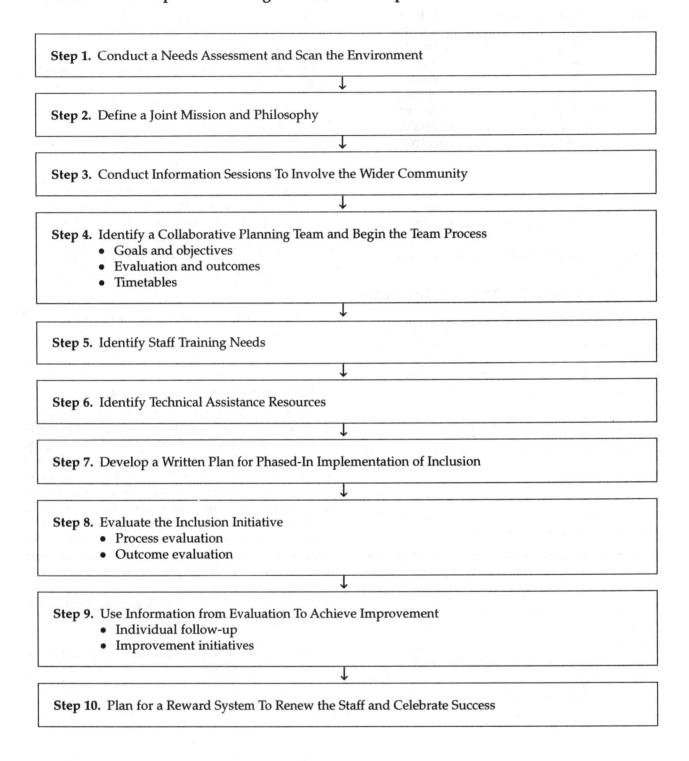

Step 1. Conduct a Needs Assessment and Scan the Environment

↓

Step 2. Define a Joint Mission and Philosophy

↓

Step 3. Conduct Information Sessions To Involve the Wider Community

↓

Step 4. Identify a Collaborative Planning Team and Begin the Team Process
- Goals and objectives
- Evaluation and outcomes
- Timetables

↓

Step 5. Identify Staff Training Needs

↓

Step 6. Identify Technical Assistance Resources

↓

Step 7. Develop a Written Plan for Phased-In Implementation of Inclusion

↓

Step 8. Evaluate the Inclusion Initiative
- Process evaluation
- Outcome evaluation

↓

Step 9. Use Information from Evaluation To Achieve Improvement
- Individual follow-up
- Improvement initiatives

↓

Step 10. Plan for a Reward System To Renew the Staff and Celebrate Success

Preplanning assessment—involves (1) defining the local "picture" or landscape of the school organization and existing services for students with special needs, in order to identify an existing foundation for an inclusion initiative or improvement of inclusive practices, and (2) determining the level of "readiness" of personnel and related services professionals to collaborate (Kochhar & Erickson, 1993).

It is important to understand that there are many kinds of collaboration required of teachers and related service personnel in schools and community agencies that serve the educational needs of children and youths with disabilities.

Readiness of Inclusion Team for Collaboration. Inclusion planners should know what each team member brings to the relationship in terms of resources, knowledge, and philosophy about inclusion. If you are just beginning the process of implementing inclusion, you may find it useful to consider some basic questions about:

1. the *structure of school and community agencies* that are collaborating
2. the *attitudes* of the inclusion team members toward inclusion and toward the population of students to be served
3. the *knowledge* of each team member about the population of students, the collaborative team process, and inclusion principles and strategies.

Strategies for Assessing Readiness for Inclusion. The following six sections offer strategies, methods, and resources for assessing the readiness of potential inclusion team members. The strategies can be used by inclusion planners or in self-assessment by individual teachers for their classrooms.

Assessment of Readiness for Team Collaboration. In an inclusion initiative, it is important to first *assess the needs of professionals who will form the inclusion implementation team.*

Assessment of inclusion team needs— the process of gathering and interpreting information about (1) the educational and support service needs of students, (2) the "goal posts," or progress measures, toward which the collaborating teachers and support personnel are working, and (3) the operational needs of the inclusion team members as they invest in real change in the teaching and learning environment (Kochhar, 1995).

Need for Periodic Assessment. The needs of students and school personnel change over time and therefore needs assessments must be performed regularly so that, as needs shift, so can the inclusion goals and procedures. The first set of goals and activities that are defined among collaborating team members will provide only a blueprint or map for defining educational needs. As student IEPs must be revisited and modified; so must the goals and procedures of inclusion teams. Ongoing needs assessments for both the individual student and the inclusion team can help teachers to remain sensitive to these changes.

Elements of Readiness Assessment. Assessment of readiness for inclusion activities involves the following elements:

- Defining the range of local services available in the school system in order to establish a foundation for an inclusion initiative
- Identifying service gaps and service needs that are currently not being met within the system
- Determining the level of readiness of teachers, support personnel, and cooperating agencies to form a collaboration for meaningful change in the service environment (e.g., changes in education, employment, health services, or social services)
- Determining the expertise and resources that each discipline or organization brings to the inclusion partnership
- Assessing the needs of the cooperating community organizations

A thorough needs assessment can help to provide important information for determining how prepared each inclusion team member or school unit is to participate in inclusion. Ongoing needs assessment is as important at the school level as it is for the individual. Also, as individual needs change over time, so do the needs of schools and school-linked agencies. As needs shift, so should the interagency goals and activities. Ongoing needs assessments can help the system remain sensitive to future change.

Levels of Assessment in Inclusion. Assessment of needs for the inclusion partnership has to do with knowing the needs of students and their families, as well as the needs of the cooperating agencies. It is also an essential step in the process of defining the goal posts that the cooperating partners will work toward.

1. **Needs assessment at the individual/consumer level** is the process of gathering and interpreting information about the educational and support service needs of students by the school and by related support agencies. Needs assessment at the individual level means identifying the range of developmental, health, academic, vocational, social, and support needs of individuals and families. On the basis of an assessment of individual needs, teachers and support personnel can establish goals and priorities for services.

2. **Needs assessment to define goalposts** means assessing the performance of students today (baseline performance), establishing performance goals for tomorrow, measuring the gap between the two, and finally, setting priorities for services and activities to move students and families toward new levels of functioning, progress, or achievement. Individual student's needs are interpreted in relation to future performance goals. It is a marriage of needs with goals and directions.

3. **Needs assessment at the interagency level** involves determining

   a. the level of readiness of cooperating agencies to form an inclusion partnership that results in meaningful change in the school environment for the benefit of all students

   b. the relative strengths and weaknesses that each group of professionals brings to the inclusion partnership.

Needs assessment at any level should not be a single event that occurs at the beginning of inclusion planning but, rather, should be an ongoing process that extends throughout the life of the partnership. Ongoing needs assessments can help the partners to remain alert to the adjustments they need to make.

Understanding what each team member can do and the kinds of commitments each can make will help the inclusion planners understand how they can *function together* as an effective team.

Collection of Planning Information. Information should be collected regarding the preparation of teachers, parents, and students for inclusion. Teachers should read and learn as much as possible about best practices in the inclusion process, especially in regard to the following questions:

- How should teachers and support personnel be prepared for inclusion?
- How should the physical environment be changed for inclusion?
- What modifications in curriculum, instruction, and student evaluation should be made?

- How should the IEP and interdisciplinary team process be used?
- What classroom supports are needed?
- How can students access available technology?
- How can students be helped to access and participate in vocational, occupational, and technical education?
- How can students be helped to participate in extracurricular school activities?
- How can students be helped to participate in community-based and community service experiences?

The Resource Environment: A Circle of Commitment. The term *circle of commitment* applied to inclusion implementors helps to define the range of resources in the environment, both human and material, that must be invested in an inclusion effort (1) to improve and support services and outcomes for students with disabilities and (2) to improve the overall learning environment. Members of the school community (key stakeholders), along with material and financial resources, form the inclusion planning team's circle of commitment, which includes the six elements found on the following page.

Six Elements in the Circle of Commitment to Inclusion

Commitment

1. **The Human Commitment:** the key personnel and advisors in the inclusion planning and implementation team.

2. **The Resource Commitment:** the financial and material resources that are committed to planning and implementation of inclusion.

3. **The Values Commitment:** A shared set of values and a belief in the "shared responsibility" for the development and education of all students in the school and community.

4. **The Action Commitment:** A shared mission, written procedures, and common set of goals for the inclusion initiative.

5. **The Outcome Commitment:** A shared set of expectations or outcomes for those who will be served or impacted by the inclusion initiative (students, teachers, families, and others).

6. **The Renewal Commitment:** A shared long-term plan to (a) continue to review the course of the inclusion initiative, (b) to recognize and celebrate the unique contributions that each group makes to the initiatives, and (c) to continue to renew those commitments (Kochhar & Erickson, 1993; Kochhar, 1995).

The circle of commitment includes the range of tools that inclusion pioneers need in order to make changes in the educational and human service system, to better serve students with disabilities and their families.

Step 2—Define a Joint Mission and Philosophy

Defining a joint mission and philosophy involves meeting with key inclusion planners, discussing a joint vision of inclusion implementation, and hammering out broad goals and strategies for achieving that shared vision. This step will help in the design of a written *mission and philosophy statement* for the inclusion initiative, as well as in the development of formal agreements with collaborating nonschool agencies. The inclusion team may think about its initiative in terms of two kinds of strategies:

1. **a classroom level strategy** or intervention that is designed (a) to improve the availability of and access to supportive services in the classroom and (b) to help solve specific problems and overcome barriers to inclusion identified by teachers in the individual classroom
2. **a schoolwide inclusion strategy** designed to assist all school personnel, both instructional and noninstructional, to understand the inclusion goals and strategies and to be a part of changing the school's "culture" to support full participation of all students.

Developing a Mission Statement for Inclusion. Each school will define its inclusion mission differently, so no two mission statements will look alike. However, a few fundamental rules should be followed in developing mission statements. A mission statement should describe the *broad purpose* of the initiative and collaborating units and the specific areas of joint responsibility. A mission statement may include one or all of the following four parts:

1. **A statement of context**—usually a brief introductory paragraph that broadly describes the initiative, how it was begun, how it addresses current educational needs of students, and how it differs, expands, or improves on the school's current practices to promote inclusion.
2. **A statement of the authority for the initiative**—an introductory section in the mission statement that refers to the legal basis for the initiative (e.g., the Individuals with Disabilities Education Act, section 504, and the Americans with Disabilities Act) and may list the local and state laws, regulations, or policies that give authority to this agreement.

3. **General statement of the philosophy, the purpose of the initiative or agreement, and the expected benefits and outcomes**—includes a broad declaration of the goals of the initiative and the anticipated benefits and outcomes for students with disabilities.
4. **Statement of broad goals, roles, and responsibilities**—defines the goals of the initiative, the roles of key planners and implementors, and cooperating agencies or community agency personnel.

Mission statements are usually supported with declarations of well-defined goals and measurable objectives.

Step 3—Conduct Information Sessions To Involve the Wider Community

Involving the community is the first step in implementing a collaborative planning process to develop inclusive practices. The success of any inclusion initiative depends on the ability of the planning team to create a supportive environment for the development of professional collaboration. This process of collaboration begins by *informing key populations within the school and wider community, particularly parents, about intentions to develop or expand inclusive practices.*

> **Informing and involving the school community**—In an environment that supports inclusion, *key stakeholders (persons who care about and are invested in seeing inclusion successfully implemented)* become knowledgeable and informed about the need for improved collaboration and the benefits of inclusion for the student, school, and community.

Under current laws, state and local educational agencies are required to increase opportunities for inclusion into mainstream classes and activities and to improve working relationships between students, families, teachers, and related services personnel concerned with the development of children and youths.

Informing the School Community. There are 15 strategies for informing the school, communities, agency personnel, parents, students, and community leaders about initiatives for inclusion. By informing the school community, inclusion planners can begin to identify future participants in the planning process. Often, community leaders must be sought out and invited into the process. Different schools will require different strategies for informing the community.

Strategies for Informing the School Community about a New Inclusion Initiative

1. *Inform parent, student, and consumer organizations*	Inform parent, student, and consumer organizations, such as the PTA, parent advocacy groups, and student organizations, about the plans for service coordination. Distribute information and solicit input into the plans and roles of these groups in the development of the collaboration.
2. *Inform educational leaders and school principals*	Inform educational leaders and school principals who have primary responsibility for any new programs or initiatives that will affect instruction or student services. Most school districts and schools establish their educational priorities well in advance (expansion of special education programs, addition of bilingual program, improving basic skills, etc.). Principals should be among the earliest to be informed of the effort and helped to see how the initiative will aid them in achieving their educational goals and objectives for students.
3. *Inform staff and directors of community and adult services agencies*	Inform staff and directors of community and adult services agencies because their support is vital to an interagency services coordination initiative (new or renewed). Each cooperating (or potential) partner needs to know about an intent to collaborate and the process for forming the collaborative arrangement.
4. *Develop concept papers and rationale statements*	Develop concept papers and rationale statements to help each potential cooperating agency understand the relationship between the collaborative endeavor and their own individual agency mission, goals, and objectives. Each must understand how the new collaboration will help them to achieve their individual agency goals, improve their services and resources, or evaluate their efforts. The mutual benefits to all cooperating agencies must be defined and stressed early on.
5. *Inform relevant teacher unions and educational associations*	Inform relevant teacher unions and educational associations about new initiatives that involve teaching staff and help them understand the potential benefits of the collaboration for the students and professionals. It is also helpful to have the county or district educational associations go on record as supporting the initiative.
6. *Conduct local education reform seminars*	Include in local education reform seminars information about or discussion of the interagency initiative.
7. *Conduct special seminars*	Conduct special seminars on interagency service coordination and co-training with members from a variety of agencies and organizations.

continues

8. *Plan teachers', principals', and parents' coffees*	Plan teachers', principals', and parents' coffees to discuss the initiative. Have students and parents share successful experiences during these sessions.
9. *Conduct highly visible brainstorming meetings*	Conduct highly visible brainstorming meetings with heads of agency personnel at all levels to discuss interagency service coordination.
10. *Develop informational brochures and materials*	Develop informational brochures and materials that explain the mission and benefits of interagency collaboration. Include information packets in the local budget documents that are distributed to educational and community agency planning boards. Develop interagency logos and brochures to inform the community of the key partners in the initiative, and to promote the interagency partnership as a distinct entity.
11. *Conduct business-education seminars*	Include in local business-education seminars information about the initiative, or in Chamber of Commerce meetings, or Private Industry Council meetings (Job Training Partnership Act). Seek community support for community-based instruction.
12. *Utilize local newsletters and newspapers*	Include in local newsletters and newspapers editorial and feature articles about the initiative.
13. *Conduct meetings with community leaders*	Conduct meetings with community leaders to assist in "championing" an initiative in interagency service coordination.
14. *Develop links with local colleges or universities*	Develop links with local colleges or universities to develop meetings or seminars related to new initiatives, or to develop grant proposals.
15. *Utilize annual reports of cooperating agencies*	Include in the annual reports of cooperating agencies descriptions of interagency initiatives and plans.

Working with School Administrators and Personnel. There should be individual meetings with teachers, administrators, and support personnel. Efforts should be made to identify current successful integration practices in the school district. A meeting should be held with the key teachers involved, and their opinions should be solicited on what the issues are and what needs to happen next. This first meeting should be an exercise in active listening!

Step 4—Identify a Collaborative Planning Team and Begin the Team Process

The concept of *collaborative planning* is helpful when inclusion planners try to determine which key individuals are needed in the planning process.

The Collaborative Planning Process. As with many educational innovations or restructuring, inclusion planning and development has been primarily viewed as a responsibility of administrators, but the inclusion planning process must be viewed as much more than an extension of administrative activities. *Inclusion planning activities should be student-centered (consumer centered) and teacher-centered, rather than "procedural."* Instead of benefiting or being convenient for administrative functions, the inclusion processes and procedures established should primarily benefit students and teachers. They should benefit the teaching and learning environment as a whole.

Outcomes: Inclusion As an Intervention.

To be successful and beneficial for teaching and learning, inclusion planning should be viewed as an *intervention—a planned effort designed to produce intended changes, or outcomes, in the target population.* This "outcomes view" requires a change in the methods used to define and measure the effectiveness of inclusion planning. The intended changes in the target population (achievement and progress of students with disabilities) must be clearly specified, and school and community resources must be focused to pursue those outcomes. An outcome orientation and a vigorous focus on measuring benefits to students and teachers and effects on the total learning environment, becomes central to evaluating inclusive classrooms and schools. *In a student-centered service system, student benefits and impacts drive the development of inclusion planning and implementation, from initial definition of the mission and goals to annual evaluation.*

Planned Change As a Management Practice.

Many forces in the school system affect the work of inclusion planning teams and the "sustainability" of the change process. Change and innovation can decay in a short time if school environment factors that support the change process are not identified and "engraved" into the inclusion planning process. *Planned change is beginning to be viewed as essential* to the planning and implementation of inclusion initiatives. *Collaborative planning* strategies can help teachers and school leaders develop planning teams to manage a continuum of inclusive placements.

Defining Collaborative Planning for Inclusion.

Two terms that are important to an understanding of the development of inclusive practices are *collaborative planning* and *planned change*. Collaborative planning relates to how teachers and administrators go about making decisions and planning actions in cooperation with one another. Planned change relates to the implementation and management of the relationships needed to implement inclusion. Both processes are essential to the change process in order to implement inclusive classrooms.

Defining Strategic Planning for Inclusion.

Strategic planning has been defined as a "disciplined effort to produce fundamental decisions and actions that shape and guide what a school or organization is, what it does, and why it does it" (Bryson, 1988, p. 5). Collaborative planning is strategic planning conducted by a team of teachers, administrators, and others in order to identify and understand how to implement an initiative within the given school environment. Strategic planning also helps inclusion planners to understand and identify ways that different parts of the school can interact to improve access to mainstream classrooms and nonacademic activities for all students. The school environment includes the political, economic, professional, and social influences that characterize and influence the school.

Planned change focuses on the implementation and management of the change process for inclusion and helps teachers to use and modify these forces to achieve a *shared mission*. The inclusion planning process must be viewed as a dynamic process that may be imperfect and sometimes not particularly orderly. The essential guiding principles and goals are of primary importance. *The planning process must support flexibility in the placement process so that schools can respond to changing needs of students and learning environments.* The concepts of strategic planning provide a foundation for understanding, creating, and implementing inclusive practices that are responsive to the needs of students and their families (Kochhar, 1995).

Pioneers: Conducting Team Planning Sessions.

The inclusion planning team must determine the most important activities that need to occur in order to improve curriculum, instruction, and support services for students with disabilities. These activities are indications of the goals and objectives the team sets.

Step 5—Identify Staff Training Needs

Inclusion requires increased awareness, thoughtful consideration, and meaningful dialogue. Teachers and parents need the opportunity to discuss the complexity and importance of diversity in the classroom and to air their concerns. Well-planned training and professional development opportunities can help the teacher to learn how to implement inclusion effectively. In addition, change can create resistance among the very people who are needed to implement the inclusion initiative. When teachers sense that the traditional ways of doing things are being abandoned, some may resist or become negative. The inclusion pioneer needs special knowledge and know-how to help champion change and transfer the spirit of opportunity to others who will be involved in the inclusion process.

Building a Sense of Ownership for Inclusion.

How can inclusion implementors foster a sense of investment or ownership in the initiative? How should teachers be oriented to the changes that the new collaboration will bring? What kinds of training are needed? How can the teachers share and "celebrate" their successes and honor those who have made important contributions?

The Adoption Plan for Inclusion. Change re-

quires teachers to adopt new teaching methods, relationships, procedures, norms, values, and attitudes. An inclusion initiative will *not* be successfully adopted or fully implemented by teachers and related service personnel unless they are *adequately trained in their field, understand the purposes of the collaboration initiative, and*

are prepared for change. New training and development activities are needed to help key personnel *adopt new practices*. Two important concepts related to preparing teachers for change are:

1. The *adoption plan* is a strategy for fostering the constructive involvement of teachers and related personnel in the development and support of the inclusion initiative. It involves preparing teachers for new practices related to inclusion, enlisting the help of volunteers, and securing the support of students and families.
2. The *knowledge-sharing plan* defines the specific areas of new knowledge and skills that teachers and related personnel need to have to successfully implement inclusion.

The knowledge-sharing plan includes a series of professional development, training, and organizational development activities aimed at ensuring that the inclusion initiative is adopted or fully accepted by all who will be involved.

SIX COMPONENTS OF THE ADOPTION PLAN

There are six important components of an adoption plan. These components are important for establishing a plan that can reach many school professionals efficiently, and they increase the likelihood that the plan will endure over time.

Strategy 1. Establish links with training programs of local and state educational agencies. Each local and state educational agency organizes in-service training days for teachers, administrators, and support personnel. Interagency planners should use these existing training activities as a vehicle for providing an introduction and orientation to the new inclusion initiative and teacher roles.

Strategy 2. Ensure participation of all cooperating agencies. The adoption plan must include all cooperating agencies in the training, for coordination of services. This does not mean that all training sessions must include personnel from all agencies, but planners should plan some regular training meetings that include staff from all key community and support services agencies. This approach increases the likelihood that, over time, action team personnel will come to share a com-

mon understanding and vision of the direction of the initiative. Representatives of cooperating school-linked agencies could be invited onto a panel with education personnel to share and discuss the mission and goals of the initiative. Families, students, and community leaders could be invited to attend and join the discussion. These are good opportunities for sharing information, presenting inclusion concepts and philosophy, and discussing the benefits of inclusion for all students. The mission statement and inclusion plan should include the schedule for training and staff development.

Strategy 3. Develop inclusion planning materials for training and distribution. Materials must be developed for use in in-service training for teachers and collaborating personnel. These materials should include specific information about the inclusion goals, strategies, teachers and students, key roles and contact persons, and mission and goals as they relate to inclusion and new support services that will be offered through the initiative.

Strategy 4. Adopt new educational and human service practices. The inclusion planners

continues

continued

must help key teaching personnel to reassess their teaching practices and adopt new ones. Once inclusion practices have been in place for one or two years, advanced training will be needed. For advanced training, the results of the past year's inclusion implementation would be used to renew and strengthen the initiative, identify barriers and weaknesses, and further define and improve the outcomes of inclusion.

Strategy 5. Evaluate the adoption plan. The inclusion team must make sure that adoption plans are evaluated. They must ask questions. Is the training having the desired effect on teachers and the classrooms? Is the training reaching all key school personnel? Is interdisciplinary training occurring? Are the teachers involved in evaluating the adoption plan and the training effort? Are the teachers satisfied with the training and is it useful? What are their recommendations for improvement? Ongoing evaluation of training should be included in the inclusion mission statement.

Strategy 6. Provide technical assistance. Inclusion planners should also ensure that they are linked with experts who can provide help and assistance during the development, implementation, and evaluation phases. Expert consultants such as university personnel, private evaluation firms, and education association personnel can be helpful on a short-term basis to

- problem solve during implementation

- develop assessment and monitoring tools

- design training material

- provide orientation to planners and related personnel

- conduct advanced training for staff after the inclusion team has been functioning for one or two years

- assist the teachers and administrators in learning how to use evaluation information to make improvements and set new directions.

Inclusion experts can also provide information about other programs and their successes and can help to link new local inclusion teams with more experienced teams. Staff development plans are discussed further on p. 63, "What Should be Included in a Staff Development Plan."

Step 6—Identify Technical Assistance Resources

Many resources are available to school districts. Universities, regional resource centers, professional associations, and state educational agencies have many professionals who will share information, professional literature, and best practices from exemplary programs. The greater the amount of information, the better are the decisions at the local level.

Step 7—Develop a Written Plan for Phased-In Implementation of Inclusion

Written plans do not have to be lengthy, but they are important to help teams to remain focused. Written plans provide documentation and set goals for achievement. The written plan has a well-defined set of activities, with accompanying time lines and assigned responsibilities.

Step 8—Evaluate the Inclusion Initiative

After inclusion is implemented, an annual evaluation should be conducted to assess the success of the initiative and to determine areas that need improvement. Without a formal review of the inclusion process and outcomes, students' needs appear to be less significant. Evaluation activities keep the student's individual needs at the focus of decision making and drive future development or modification of the initiative. Part III contains resources useful in designing evaluation strategies.

Step 9—Use Information from Evaluation To Achieve Improvement

No program is static. Adjustments are part of the educational process. For example, a high school in a suburban area conducted a self-evaluation of the special education program. Administrators identified six goals that needed to be addressed. Consequently, they contacted a local university for technical assistance and support in restructuring their services. They set in operation a teacher training program and an inclusion initiative.

Step 10—Plan for a Reward System To Renew the Staff and Celebrate Success

Inclusion planners recognize that there is a need for reward and recognition of all collaborating personnel. Celebrations of individual and program successes become important experiences in the lives of those committed to the mission of service coordination. Recognition serves to strengthen commitment and to help develop camaraderie and a team spirit. Plans for such a reward system should be built into the annual action plan from the state.

Staff rewards and celebration of success include activities, gifts, or tokens given to staff to thank them for their effort and participation. Reward and celebrate also include:

- reminding staff that they are valued contributors
- strengthening and ensuring their continued commitment
- recognizing individual success stories of participants
- encouraging the participation of new staff and volunteers.

There are as many ways to reward people as there are people with imaginations. Here are a few common examples of ways to offer rewards and celebrate success.

Suggested Incentives and Acknowledgments

- Use of local media to make special announcements about new programs or special successes of consumers and families; includes cable TV and radio.
- Newspaper articles about the program or individual teacher members.
- Articles in local educational agency newsletters, business newsletters, annual reports, and community agency newsletters and bulletins.
- Principal's breakfasts and "coffees" in which special recognition is made to teachers, students, or parents.
- Reward banquets associated with PTA activities.

- Plaques for individual achievement and service.
- Certificates for outstanding contribution and performance by teachers.
- A program which offers "volunteer or parent of the month (or year)," or "most valuable player" awards.
- Pins and buttons with an inclusion partnership logo.
- Dedications of sites or equipment in honor of a staff member.
- Small gifts or mementos.
- Photograph displays in schools and community agencies.

Staff Renewal. The concept of *renewal* is related to reward but differs because it is directed at teachers and related personnel who have been involved in the inclusion team for a substantial period. Sometimes, key staff who have worked particularly hard in the effort may need to be "re-energized" or reminded of the mission of the initiative and the value of their role. Often, these key individuals include the first champions for inclusion who have done more than their fair share in leading and promoting the initiative. They may simply be tired, feeling as though they have reached a plateau. They may have seen many changes and new directions and may no longer feel that their role is valued or appreciated. They may feel that their role as initiators and developers has now given way to routine operations, policies, and procedures. *In short, they need to renew their sense of commitment, spirit, and purpose with the initiative.*

Staff Renewal—Activities aimed at reenergizing inclusion team members, reminding them of the mission of the inclusion initiative and the value of their role, and renewing their sense of commitment and purpose.

Strategies that can promote renewal of commitment and dedication in valued team members include:

- using rewards discussed earlier
- conducting special retreats in which key personnel share experiences, review the mission, goals, successes, contributions of teachers over the past years in the partnership, and set new directions for the inclusion initiative
- developing a video or television production that chronicles the development of the initiative, its accomplishments, and the contributions of its key players. Such a production should focus on impacts and benefits for consumers and families, as well as improvements in the effectiveness of service coordination
- changes in previous roles and opportunities for new experiences or responsibilities
- offering an individual a more prestigious role in the views of the team, such as a role in the evaluation or in public relations or allowing staff to help other classrooms or schools develop or improve inclusion practices.

Universities Assist in Planning for Inclusion

Local colleges and universities can provide many resources to assist schools and administrative agencies at the local and state levels to plan for inclusion. Universities with departments in special education, vocational education, social work, or rehabilitation counseling can be of special assistance. Some universities have interdisciplinary programs that can offer expertise in collaborative planning. Specialized programs such as the following can provide linkages with academic expertise:

- special education and teacher education programs
- vocational education and evaluation programs
- early intervention specialist training programs
- special education programs for at-risk students
- learning disabilities training programs
- rehabilitation counselor training programs
- social work services
- nursing and health services administration
- business-education partnership programs.

College and university programs may participate in subcontracts for services or provide technical assistance to individual faculty members in activities such as the following:

- technical assistance with the evaluation of the local education agency (LEA) improvement initiatives, reporting on LEA activities, and collection of achievements and best practices that could be shared statewide
- development of instructional, curriculum, and in-service training materials for LEAs and local service providers implementing inclusion
- assignment of graduate students to LEA or state level inclusion planning, implementation, and evaluation activities for internship credit
- design and provision of inclusion in-service training, special seminars, and institutes for LEA professionals
- assistance with development of state, federal, or private funding to support inclusion initiatives.

Working relationships should be developed with college and university faculty, and these faculty members should be included in advisory and planning meetings. They are often knowledgeable about resources related to inclusion models and practices in other localities and states.

In summary, the partnership *adoption and knowledge-sharing process* includes the broad range of activities aimed at recruiting, orienting, educating, preparing, and renewing personnel who will be key players in inclusion planning and improvement. *Frequently, those who resist change in the beginning are the most likely to call themselves pioneers as the initiative expands!*

16. What Should Be Included in a Staff Development Plan?

Teachers need strategies to develop and implement inclusion planning and implementation, and they are prepared for the challenge. The more strategies they use, the better the planning process, and the better the opportunity for success for all involved. *(For a listing of topics for professional development of inclusion planners, see Part IV, "Sample Plan for Staff Development.")*

Developing a Knowledge-Sharing Plan	
KNOWLEDGE-SHARING NEED	**STRATEGY NEED**
Teacher training and orientation to the inclusion initiative	**Include in teacher training and orientation the following content:** a. the inclusion philosophy, concept, and strategies, b. the inclusion development process, c. the concept of collaborative planning, d. the process of change and restructuring to develop inclusive practices, e. overcoming resistance to change, f. the elements of collaboration and communication, g. strategies for problem solving, and h. key roles and responsibilities of personnel for inclusion.
Personnel training in the inclusion change process	Provide special sessions related to the change process. Ensure that cooperating teachers and related personnel are oriented to the principles and processes of inclusion, collaboration, and strategic planning centered on student needs and outcomes.
Promoting teacher leadership in inclusion planning	In addition to basic staff training and orientation to new roles, it is important to help teachers understand the broader impacts of the inclusion initiative upon the students and their families, the agencies, and the community as a whole. Share with them what the inclusion team is expecting from its effort and what changes are sought in the school and classroom environment and in student outcomes.
Promoting professional collaboration	Communicate the goals of the initiative to all personnel in the school, including noninstructional personnel, as well as those in collaborating school-linked service agencies. Within the school this might include the math department, English department, special education, vocational/technical education, English as a Second Language, and others. Make sure all are aware of the inclusion goals and are prepared to work together.
Promoting cooperation among school-linked service agencies	Ensure that the relevant school-linked service agencies are prepared to work together. Plan for joint training and orientation seminars with school staff, rehabilitation agency staff, social services, and others.
Promoting constructive change	Ensure that teachers and related personnel are knowledgeable about the change process and their roles in it, and they endorse the shared mission for the inclusion initiatives.

Key personnel in collaborating agencies need a common understanding of the goals of the initiative and of the individual roles that teachers will play. *This understanding is also essential to the acceptance (adoption) of the new relationships, to fostering a sense of ownership of the new initiative and its goals, and to the ultimate success of inclusion.*

What Should Be Included in Staff Training and Orientation?

Seven important areas of new knowledge and skills are needed by partnership planners and anyone else involved in achieving the goals of a partnership. These areas include information about:

- the philosophy and legal foundations and authorities for inclusion, including local, state, and national education and service goals
- the elements of inclusive services and collaborative team planning
- the concept of strategic planning for change and a range of strategies for implementing inclusion
- strategies for promoting collaboration and communication with the wider community

- strategies for problem solving and overcoming resistance to change
- increasing involvement of students and families
- using evaluation to renew or strengthen the inclusion initiative, improve practices, and outcomes.

These topic areas are suggested as a guide and not a prescription. They are not necessarily inclusive of all of the information or material that should be covered in orientation and training sessions. Each school may want to develop unique training strategies and materials to meet the needs of its students and teachers.

Inclusion Implementors Orientation and Training	
Area of Knowledge and Skills	**Example Training Objectives**
1. Philosophy and legal foundations for inclusion, including local, state, and national educational goals	• Inclusion philosophy and principles of student-centered services • Legal authority for inclusion in the locality and state • National and local education goals • Defining priority goals for inclusion for the locality and state
2. The elements of collaborative team planning and school-linked interagency cooperation	• Introduction to the interdisciplinary team planning process • Assessing student needs and the classroom environment • Introduction to the key inclusion partners and how the linkages are established • Overview of the cooperative agreement of the partnership, its mission and goals • Relating the mission of the collaboration to improvements in the teaching and learning • Overview of the inclusion plan and implementation schedule
3. The concept of collaborative planning for inclusion	• Overview of the concept of interdisciplinary team collaboration • Overview of shared and collaborative planning • Introduction to the inclusion team approach to instruction and classroom management
4. The elements of orientation training and communication for inclusion	• Communicating among school units and personnel • Strategies for improving communication and sharing information among teachers, readministrators • Conducting effective training sessions and planning meetings • Understanding different perspectives on inclusion
5. Strategies for problem solving and overcoming resistance to change	• Overview of problem-solving strategies and use of educational approaches in problem solving • Selecting the right strategy to match the problem • Identifying staff resistance to inclusive practices • Managing conflict and resistance to change

continues

continued

Area of Knowledge and Skills	Example Training Objectives
6. Involvement of consumers, families, and volunteers	• Overview of the importance of family involvement in inclusion education • Roles of consumers and families in evaluating service coordination
7. Using evaluation to "renew" or strengthen the inclusion initiative, and improve its practices and its outcomes	• Introduce the inclusion evaluation plan and the expected outcomes • Highlight outcomes related to improving inclusive services • Review the actual results of annual evaluations • Discuss strengths and weaknesses of the initiative and develop a "new directions for inclusion" forward plan for improvement

17. What Factors Are Most Important in Planning for Inclusion?

Certain elements are critical to the planning process. Successful inclusion is the result of deliberate, focused planning efforts. The better the planning is, the better are the results. Several factors require attention in planning for inclusion.

Administrative Sensitivity and Support. Administrators provide instructional leadership, and they set the "climate" for acceptance and a positive approach to including students with disabilities in general education (Dalheim, 1994). Among the most important factors in the success of inclusion are interpersonal relationships and support. Teachers who are regarded as supportive demonstrate qualities of interpersonal communication that include good rapport with others, enthusiasm, positive attitude, flexibility, and a low-key and nonthreatening manner. *Teachers need to know that the administrative staff notices and appreciates their efforts and considers the time and energy spent in advancing inclusion as necessary and meaningful to the educational process.*

Planning Time. Inclusion requires additional planning time to develop meaningful curriculum, modify instruction, consult with parents, meet with school personnel, plan community-based instruction, and train peer tutors to work with the student(s) with disabilities. Teachers should work as a team and take a problem-solving approach. They need to implement collaborative student-centered planning teams and develop good communication between general and regular education teachers.

Collaboration and Support. General and special education teachers need to become informed about how to integrate students' abilities, needs, and goals. They should communicate with students about their disabilities and their strengths and weaknesses. Mutual planning and cooperation are essential. Input should be obtained from general education teachers about where and when integration of abilities, needs, and goals is appropriate, when assistance is required, and the availability of special education consultants when they are needed. Special education teachers should coordinate the process and remain accessible.

Teacher Incentives. Teachers have not traditionally received high salaries. While increased pay for inclusion activities would be ideal, it is generally not provided in most school districts. Teacher incentives are a way to acknowledge the importance of inclusion. Examples of teacher incentives are:

- professional leave to visit other inclusion classrooms
- assistance of substitute teachers to release regular teachers to meet with other professionals involved in planning
- support of an aide in the classroom to assist with additional activities
- summer stipends to attend graduate training courses.

Staff Development. Training and preparation of administrators, teachers, and parents are essential for inclusion. Staff development comes in many forms including workshops, technical assistance, graduate training, federal or state grant programs, and mentoring by master teachers.

Support Services. Several types of support services that can contribute to inclusion efforts are available. *Inclusion is not the sole responsibility of one teacher, but rather a collective responsibility of the whole school.* Examples of support service personnel are the school nurse, counselor, physical therapist, speech therapist, reading teacher, rehabilitation case manager, music teacher, social worker, librarian, vocational resource educator, interpreters, support service personnel, and technology assistants.

Technical Assistance. School districts involved in inclusion efforts frequently call on outside consultants for assistance in planning, organizing, and/or conducting staff development needed for successful inclusion. In addition, outside consultants can be invited to observe classrooms, meet with teachers, and answer their technical questions. Consultants may also be involved in program evaluation activities, such as designing teacher and student surveys, analyzing student achievement data, describing successful practices, and developing reports.

Teacher Team Relationships. *The personal relationships of the individuals involved in inclusion are the cornerstone of a successful inclusive classroom.* The most powerful of these relationships occurs among those closest to the students (teachers, instructional support staff, and volunteers). Often, both the successes and difficulties with the inclusion process can be traced to problems in individual relationships. Collaboration for inclusion is much more effective if teachers are familiar and alert to these barriers to cooperation. Fears and perceptions can arise among school personnel as they work to develop teams for inclusive education.

Common Fears Related to Collaboration

Fears Related to the Environment for Inclusion

- No funds available for collaborative activities
- Feuds based on personalities and tradition of organizational prejudices and broken trust
- Competition for students and resources

Fearful Attitudes about the Impacts of Inclusion

- Fear of being influenced or controlled by the professionals or school units
- Fear that failures or inadequacies will be discovered and exposed to the school community
- Fear that administrators will not approve new collaborative arrangements and will end support
- Fear that exchanging resources will mean losing them or receiving less than one gives
- Fear that innovation or change will mean more work or may threaten positions
- Fear that students will not receive adequate services or information as classrooms are restructured
- Fear that the quality of education and the teaching environment might be compromised
- Belief that students might be rejected by their peers

Lack of Knowledge and Communication Skills

- Lack of awareness and understanding of other professionals, their disciplines, functions, and resources
- Lack of broad understanding of students' needs or options, because of inability to "see" outside one's specialty or discipline
- Drained energy from dealing with a complex restructuring initiative
- Lack of staff planning for cooperation and inability to see possibilities for cooperation because job demands exceed time and resources

Source: Adapted with permission from Hiltenbrand, D., Brown, D., & Jones, E., in Kochhar, C. (Ed.). (1995). Training for interagency interdisciplinary service coordination: An instructional modules series. Des Moines, IA: Iowa State Department of Education and the Mountain Plains Regional Resource Group, Drake University.

18. What Is an Appropriate Class Size for Inclusion?

Class size issues are relevant for all classrooms in all school districts, but it is rarely discussed because of its implications for educational funding in today's schools. Class size becomes an important issue for inclusive classrooms because teachers must attend to the needs of a very diverse group of students. These new student challenges include substance abuse, aggressive and violent behavior, disrespect for property, school code violations, and nutritional problems. In addition, teachers have very bright and committed students in the classroom. The teacher is expected and required to make accommodations and produce reasonable outcomes in the classroom, despite today's challenges. The teacher is also expected to design curriculum and to use cooperative learning groups, technology in the classroom, alternative assessment, and interdisciplinary instruction.

Class Size and Inclusion. Few resources on inclusion address specific issues of class size. When Sailor (1991) outlined six components for inclusion, he suggested a "natural proportion" of students with disabilities in schools and classrooms. According to Sailor, one of the characteristics of an inclusive school is that the population of students with disabilities and students without disabilities reflects the population of the community as a whole. He also applied this natural proportion to classroom placements. Therefore, if the community had approximately 10 percent students with disabilities, then each classroom should have no more than 10 percent of such students in a classroom (2 or 3 in a classroom of 25 to 30). Also, rather than concentrate students with disabilities in a few selected classrooms, it is preferable to distribute them equitably among all educators. This approach equalizes the responsibility within the school and allows greater opportunities for social interaction among students with disabilities and nondisabled students (Turnbull, Turnbull, Shank, & Leal, 1995).

National Education Association Recommendations. The National Education Association (Dalheim, 1994) recommends a much higher placement proportion of students with disabilities than Sailor suggested. The NEA reported recommendations from teachers who conducted research on the inclusion of students with disabilities. Teachers have recommended that class size not exceed 28 students and that the number of boys and girls should be roughly equal. In addi-

tion, these teachers recommended that the proportion of students with disabilities should not exceed one quarter, or 25 percent, of the class. The remaining three quarters should be a heterogeneous group of both talented and general education students. They also suggested that the balance between boys and girls improves the experience for all students (Dalheim, 1994). Thus, for a class of 28 students, 7 could be students with disabilities, depending on the type of disability and other environmental factors.

Most students with disabilities being placed into general education classes are coming from smaller special education classrooms. The experience of the large general education classroom is often a major adjustment for these students. It is also an adjustment for the teacher, who now has an additional challenge in time and classroom management, to ensure that the students with special needs receive the time and attention they need. *The specific percentage of students with disabilities is not as important as factors in the classroom environment such as teacher and peer acceptance, administrative support, support services, instructional aides, and planning time.*

Strategies for Managing Large Inclusive Classrooms. Teachers have found several strategies to be successful in management of large classrooms that include students with disabilities. These strategies include the following (Dalheim, 1994; Putnam, 1993):

- team teaching in which teachers share their ideas, knowledge, and techniques
- using "learning teams," by grouping students who are academically different from the student with disabilities (Team sizes are determined by the nature of the activity, with teams of two, three, or four most commonly used.)
- using alternative assessment tools to evaluate the achievement of the students in the groups (project evaluations, student exhibitions, performance demonstrations, science "fairs," and other performance-based or nonpaper and pencil assignments)
- providing special reminders to students or calling them at home to remind them to complete their homework
- checking notebooks regularly to make sure students with disabilities are able to maintain them in an organized fashion

- using assignment schedule books which students write in each day.

These strategies are generally beneficial for non-disabled students as well.

Considerations in Determining Student Ratios. In determining acceptable classroom ratios of students with disabilities to nondisabled students, school district administrators should consider several factors related to students and classroom environments:

- severity of the disabilities of all students identified for placement in a specific classroom
- funds available for classroom restructuring
- resources and support services available in the classroom
- teacher access to support services in the school and community.

Severity of Disability. School administrators must be realistic about learning environments for all students, including those with disabilities. The severity of the disability must be considered in determining the ratio of students with disabilities to nondisabled students in a classroom. More severe disabilities require additional supports, planning time, and physical accommodations.

Funds Available for Classroom Restructuring. Special education funds are required to directly support students in the classroom. Special education allocations for students should provide additional financial assistance to the classroom teacher as needed. In some cases, additional funds may be needed for specific equipment, resources, or instructional supports. Whether these resources benefit all students is less relevant than whether students with disabilities have access to them.

Resources and Support Services. The availability of resources, support services, equipment, and technology is an important consideration in determining appropriate placement. The teacher has a right to expect to be informed in advance about the placement of a student with a disability into the general education classroom. Adequate advance notice enables teachers to understand and plan for modifications that will be needed in the physical setting, curriculum, and instruction. Teachers also have a right to know the nature of the new student's disability and if the student has a physical, medical, emotional, or behavioral problem that might result in the need to make special accommodations, such as taking emergency action. The IDEA promotes the inclusion of children with chronic health impairments and those dependent on medical technology in the regular classroom within reasonable limits. An unreasonable situation is one in which no classroom aid is available and the teacher is required to perform physical assistance activities to the detriment of instruction of all students in the classroom. However, the teacher should have in writing, or in the IEP, specific expectations in the classroom for physical assistance or the assistance of an aide.

Teacher Access to Support Services. Teachers expect technical assistance and support services in order to accommodate students with disabilities. The teacher team has the right to expect that information about the student will be confidential and that they will be able to access the range of needed student support services in general education classrooms. These services should include:

- guidance and counseling
- consultation with the school psychologist or social worker
- collaboration and support from teachers who coordinate peer mediation and conflict resolution services (these teachers often have special knowledge and background and could help to promote positive peer relationships)
- health services or consultation of the school nurse
- consultation with special education teachers and specialists to facilitate understanding of the implications of the disability for student learning and for teaching modifications
- consultation with vocational teachers and career counselors to learn about how to make the academic curriculum relevant for student career interests and preferences
- access to transition services and job training and placement opportunities for youths
- assistance in promoting the student's participation in the extracurricular opportunities generally available, including student clubs, sports (as appropriate), drama and theatrical productions, chorus, debate teams, trade-related clubs, student governance organizations, booster clubs, and student fundraising activities
- assistance and consultation for promoting students' access to technology in the classroom, libraries, information centers, technology laboratories, and school-based weather stations
- assistance and consultation for making accommodations in such centers
- adaptations to equipment that may be necessary for use of the technology and participation in student group activities that rely on the use of computers or other technology.

19. What Curriculum Modifications and Instructional Strategies Are Considered Best Practices for Inclusion Classrooms?

Inclusion and Curriculum. Several curriculum modifications and instructional strategies have been consistently found to be part of exemplary inclusion programs. Curriculum experts recommend that teachers consider the following twelve assumptions when they explore curriculum modification in order to accommodate diverse learners.

Twelve Assumptions for Modifying Curriculum

1. Expectations for schools need to be raised by students, parents, teachers, educational administrators, and the community. Accomplishment and progress should be expected of all students—everybody counts.

2. Learners need a curriculum that is systematically integrated and not fragmented, with greater coherence and with more interrelationships and connections among subjects and disciplines.

3. Curriculum decisions should be focused not only on "what to cover," but also on how the material fosters the ability of the learner to use and apply knowledge resourcefully.

4. Learning must be placed into contexts of the real world, so the material makes sense in the world of the learner.

5. Although not all learners are alike, think alike, or learn alike, attention needs to be directed toward common general standards of achievement in learning and using knowledge.

6. Evaluation of the learner should focus on non-traditional evaluations of performance, through strategies such as "exhibitions," which call for the resourceful *application* of new knowledge rather than its display. The National Assessment of Educational Progress (U.S. Department of Education, 1994) urges engagement of the learner in concrete experiences.

7. Learners need the opportunity to be engaged in advanced academic work to prepare them for college placement.

8. Teachers need to become facilitators of learning, and learners need to become active doers and thinkers in the classroom, rather than passive recipients of information.

9. Each learner needs an advisor, advocate, or coordinator with whom the learner plans an academic program.

10. Current technology must be integrated into the curriculum and all learners brought to proficiency in the use of computers for communication, computation, and research.

11. Learners should have the opportunity to engage in advanced study through structured apprenticeships that are patterned after work-study arrangements in either traditional or new occupational fields. These advanced occupational opportunities serve as a bridge between secondary school and college or employment and provide for an organized transition into occupations for those learners who elect a career education path.

12. The critical transition to college or work after graduation requires additional planning and supports for the learner.

Effecting these changes requires different responses on the part of the schools and community. The existing familiar routines of schedules, courses, and teaching styles may not be adequate to reach these ends.

Who the Learner Is. Inclusive models for educating all children require changes in the ways learners are viewed and curriculum is structured. Inclusive education requires a reexamination and reformulation of (1) our view of who the learner is and (2) how curriculum, instruction, and learning environments must be restructured to accommodate this view. We are talking about preparing all members of the school system (e.g., teachers, students, parents, administrators, guidance counselors, and specialists) for a new kind of work that integrates our understanding about the learner and what we know about the promise of technology. As Jean Jacques Rousseau pointed out in 1911 (Emile), education comes to us from many sources in nature, from each other, and from our experience and environment. Over the century, educational theorists have explored the concept of individual differences in the learner. Gardner (1983, 1992) and others have built on the works of many theorists over the past century to develop new understanding about human intelligence and the various ways in which information is learned and understood.

New Ideas about Intelligence. Gardner (1983) has questioned the assumption that intelligence is a single general capacity and that it can be measured by standardized verbal instruments commonly used today. He defines intelligence as the ability to solve problems or create products that are valued within one or more cultural settings. Human development is flexible and elastic. Intelligence involves a set of skills for problem-solving potential for finding or creating problems, thereby laying the groundwork for the acquisition of new knowledge. Gardner (1992) clustered the broad range of human abilities into seven "intelligences," each of which is independent of the others:

1. **Linguistic intelligence**—rooted in the visual and auditory realms
2. **Musical intelligence**—rooted in the auditory realm
3. **Logical-mathematical intelligence**—rooted in the sensory-motor realm
4. **Spatial intelligence**—not rooted in any particular modality
5. **Bodily-kinesthetic intelligence**—rooted in the kinesthetic realm
6. **Intrapersonal intelligence**—sense of self and access to one's own feelings
7. **Interpersonal or social intelligence**—ability to make distinctions among other individuals.

Inclusion efforts must be built on an understanding of different intellectual strengths (domains) and their variability within different environments. Gardner's system for understanding the learner demands that we raise questions about different learning rates and styles and the interactions among the characteristics of the learner, the way we teach, and the characteristics of the learning environment. Examples of these issues related to learner characteristics include the following:

- **Use of symbols and different styles of learning.** Since we rely on symbol systems to communicate meaning (e.g., number systems, musical notes, chords, and symbols), a central question that arises from the recognition of multiple intelligences is whether information received in one medium is the "same" information when transmitted in another medium. We are challenged to explore different patterns and styles of learning and of conveying information to different learners.

- **The cultural context of cognitive accomplishments.** Cognitive accomplishments may occur in a range of domains. Some (logical-mathematical) are universal, and others are shaped and influenced by certain cultures. For example, social intelligence is a lot more important than mathematical or linguistic intelligence in some cultures. The question for teaching practice is: To what extent should we consider the cultural context for learning in determining what should be learned and how it should be applied?

- **The context for learning.** The understanding of the variety of cognitive abilities and patterns of learning requires careful consideration of the classroom environments and methods that are most appropriate for delivering information to different learners. Concrete and abstract learning should be combined by using a variety of learning opportunities, such as the following:
  - direct, unmediated learning or direct observation, in order to develop deeper knowledge through concrete experience
  - opportunities for active learning, including new technologies for learning
  - imitation with observation—"know that" joined with "know how"
  - learning opportunities in real-world settings
  - novel or unique settings for learning
  - transmittal of knowledge through use of a variety of tools and techniques.

Relating Concepts to Teaching. The assumptions we make about exceptional learners (and all learners) and the learning environment affect how we teach. Several assumptions that underlie the seven knowledge domains are important for developing effective instruction for inclusive classrooms.

Five Assumptions about the Seven Intelligences

1. Within each knowledge domain and the sphere of its application are a series of steps or stages ranging from the level of novice to expert or master.

2. Individuals differ in the speed with which they pass through these domains.

3. Success at negotiating one domain entails no necessary correlation with speed or success in others.

4. Progress in one domain does not depend entirely on the individual's actions within his or her world. Much of the information about the domain is better contained within the culture itself, because the culture defines the stages and fixes the limits of individual achievement.

5. The culture can mold or exploit capacities differently. The media through which the information in a domain is transmitted or communicated affects the rate of progress and this difference leads to different learning styles or responses to different media (Gardner, 1992).

This new understanding of the learner requires different responses from teachers, including those mentioned in the "Inclusion and Curriculum" section, and the following:

- Technology must be integrated into the curriculum, and all learners must be brought to proficiency in the use of computers for communication, computation, and research.
- Teachers need to become facilitators of learning, and learners need to become active doers and thinkers in the classroom, rather than passive recipients of information.
- Principals and teachers should think of themselves first as "generalists" in general educational strategies and second as "specialists" in their particular disciplines.

- The critical transition to college or work after graduation requires additional planning, supports, and resources for the learner.

Mathematics-Science and Inclusion. Students with disabilities are often counseled out of mathematics and science classes. Inclusion planning should emphasize the role of guidance counselors in promoting access and participation in mathematics and science classes, as well as access to special enrichment opportunities offered by the schools, such as "hands-on-science" after-school classes. Teachers should also offer examples of leaders in mathematics and science who have disabilities; such role models can provide a sense of "possibility" for students with disabilities. Special resources will also be needed to help teachers focus on curriculum modifications in mathematics and science in order to accommodate students with disabilities.

Curriculum Design. The student placed into the general education classroom should be expected to benefit and gain from the general education curriculum, with reasonable accommodations and adjustment in that curriculum. These reasonable adjustments are made to help a student with a disability catch up with his or her peers or to modify the expectations for the student but permit him or her to work in parallel with peers. Curriculum modifications can take many forms.

The Modular and Thematic Approach. The modular,* thematic† approach provides opportunities for success at many levels of academic or vocational skill training for every student, while allowing constant supervision and modification in the appropriate areas, as needed. The advancement of integrated curriculum is also assisted by the very nature of the cross-curricular model. The thematic approach provides a means to constantly upgrade the curriculum, but it is the student who receives the greatest benefit. This approach gives each student a chance to achieve at an individual learning rate, providing for immediate feedback on each activity. The thematic approach promotes a cooperative learning atmosphere by teaming students and faculty members, giving the staff an opportunity to learn more about each student. It reflects a holistic view of the student as a learner, allowing more intensive individual or small group learning sessions for remedial support. The use of the modular approach to introduce information allows for a synthesis of the materials and methods that are most suitable for instruction of students.

---

*Modular approach—small unit of instruction that can be thematic or functional or strictly academic
†Thematic approach—integrated academic subjects

Many students with special needs are hands-on learners who are trapped in a dominantly verbal environment. The incorporation of multimedia instruction, using current technology provides students with a variety of methods with which to achieve success. Using interactive technology also gives the student the hands-on experiences he or she needs to be prepared for authentic work environments.

The following are examples of curriculum modifications:

- inclusion of functional skills and applied academics in the curriculum
- community service activities built into the curriculum
- flexible schedules for completion of assignments and for meeting annual curriculum objectives (including summer)
- alternating performance-based assessment for grading students
- integration of computer-based learning activities
- access to technology and technology laboratories for all students
- open enrollment for vocational and community-based work experience programs
- curriculum modules or units that permit flexible enrollment
- integrated academic and vocational instruction (academic instruction embedded in vocational-technical education and work-based programs)
- alternative certification for vocational skill proficiencies, including certification of levels of skill attainment.

Social Aspects of the Curriculum. It is essential to provide information and awareness about disabilities to the nondisabled students in the classroom. Teachers can use numerous activities for explaining to nondisabled students the importance of integrating students with disabilities and their nondisabled peers into the learning environment and why modifications in curriculum are needed.

- Teachers can invite members of the community who have disabilities into the classroom to discuss their abilities and how they have overcome the challenges in their lives.
- Teachers can assign students to interview someone they know who has a disability and report to the class.

- Students can identify a famous person or celebrity who has a disability and discuss how they have overcome it and how society has perceived them.
- Teachers can have students role-play and can arrange simulations of disabling conditions in order to achieve awareness of disability (e.g., use of a blindfold or a wheelchair or binding of the legs or fingers).
- Teachers can ensure that students with disabilities are included in cooperative learning teams and are given responsibilities as members of those teams.
- Teachers can pair students for social as well as academic activities.

Classroom Modifications. Many strategies are available for making reasonable accommodations in the classroom environment. They include the following:

- creation of barrier-free settings for classroom access, including libraries, resource areas, and technology or learning laboratories
- modification in physical groupings of desks
- modification of seating arrangements to permit improved access and viewing for those with physical and/or visual disabilities
- rearrangement or enlargement of visual tools or resources
- use of audiotape equipment or alternative communication devices for students with communication difficulties
- rearrangement of classes, with consideration to their relationship to school building entrances and exits.

Instructional Strategies. The teacher can use many strategies to maximize the adjustment and learning of the student with a disability who is placed into the classroom with an expectation of reaching near-grade level with his or her peers by the close of the school year. Consideration should be given to variations in basic instructional methods.

- **Task analysis to break down instructional objectives into smaller units.** Task analysis provides a way of dividing larger units of instruction or student objectives into smaller, manageable activities and assignments. The teacher facilitates the step-by-step process. This is particularly effective for students who have short attention spans and who have trouble organizing and completing assignments. Task analysis provides more frequent opportunities for teacher feedback and for successful completion of assignments.

- **Strategic instruction.** Use of multiple instructional strategies aimed at matching the student's individual learning style to specific skill acquisition increases the opportunity for success.
- **Hands-on instruction.** Increasing students' opportunities to participate in active learning enhances the potential for success in the inclusive classroom. Active learning involves more hands-on instruction, which is particularly beneficial to students with disabilities, because it adds the kinesthetic learning modality to the visual and auditory modalities.
- **Collaborative team teaching.** The team teaching model offers an alternative instructional approach and is generally preferred over simply putting several students with disabilities into a traditional academic setting without support. Two or more teachers collaborate in the joint planning and the delivery of curriculum. This collaboration provides additional support for both the academic teacher and the special education teacher, as well as the students in the class.

Supplements to class instruction can be effective in enhancing learning abilities. These include the following:

- **Use of special materials or computers for one-on-one instruction and programmed instruction.** A vast array of commercially available instructional materials as well as software are available to supplement classroom instruction. This type of software is self-paced and allows students to feel a sense of control over their learning. Self-paced computer learning programs have helped many disabled and nondisabled students to achieve academic success. Students are often visually stimulated by computers and are motivated to achieve more in the classroom through computerized integrated learning systems, software for drill and practice, simulations, and electronic networks.
- **Use of peer learning teams in project activities.** Student group projects are becoming popular in today's classrooms because such projects help students to learn cooperatively and to share each other's talents and special abilities. Webbing and learning teams are one example of peer learning. Students are required to read chapters in the text and then to web the basic concepts on large newsprint or paper. Each student is responsible for web-

bing notes on a particular section of the chapter, and all the notes are brought together in the web. Students then assist and check each other's notes to make sure they are complete. This activity combines the abilities of the strong students with those of the students who are not as academically strong. Students are then given a group grade, as well as an individual grade based on their ability to answer questions related to information in their individual portion of the web.

- **Use of visual diagrams to reinforce classroom instructions.** Many students learn better through the visual modality. Therefore, teachers may use ready-made visual materials, as well as student-constructed visual materials to supplement classroom instruction and readings. One of the best examples of a visual diagram to reinforce instruction is the use of visual pictures to teach fractions and mathematical concepts. Homework projects that emphasize construction of posters, collages, visual models, and diagrams are particularly effective.
- **Writing and learning.** Teachers can help students with disabilities to improve their *writing skills* and to learn from their experiences by providing more opportunities to write about *learning experiences*. Such assignments could include the following:
  —Write about what they already know about a topic before a unit begins.
  —Write about experiences with activities they have completed in class.
  —Write responses to field trip experiences.
  —Write about films seen in class.
  —Write about the participation in learning teams or computer laboratory groups.
  —Write about the students with whom they completed an activity.
  —Write about homework experiences and how they believe they learn best.

Finally, teachers should encourage students with disabilities to complete a *job profile* before completion of high school and to participate in interviews with prospective employers as part of their job search activities. The job profile and portfolio involves a process that includes

—writing about a career interest or occupation
—participating in job search activities
—writing letters of interest
—obtaining letters of reference
—completing a job resume
—completing job applications

—participating in interviews

—writing the follow-up letter

- **Partnerships as instructional supports.** There are several ways in which relationships can provide *additional support* for students with disabilities in inclusive classrooms. They include the following:

- **Peer mentoring to support students with special needs.** Each student is assigned to a peer-mentor team of two students. The participant's peer-mentor provides support and encouragement and enables the student with disabilities to solve problems, make decisions, and adjust to the classroom and to new expectations. Peer teams also help (enable) each other to prepare for performance demonstrations and exhibitions. Sometimes group sessions are conducted by the psychologist, career counselor, and teacher-advocates to prepare or support peer-mentor teams.

- **Teacher-student mentor relationships.** Teacher-student mentor relationships provide additional support to students in inclusive classrooms. These relationships provide emotional and social support and help to link the student with needed support services. A student is assigned to a teacher-advocate who provides guidance, support, crisis assistance, and linkage with other professionals. The teacher-advocate is responsible for a group of students and meets with them on a regular basis.

- **Paraprofessionals and teacher aides.** Additional support from paraprofessionals and teacher aides within the classroom is always a benefit. Such support is particularly welcome and necessary in order to meet the demanding challenges of the inclusive classroom.

- **Volunteers.** Parents, the Parent-Teacher Association, and community representatives can volunteer to support instruction. Typically, they assist by providing tutoring, special lectures, duplicating instructional materials, gathering resources, developing student materials, and performing any other services helpful to teachers in the classroom.

- **Peer tutors.** Students in the class can also assist other students in the learning process. Students can also lead discussions or project teams. However, peer tutoring does not mean simply pairing students together. It means matching students with common interests, outlining the purpose of the peer tutoring with the student tutor, and providing ongoing supervision of the peer tutoring process. Peers can tutor individual students or in teams.

- **Service coordination.** For assistance with coordinating a range of services to students with disabilities, some schools assign a teacher-advocate who is responsible for knowing the student, determining additional service needs, and making referrals for needed support services. The teacher-advocates work closely with the school social workers, psychologists, and others to identify and link the student and/or family with needed services in the school and community.

Modifications in Student Assessment. Many teachers are experimenting with nontraditional methods of assessing student learning through use of student portfolios of completed work and exhibitions of student work products and performance. By increasing variety in student learning assessments, teachers have a better opportunity to determine student progress in acquisition of specific skills. Authentic assessment, that is, assessment of students in performance-based activities, will enhance the learning experience in the inclusive classroom for all students. Examples of these approaches include the following activities:

- **Completion of a project portfolio and presentation of the portfolio before a panel of peers or members of the community in special demonstration sessions.** A portfolio is a collection or compilation of a series of assignments or projects designed to integrate academic learning. Demonstrations require students to actively present their work and to discuss the process and products. Portfolio development can be directed by the teacher or the student and can involve teams of students using resources in the community. Portfolios can also be used at the end of the year to present student homework or special projects. Demonstrations and exhibitions can be used to evaluate individual and group learning and performance. Students can demonstrate proficiency in a variety of skill areas in either academic or vocational areas.

- **Participation in "leadership activities."** Leadership activities require students to cooperate in the planning and performance of a classroom demonstration or exhibition. Students may form teams to organize a science exhibit or a multicultural fair or to produce a photographic exhibit, a videotape of an activity or process, preparation of graduation materials for print, or a presentation to parents attending the exhibitions.

20. What Support Services Are Needed for Inclusive Classrooms?

There are several related or support services that enable school districts to provide effective inclusive classrooms.

> **What are related services?** Related services are supportive services that enable a student to participate in and benefit from placement in an inclusive classroom. They assist the student with a disability to learn in the general educational setting. Related services include early identification and assessment of disabling conditions, transportation, developmental and corrective services, such as speech pathology and audiology, psychological services, social work services, physical and occupational therapy, recreation therapy, and medical and counseling services. Such services may be required in order to assist a child with a disability to benefit from education.

Each support service by itself cannot guarantee success in the general education classroom, but these supports in addition to adequate individualized educational planning can be a positive step forward in the inclusion process. The following are examples of related or support services that may be available in the school or community:

- **Medical and health services.** Reviewing existing medical and health reports provides important information that is needed when the student's daily schedule is changed, to determine any possible emergency arrangements, set up classroom guidelines, or alert family members to any medical concerns the school district may have.
- **Social and family support services.** Contacting appropriate social service agencies to make arrangements for services can be helpful to students with disabilities.
- **Emergency management supports.** Planning for unforeseen emergencies can establish a safety net and a backup plan for school personnel.

- **Rehabilitation counseling.** Determining the eligibility of the student for vocational rehabilitation services can be crucial to the future of students with disabilities.
- **Personal counseling.** Providing personal counseling for students and/or family can assist in the inclusion process. Frequently, circumstances that are beyond the control of the school must be addressed so that learning can proceed.
- **Job coach and job placement services.** Providing vocational training for students with moderate or severe disabilities often requires the skills of a job coach. A job coach provides one-on-one assistance during the occupational training. Job placement services identify potential job placement sites. This task requires a concentrated effort to know the community, the availability of job openings, and the labor market needs at the local, state, and regional levels.
- **Occupational therapist.** Providing physical therapy can improve work mobility for on-the-job performance. Occupational therapists assess the physical capabilities of students or workers and provide suggestions for job accommodations.
- **Reading specialist.** Providing additional reading tutorial assistance is designed to improve reading skills, comprehension, and academic performance.
- **Physical therapist.** Providing physical therapy helps in preventing, correcting, relieving, or strengthening physical conditions.
- **Speech therapist.** Providing speech services helps to remediate articulation problems, voice fluency disorders, and general language problems and to foster the communication skills of students within the classroom environment.

Inclusive school teachers recognize that for students with disabilities who are transferred from segregated schools or other locations, there are often many barriers to participation in general education classrooms. A supportive environment is essential to the success of inclusive classrooms.

21. How Do Interdisciplinary Teams Coordinate Services for Effective Inclusion?

Students with disabilities have many unique needs and often need the services of a variety of professionals in order to succeed in the general classroom. Therefore, students require an interdisciplinary approach to developing and monitoring their individual educational programs (IEPs).

Interdisciplinary Planning and Coordination for Inclusion

As discussed earlier, students often need a variety of support services to successfully participate in an inclusive classroom. Therefore, implementing the IEP requires a special kind of coordination among members of the IEP team. *The purpose of inclusion coordination is to develop processes and procedures that help professionals collaborate to address the multiple needs of children and youths in mainstream educational settings and to help them achieve their maximum potential in the full range of functional areas.* Inclusion implementors are interested in what teachers and support service personnel can do to better coordinate and link services for these students. Assessment of student needs in collaborative programs requires two elements.

1. A common target group of students with a range of needs in the variety of functional domains (physical development and health status, independent functioning, social functioning, family relationships, behavioral functioning, emotional and psychological functioning, academic and vocational functioning, employment skills and recreation/leisure functioning) to be served by collaborating team members (e.g., special education and general education teachers, and related service professionals), and
2. A common goal of linking the educational and support services in a continuum of opportunities that can increase the chances of success of these students.

The next step is to outline the common needs shared by students and identify the collaborative activities used by interdisciplinary team members to build a range of options for meeting these needs.

Individual needs of students require a team approach. *The multiple needs of individual students require interdisciplinary team planning and collaboration.* It is helpful to review the variety of collaborative team activities that define interdisciplinary coordination for inclusion. The mechanism that schools create to meet the needs of students integrated into inclusive classrooms can be called "inclusion coordination functions." They include:

- information and placement referral
- review and screening
- assessment and diagnosis
- IEP planning and development
- support service coordination and linking
- IEP monitoring and follow-along
- inclusion advocacy and support
- inclusion evaluation and student follow-up.

In assessing the school's readiness for inclusion, it will help to determine the capability of personnel to perform these core functions. Such an assessment should result in recommendations for what each person must do to strengthen inclusion coordination.

Assessment and the Interdisciplinary Team

The assessment of each student culminates in an IEP and/or an individualized education or school-to-work transition plan (ITP). Some school districts prefer to develop ITPs during the last two years of high school. The IEP is developed (1) to ensure that each student achieves the required standards established by the state for learning in academic and vocational areas, (2) to engage students in the planning process for their education, and (3) to motivate students to achieve their maximum potential. Core education skills combine development of academic and vocational-technical skills in a curriculum that also emphasizes:

- social responsibility
- technology (the curriculum makes effective use of technology, developing in students both the com-

petence and the confidence they will need in technologically enriched work environments)

- problem solving, critical thinking, analysis and synthesis, creativity, and application of knowledge
- integration and interrelatedness of knowledge
- comprehensiveness (addresses multiple learning styles and multiple levels of intelligence)
- developmental appropriateness
- curriculum relevance to work-based standards
- flexibility and collaboration

No ambiguity about whether students must be invited to IEP meetings. The U.S. Department of Education's regulations for implementing the Individuals with Disabilities Act (1990), states that the student should be invited "if appropriate." The final rules state that

> . . . if the purpose of the meeting is the consideration of [educational or] transition services for a student, the public agency *shall* invite the student and a representative of any other agency that is likely to be responsible for providing or paying of transition services. If the student does not attend, the public agency shall take other steps to ensure that the student's preferences and interests are considered. If the agency invited to send a representative to a meeting does not do so, the public agency shall take other steps to obtain the participation of the other agency in the planning of any transition services. (Section 300, 18, U.S.C. 1401)

Basic Functions of Inclusion Coordination

This section defines the essential elements or functions of inclusion coordination. These functions have been adapted from traditional service coordination models in human services agencies. Although many researchers have identified different elements of coordination, a synthesis of the literature reveals that there is agreement on the eight basic functions or clusters of activities listed. These eight functions represent the procedures and activities that schools create to address the common needs of students in inclusive environments.

Eight Basic Functions of Inclusion Coordination

1. Information and referral for classroom placement
2. Review and screening of student needs
3. Assessment and diagnosis of disability and educational needs
4. Planning and development of individual educational plan (IEP)
5. Coordination and linking of support services
6. IEP monitoring and follow-along
7. Inclusion advocacy and support
8. Evaluation of inclusion program and follow-up of student (Kochhar, 1987, 1995)

Studies of service coordination show much variety in the types of activities that are included in each of the eight functions. The following definitions have been synthesized from the experiences of many coordination programs in operation in human services today (Kochhar, 1987, 1995). These functions are being transferred for use in schools in order to coordinate support services to students who need special supports to succeed in the home school.

Function 1: Information and Referral for Classroom Placement. Procedures for providing information and placement referrals vary widely among schools. The information and referral function is defined in two ways:

1. **narrowly**—as the giving of information to teachers receiving students into inclusive classrooms
2. **broadly**—to include activities of inclusion planning teams or principals to gather information about general changes in placement policies, extensive outreach activities, parent orientation, and information to identify students who might be appropriate for placement into inclusive classrooms or for placement from segregated schools to home schools.

When students with severe disabilities and complex needs are considered for placement into inclusive settings, aggressive and creative attempts at outreach to families are needed. Individual information and referral includes activities such as:

- identifying and conducting outreach to students' families
- disseminating information to the community about inclusion goals, philosophies, and benefits
- developing a single point of entry or a coordinator for teachers and families, to facilitate discussion and problem solving for students being transferred into inclusive settings
- managing classroom placement referrals and follow-ups
- decreasing the amount of time between the family's initial contact for information or assistance and coordinator or teacher response
- managing expanding student caseloads.

Many schools are working toward improved identification and referral procedures for students who could successfully be placed into more inclusive settings. When families learn about inclusion efforts through an organized and coordinated information and referral strategy, the school is more likely to be perceived by families as accessible, responsive, and supportive.

Function 2: Review and Screening of Student Needs.

At the *individual level*, intake and screening involve procedures (1) for determining the appropriateness of placement in an inclusive classroom and (2) for matching student need for support with relevant services and teacher teams. Screening activities may include:

- understanding prevalence rates for different disability groups
- developing meaningful quality standards for inclusive classrooms
- developing appropriateness criteria for placement into inclusive classrooms
- making support services accessible to students in the classroom, library, laboratory, and other settings
- obtaining and documenting informed consent for placement, given by the student and family
- developing and maintaining student records
- understanding the needs of and communicating with families.

At the *administrative level*, screening can mean developing processes for schoolwide data collection and determination of placement. Through data collection, schools can compare information about different groups of children and youths served in different inclusion options and can help each other anticipate classroom needs. Schools can share enrollment and placement and can help each other to match individuals to classroom environments, and related services, and to project future service and budget needs.

Function 3: Diagnosis of Disability and Assessment of Educational Needs.

Needs assessment is a process by which information is collected and analyzed in a collaborative way among educational personnel, support service personnel, and students, in order to answer six key questions:

1. What is the current functioning of the student in the range of functional domains (e.g., social, intellectual, and physical)? What are the student's strengths and needs?
2. What features of the student's environment or classroom milieu support or inhibit improved functioning?
3. What goals and objectives for improved functioning in the range of domains should be identified and included in the IEP? What are the priorities?
4. What resources and support services are necessary to accomplish these goals and objectives in the classroom and in activities outside the classroom?
5. What procedures and schedule will be used for monitoring progress toward these goals and objectives inside and outside the classroom?
6. What outcome criteria will be used to evaluate results of the inclusive placement?

Function 4: Planning and Development of the IEP.

The development of IEPs is an essential function of inclusion coordination. Written plans are essential for students and families in inclusive classrooms, because they represent the service "agreement" or contract between the student and the instructional personnel. An IEP documents the planned activities and responsibilities of the student, teachers, related and support service personnel, family members, and others concerned with the student's development. It also indicates the criteria by which all parties will determine if the student's educational and other goals have been achieved and if the required support services have been provided. The plan is based on information obtained from the individual assessments described earlier.

The IEP team is made up of a variety of professionals who are responsible for providing the special educational and support services that the student may need. The IEP team also includes the student and his or her family. As part of their ongoing role, the team initially identifies students who are ready for appropriate placement into an inclusive setting. In designing the IEP for a student, a team must determine the curricular emphasis a student should receive and the least restrictive environment for instruction. Consequently, the identification of a student's readiness for inclusion begins with the IEP. Each student's needs are discussed on a case-by-case basis and not as part of a general policy or movement. *However, in school districts where inclusion is supported and encouraged, it is easier for an IEP team to make a recommendation for placement in a general education classroom.* The team can also identify services the student may need from outside agencies and provide coordination of such services.

Individual program planning activities include:

- engaging the interdisciplinary team in educational planning
- developing support service plans related to the range of functional domains
- providing for the necessary linking services or transition services as the student moves from one school or setting to another or from one level to another (e.g., middle school to high school)
- ensuring regular review of IEPs
- ensuring the active participation and decision making of students and their families in IEP planning and review
- communicating with students and families about adjustments or revisions in IEPs.

Components of an IEP

1. Date of entry into the inclusive setting, date of IEP meetings, and placement information
2. Identifying information (e.g., name, date of birth, address, sex, and grade level)
3. Assistance needed (1) to establish appropriateness for placement and eligibility for special educational services, or (2) to apply for other needed services
4. Name of service coordinator or program advocate and parent or guardian
5. Names of individuals and agencies represented in the development or review of the plan
6. Summary of assessments and observations of the student that indicate strengths, needs, and needed services
7. Types of support and advocacy services the student and his or her family are receiving
8. Names of persons providing services
9. Short- and long-range measurable objectives for the services and service priorities in all relevant functional areas
10. Objectives for vocational-technical training, on-the-job training, and/or employment assistance
11. Methods or strategies of service delivery, including names of responsible persons and agencies to which the individual may be referred
12. Service coordination supports needed and methods of monitoring the receipt of services
13. Special supports needed by the student to participate in the service (e.g., transportation, assistive devices, and/or financial help)
14. Criteria for evaluation of services, with explicitly stated and measurable outcomes
15. Expected and realistic dates of completion for each service to be delivered
16. Potential barriers to accessing or using services recommended in the IEP (e.g., placement criteria, enrollment procedures, unavailability of services, attitudes of the individual, and lack of family agreement or support)
17. Services or supports needed to exit from the placement and to make a transition to an alternative placement or program, if appropriate
18. Signature of student, parents, and professionals participating in the planning meeting

Note: Synthesized from a review of many individual service plans and IEPs from several states and localities.

Inclusion planning occurs at the student level and results in development of an IEP. When inclusion planning occurs at the *team or school level*, it often results in the development of an *inclusion coordination agreement* among professionals or agencies. The coordination agreement is written to guide the inclusion planning and implementation team and typically includes the mission statement, inclusion goals and objectives, and a timetable for activities. The mission statement describes the *broad purpose* of the agreement and broad areas of joint responsibility of professionals who will be involved. The statement provides the broad parameters for the collaboration and is a declaration of what the team members or school units will and will not provide.

An inclusion mission statement may include one or more of the following parts:

1. **A statement of context or history of the agreement or a brief introductory paragraph** that defines how the cooperative arrangement differs from or expands on what has been in place before
2. **A declaration of the authority for the cooperative relationships,** which describes the legal or policy basis for the agreement and typically lists the local, state, and federal laws and the statutes and regulations that may give authority to this inclusion initiative and agreement
3. **A general statement of purpose of the agreement and expected outcomes,** which offers a rationale for entering an inclusion coordination agreement to advance the goals of inclusion and broadly defines what benefits and outcomes the inclusion team hopes to achieve
4. **The broad goal or outline** of what the agreement provides, which lists the specific goals and objectives of the agreement

The inclusion coordination agreement defines the scope of activities, responsibilities, and contributions of each team member or agency and the expected outcomes for each participating partner.

Coordination agreements should address four essential functions of interagency planning:

1. Identify resources to support the inclusion initiative.
2. Identify activities of the inclusion planning and implementation team.
3. Identify expected results of the inclusion initiative.
4. Establish timetables for the inclusion initiative.

The statement of goals and shared activities of "first time" inclusion planners and implementors provides only a blueprint for defining new relationships and procedures. These agreements must be modified annually or at least periodically.

Function 5: Coordination and Linking of Support Services. Linking of services identifies appropriate disciplines or providers of related services who can deliver support services required by the IEP. For example, it may mean providing a central point of contact in the school for help to families of at-risk students in locating needed community services (e.g., health services, mental health services, family counseling, or assistive devices or equipment for home health care). For individuals with chronic health needs, it may mean providing information and linking with health clinics, physician services, and providers of in-home health-related and adaptive equipment. For youths preparing for post–secondary school placement, it may mean providing additional linking services in the event that the first post–secondary school linkages or planned placements are not achieved. Linking activities may include:

- establishing a school coordinator or point of contact for each individual or family
- identifying and contacting needed services within the school district or outside, if appropriate
- arranging for contacts or visits to the school for the student and family
- arranging special support services for students who are transferring from more restrictive settings to inclusive settings or from segregated to inclusive schools (This may mean arranging visits to the school and classroom before the transfer occurs, providing extra counseling or guidance during the transfer or transition, providing information about the new environment and expectations, and arranging meetings with new teachers.)
- tracking and documenting changes in student placements or movements among schools or classrooms
- documenting support services used by students and families
- documenting referrals to other related agencies for assessments or additional services.

At the *administrative level*, coordination of inclusion through linking services means sharing resources among schools and community agencies. In times of economic austerity, schools are more likely to share resources in order to preserve and enhance services to students. Shared resources include personnel financial and material resources that belong to the schools and cooperating agencies, but that could be dedicated to inclusion activities. Linking of interagency activities can help prevent duplication of services in schools and community agencies. Such reductions can save costs and make the educational system more efficient.

Linking functions also join professionals from different disciplines in common goals and activities. This sharing not only results in combined service efforts, but also creates a "cross-fertilization" of ideas that enhances problem solving and can accelerate the process of improving services. Staff from different agencies can complement each others' talents and skills. For example, several agencies might benefit from a specialized talent of a particular staff member in one cooperating agency.

Function 6: IEP Monitoring and Follow-Along.

IEP monitoring and "follow-along" are essential functions of inclusion coordination. At the *student level*, the purposes of IEP monitoring are (1) to evaluate the student's progress in achieving the goals and objectives in the IEP and (2) to ensure that the student is receiving the services and accommodations that are required by the plan and that are appropriate to enable the student to benefit from the educational program in the general classroom.

Monitoring requires that the teachers maintain ongoing contact with the student in the inclusive classroom and with the professionals providing support services (McCoy, 1995). Monitoring of the IEP also enables the teacher to observe and gain direct knowledge of the types and quality of the support services received by the student. Another important aspect of monitoring is that it allows the student to evaluate the services that he or she is receiving and allows the teacher to understand those services from the student's perspective. Monitoring of activities may include:

- documenting and maintaining a chronological record of support services received by each student
- measuring and documenting progress made by students in their academic achievement, vocational skills development, social and family relationships, or independent living skills
- documenting student achievement of educational goals included in the IEP and modifications of the plan
- documenting services actually received, services not received, and reasons why services were not received

- documenting gaps in services for the student and efforts to locate services outside the school
- documenting barriers to services for the student
- maintaining continuity in communication and the coordination of support services.

Monitoring of services at the *administrative level* means observing the educational progress of students and monitoring the delivery of support services for inclusive classrooms. It means ensuring that such services:

- are being provided according to the intended schedules
- are reaching the students they were intended to reach
- are being provided in a manner that complies with established local, state, and national regulations, guidelines, standards, and ethics
- are being provided with an acceptable level of quality.

Monitoring activities at the *administrative level* include:

- documenting the progress and performance of collaborating personnel and school units, as well as the achievement of goals, objectives, and timetables of the inclusion team
- collecting information from students about how they perceive the quality, appropriateness, and accessibility of educational and support services in their new classrooms
- examining and improving (1) policies on inclusion that are related to placement criteria, assessment procedures, and termination criteria and (2) policies governing support services that are designed to benefit students with disabilities and to facilitate their participation in inclusive classrooms and in nonclassroom activities
- conducting projections of needs for support services and for personnel and additional spaces in inclusive classrooms.

The monitoring function can offer valuable information about the quality and effectiveness of inclusion practices.

Follow-along activities are an important part of the monitoring function. In some schools where the number of students with disabilities in general education classrooms is high, the monitoring function is often a paper-tracking activity. In others, monitoring includes ongoing and close contacts with the student and family to provide direct support. The follow-along function includes activities of the teacher or coordinator that provide emotional support, foster relationships of trust with the student, and maintain close contact and communication with the family. Follow-along activities include:

- home visits to families with students who have special needs
- visits to youths in their school or work-based programs
- visits with students in their classrooms or in nonclassroom activities
- informal counseling with students or families
- supportive counseling with families and siblings
- face-to-face contact with a school counselor or coordinator on a regular basis
- involvement and communication with the family
- behavioral (or other) crisis intervention.

The follow-along function represents the personal support component of inclusion coordination and is extremely important for increasing the retention of students placed in inclusive classrooms (i.e., preventing a student from dropping out).

Function 7: Inclusion Advocacy and Support.

Definitions of "advocacy" are not always clear and are often circular. For example, "advocacy is any attempt to advocate for services." Advocacy is a broad term that has evolved over the past few decades to mean different things, but it is a particularly important function of inclusion coordination.

This discussion of advocacy can be divided into two aspects: (1) *advocacy for student inclusion*, and (2) *advocacy for schoolwide inclusion*. At the *student level*, advocacy can mean advocating *on behalf of an individual student* for inclusion into a more inclusive setting, or it can mean assisting the student to advocate on *his or her own behalf* for an inclusive placement or supportive services (self-advocacy). Student advocacy more recently has come to mean ensuring that schools promote student *self-determination and informed decision making by students and their families*.

> **Self-determination**—the act of making independent choices about personal goals and directions, based on accurate information about one's own strengths and needs and the available placement, service, or program options. Self-determination is most effective and rewarding within an environment that promotes and facilitates independent decision making (Racino, 1992).

Self-determination does not mean "going it alone" or relying only on oneself. Rather, the idea should be placed within the context of shared decision making, interdependence, and mutual support (Racino, 1992).

Teachers can perform student advocacy activities on behalf of students or to assist students to advocate on their own behalf. Advocacy should actually be viewed as two poles of a *continuum*, rather than as "either-or" activities (Exhibit II–4). Teachers of inclusive classes continually strive to maximize the extent to which students and families are empowered and enabled to make decisions and to manage their educational experiences and personal affairs in a manner as independent and self-sufficient as possible.

Advocacy at the school level means advocating on behalf of whole groups of students by using the same methods used to advocate for individuals. Advocacy activities on the school level include:

- developing a schoolwide understanding of the needs of groups of students with disabilities
- addressing multicultural and multilingual issues with teachers and related service personnel to negotiate the development of special supports or accommodations
- identifying and targeting students in the greatest need of inclusive programs and support services
- communicating service barriers and service gaps to principals and other decision makers
- communicating and protecting human rights and due process procedures for groups of students
- promoting an emphasis on self-determination and informed decision making for students and their families

Exhibit II–4 Student Advocacy Activities: Two Ends of a Continuum

Advocacy on Behalf of the Student	Assisting the Student in Self-Advocacy
• Assisting the student to receive all the benefits to which he or she is entitled	• Assisting the student (1) to request information about the variety of benefits to which he or she is entitled and (2) to make decisions about which benefits to apply for
• Intervening to ensure that individual human rights and due process procedures are protected	• Providing information about human rights and due process procedures to the student or family for their own self-advocacy
• Helping the student gain access to a service from which he or she has traditionally been excluded	• Offering strategies to the student to help him or her independently gain access to a service from which he or she has been excluded
• Directly intervening on behalf of the student to negotiate enrollment in a service or program	• Offering strategies, information, or coaching to help the student negotiate admission to a program
• Negotiating with a service agency to provide special support services or accommodations that will enable a student to participate in a service	• Offering strategies, information, or coaching to enable the student to negotiate with a service agency for special support services or an accommodation that will make it possible to participate in a service
• Helping to educate the family, allay fears, and encourage cooperation and participation in instances in which the family is fearful of having their son or daughter participate in a needed support service	• Offering strategies, information, or coaching to help the student negotiate with the family to support participation in services or a program or to agree to enroll as a family in a needed service
• Helping an agency understand the special language or cultural conditions that prevent enrollment and participation in education and helping to negotiate special supports for a student with such problems	• Offering strategies, information, or coaching to help the student explain the special language or cultural conditions or barriers that prevent enrollment or make it difficult to participate in a service or program
• Intervening with a potential employer to provide information about an individual and explaining his or her skill training and needs for supervision	• Providing coaching to help the student/future employee describe his or her own strengths and weaknesses, relevant job skills, and training needs

• linking students with advocacy organizations or working with local agencies to help them meet new inclusion goals and requirements

• providing attitudinal leadership to improve school and community attitudes toward students served in inclusive settings and their families

• working to increase supports during the movements or transitions between schools, programs, or classrooms

• reinforcing the family and the informal support network.

Reducing conflicts of interest. As schools respond to new requirements for inclusion, advocacy can help build a shared capacity to meet the multiple needs of students and their families. Advocacy activities can help to stimulate creative approaches to reducing resistance and barriers to inclusion and collaboration. In addition, *advocacy can lead to reduction in conflicts of interest for the teacher*—an issue raised by many teachers in inclusive classrooms. For example, teachers employed by large school systems that contract for related and support services are often caught between the student and the administration, which controls funding to all parts of the system. The independence and authority of the teachers to advocate effectively on behalf of the student can sometimes be compromised by forces within the school. If this occurs, advocacy becomes an ideal that is written into every mission statement but is seldom realized. *When teachers and related services personnel set goals for the advocacy function, an emphasis on the benefits and outcomes for the student may help to empower and focus the advocacy effort, bringing it closer to students and their individual needs.*

Function 8: Inclusion Evaluation and Follow-Up of Student.

Evaluation and follow-up services are essential to effective inclusion coordination. Although program evaluation may be a *final step* in assessing the value and quality of inclusive services to students, it is the *first step* in their improvement. It may be helpful to view the evaluation process as a continu-

ous spiral that gradually lifts the inclusion initiative upward toward greater improvements.

Why is inclusion coordination important?

Resources to plan, develop, implement, evaluate, and sustain inclusion practices are usually difficult to obtain. *When educational and human services budgets are being reduced, coordination activities are carefully scrutinized and may be the first activities to be eliminated.* In many state and localities today, support services, service coordination activities, and state and local interagency cooperative teams and activities are falling under the budget ax. Sound and comprehensive needs assessments can prevent this from happening. Decision makers will ask for sound rationale for inclusion coordination activities, especially to justify additional personnel positions. The inclusion planner needs to be able *to show a clear relationship between the mission of the inclusion initiative and the contributions and needs of each team member.* The budget decision makers are likely to appreciate how collaborative activities address mutual needs and help pool resources for efficient and effective services for students and their families.

22. What Are Important Considerations Related to the Use of Technology?

In schools, there is an increasing gap between the technological "haves and have nots." Students with disabilities have a right to access the full range of technologies that are available in the classroom for instruction, including computers, libraries, information centers, technology laboratories, school-based weather stations, and other resources. Whether or not a school has a lot of technological resources, access to available technology by students with disabilities is generally more limited than that for their nondisabled peers. The same holds true for student access to computers in the home. Questions of access and equity are unavoidable when we consider the high cost of computer equipment adaptations for students with disabilities and of assistive technology, much of which has to be customized to the needs of individuals. Access to these devices and financial support for purchasing them are

lacking for many students with disabilities. For these students, it is essential to provide special attention to computer station adaptations and instruction and training early in the school career. This form or *"early intervention" for technology access* promotes independence long before the individual reaches adolescence and begins the process of preparing for transition to the work world or to post–secondary education.

Technology Integration and Access.

Billions of dollars are spent each year on educational technology that lies unused in our schools, while research demonstrates exciting links among technology, literacy, achievements for students with disabilities, improved student motivation, and performance. Over the past decade, the school improvement efforts have focused on using technology in the classroom. However, its effective use remains an elusive goal for most teachers and *also for most students with disabilities*. Reasons for this include:

- inadequate staff training for effective integration of technology into instruction
- lack of support services
- lack of incentives for schools to accommodate technology
- little understanding of how to use technology in order to accommodate diverse students in regular classrooms.

Technology can increase the likelihood that students with disabilities can also achieve the outcomes related to the national education goals: *that all students will participate in educational programs designed to meet their present and future needs within a global community*. (National Education Goals Panel, 1993; U.S. Department of Education, 1994a). Educators need to advance their understanding of the benefits for students with disabilities who are mainstreamed and included in regular classrooms.

Technology in the Classroom Supported by National Initiatives. Several national education and training initiatives have placed instructional technology at the center of education and employment training policies. One of these—the Goals 2000 initiative—establishes broad national education goals and challenges each state to achieve them by the year 2000 (National Education Goals Panel, 1993). Goals 2000 requires that all students be prepared for work and technologically literate. Goal 5, adult literacy and lifelong learning, specifically highlights technology in education, stating that "by the year 2000, every adult American will be literate and will possess the knowledge and skills necessary to compete in a global economy and exercise the rights and responsibilities of citizenship." (National Education Goals Panel, 1994, p. 10). These national educational goals and objectives require that children should become technologically literate as early as possible in their educational programs.

Including Children with Severe and Medically Related Impairments. P.L. 101-476 (the IDEA) promotes the inclusion of children with chronic health impairments and those dependent on medical technology into the regular classroom. Schools are required to include children who are in transition from medical care to special education, including those with traumatic brain injuries and chronic health impairments and those dependent on medical technology, who may require individualized health-related services to enable them to participate in or benefit from education. These in-

clude those that could be provided by nursing personnel or others with appropriate training, such as sectioning, tracheotomy care, administration of oxygen or intravenous medication, intermittent catheterization, and gastrostomy or nasogastric tube feeding. Students with severe disabilities may also require technological devices (assistive technology) that assist them in classroom participation.

Assistive Technology

Assistive Technology Device—any item, piece of equipment, or product, whether acquired commercially or off the shelf, modified, or customized, that is used to increase, maintain, or improve functional capabilities of individuals with disabilities.

Assistive Technology Service—any service that directly assists an individual with a disability in the selection, acquisition, or use of an assistive technology device. Such services include

- evaluating the needs of a student with a disability, including a functional evaluation of the student in his or her customary environment
- purchasing, leasing, or otherwise providing for the acquisition of assistive technology devices by individuals with disabilities
- selecting, designing, fitting, customizing, adapting, applying, maintaining, repairing, or replacing assistive technology devices
- coordinating and using other therapies, interventions, or services with assistive devices, such as those associated with existing education and rehabilitation plans and programs
- training or technical assistance for a student with a disability or, when appropriate, for the student's family
- training or technical assistance for professionals, employers, or other individuals who provide services to, employ, or otherwise are substantially involved in the major life functions of individuals with disabilities

The Technology-Related Assistance for Individuals with Disabilities Act; P.L. 100-407, 1988, 34 CFR, Part 300, Section 300.6.

Inclusion plans that include technology integration should be responsive to the Technology-Related Assistance for Individuals with Disabilities Act of 1988 (PL. 100-407) and IDEA regulations, which incorporate assistive technology. These laws address the need for access of students with disabilities to the range of technology and media supports available within schools.

Successful Inclusion Supported by Technology. With increased use of technology in the educational and work environment, individuals are spending much more time at the computer. Maximizing an individual's performance by ensuring proper access and comfort at the computer are important for enhancing the productivity of the individual. For persons with disabilities, issues of access and comfort often make the difference between success and failure in use of technology. The use of assistive technologies for persons with disabilities can also help to eliminate barriers that previously prevented access and success in schooling and work. For example, adapting the computer through a DOS extension software program can open doors for a one-handed typist or mouthstick user. Similarly, using a wrist rest can help an individual with muscular dystrophy or rheumatoid arthritis to access keyboard keys and thus can facilitate increased work productivity.

Many Uses of Technology for Inclusion. Many uses of technology can support the successful inclusion of students in the classroom Adaptive technologies and equipment enable students with disabilities to access technology for assessment purposes, for IEP decision making, and for instruction. Students can incorporate technology in developing their vocational-technical skills for future employment and inde-

pendent living. For example, for a student with a severe disability, a multidisciplinary team might consist of a general education teacher, special education teachers, an assessment specialist, and an augmentative communication specialist, in order to determine individual needs and access to technology. Students can use keyboarding, word processing, a database, and graphic tools, in addition to classroom-related software, to reinforce learning. Again, for students with disabilities, it is essential to provide such adaptations, instruction, and training to promote independence while the learner is still in school.

Students with more severe disabilities *would be unable to compete* in society without access to technology for basic communication and productivity. For example, students with cerebral palsy, brain injuries, vision impairments, epilepsy, and degenerative muscular disabilities must be involved in such early interventions in order to have access to technology. Each student's unique cognitive, motor, and sensory needs present challenges in the classroom, because learning stations need to be customized to match the experience, capabilities, and career interests of the student.

Types of Equipment Modifications for Technology in the Classroom. Special education means adapting curriculum and instructional methods to enable the student to learn. Educators have realized for some time that computers are able to incorporate many of the best practices of instructional methods of special education. Computers can also provide a means of helping students with disabilities to remain in the general education classroom. Behrmann (1984) outlined six reasons why computers are valuable instructional media for teachers.

Six Reasons Why Computers Are Valuable in Instruction

1. **They can be used in individual or group instruction.** Computers can assist teachers with many of the tasks designed to provide individualized and small group instruction and to free the teacher to work on children's needs (e.g., as indicated by social interaction or withdrawal). The computer can present information to groups or individuals. Some activities combine use of the computer with experiential activities in small groups or teams.

2. **They can provide immediate feedback and reinforcement to students.** Computers are intrinsically motivating because they provide immediate feedback, allow the student to work at his or her own pace, and can present information in a game format. Computers can also be programmed to provide the student with personalized reinforcement and to call the teachers' attention to good work.

3. **They can collect and analyze student performance data.** The IEP requires a plan for evaluating student progress toward short-term and long-term goals. Computers can be helpful in evaluating student performance data on such things as rate, accuracy, duration, and frequency of responses. Computers can also be used to store data collected by the teacher about other student behaviors such as seat behavior, social behavior, and tardiness.

4. **They are flexible in terms of level of instruction and type of child-computer interaction.** Computer programming can be varied to customize the way information is put into the computer by the learner (input) and the way it is taken out by the learner (output). For example, students put information into the computer by keyboard. For students with severe physical disabilities, who may have no cognitive disabilities, the keyboard can be adapted so that only one key is used for input. Information can also be entered into a computer by electronic pads or communication boards or adapted switches or sensors that can detect touch, movement, light, sound, or temperature. For example, sensors are being used to control wheelchairs by head movements, and computers are being activated by voice commands. Information provided to the student by the computer can be in the form of graphics, text, or voice. In this way, the computer varies the output or may combine the output (text and voice). The computer also varies the mode of presenting information so that it can be adapted to different learning styles of the student. For improved visual learning, computers can also be connected to peripheral devices such as video disc, videotapes, and filmstrips. For improved auditory learning, computers can use voice synthesis to control tape recorders, record players, and other devices.

5. **They allow self-paced instruction.** Computers allow students to work at their own pace, to slow down the learning or to speed it up. Computers are infinitely patient and allow the student as much time as he or she needs to respond to questions without pressure or anxiety.

6. **They allow errorless practice.** Computers allow a student time for as much practice as he or she needs to master a skill or understand a concept. It provides errorless practice for students who need more practice than others. Teachers can determine the mastery level needed by students, and the computer can then use that information to decide whether to move to the next level of instruction, provide more time to practice a skill, move to a remedial level, or alert the teacher that the student is having difficulty.

Source: Information from Behrmann, M. (1984). *Handbook of microcomputers in special education*, San Diego, CA: College-Hill Press, pp. 30–39.

Modifications for accommodating students with disabilities in the classroom equipped with computers and other types of technology include the following:

- access to technology laboratories and learning laboratories for all students
- use of visual timers or alarms on equipment in vocational laboratories or centers
- peer teaming for use of equipment or for projects requiring use of equipment

- simple modification of equipment
- relocation and reorganization of equipment in classroom or shop
- modification to provide larger spaces between pieces of equipment
- access to visual and diagrammatic instructions for safety and use of equipment
- modifications to allow lowering and raising of height of equipment or computers
- use of auditory and visual alarms or timers.

---

23. How Can Parent Participation Be Promoted?

Role of Family in Successful Inclusion. Over the past century, parents have been among the most powerful advocates in initiating inclusive services for children and youths with special needs. Parents have also stimulated major change in education and human service systems nationally and locally. Many educators and human service professionals believe that the *participation of parents and families is the most crucial factor in the success of students with disabilities in inclusive schools.* According to Henderson (1987), the main barrier to parent involvement is not parent apathy but lack of support from educators.

Parents As Partners. The IDEA emphasizes the role of the family in planning and coordinating services for individuals with disabilities (Wiel, Thomas, Callahan, & Carolis, 1992). Specifically, part H of the act states the following:

> The Secretary recognizes that parents (1) must be actively involved in making sure that their eligible children and other family members receive all of the services and protection that they are entitled to under this part and (2) are major decision makers in deciding the extent to which they will participate in, and receive services under, this program (54 Federal Register, 26331, 1989).

The IDEA regulations emphasized the choice and voluntary participation of the family and the responsibility of the service system to protect the individual rights of individuals and families. The 1990 language (P.L. 101-476) conveyed two very important messages to parents and service providers:

1. the importance of the parent-professional partnership and a recognition of the important relationship between parent and family participation in educational services and service outcomes
2. the movement to include the family unit as well as the student as a focus for support by educational and human service agencies.

Themes for Participation of Parents and Families. New provisions in special education, health and human services, vocational services, and disability rights legislation have increased support for children and youths in integrated settings in the schools and the community. Several family-related themes are conveyed in such laws.

- **Parents and Families As Partners.** Parents and families are partners with teachers and related professionals in the educational process and must be viewed as collaborators. As collaborators, parents and families accept a shared responsibility with teachers for educational outcomes. The assumption of parent-professional collaboration fosters a perception that parents and families are *active not passive* in the educational planning process and should enjoy equal status with professionals in the team decision-making process. Teachers and administrators should emphasize special communication and support to help parents understand and accept their role as partners with teachers and principals.

- **Responsibility of Parents for Their Children.** The parent has the responsibility for the educational progress of the child and for protecting the student's rights to appropriate education under the IDEA. Good communication between teachers and parents is an essential element in inclusive education. When the parents' access to information is diminished, their power as partners with teachers in the child's progress is diminished.

- **Parents and Families As Team Members.** Parents and families need to be involved in the assessment of the child's needs and must participate with members of the interdisciplinary team in developing individualized service plans. Schools are required by law to invite parents to participate in each annual IEP meeting for the child who needs special services. Parents or guardians should also be helped to reinforce learning in the home and to support the social goals of the student. They should also be integrally involved in any decision regarding a change of placement or a change in level of services. Special education law requires that parents be notified in advance of a placement change for their son or daughter and that they receive information in advance about the placement. Parents should be included in the processes for inclusion planning, policy development, and evaluation and in the planning for training of teachers, parents, and others (Hausslein, 1992).

- **Parents and Families As Decision Makers.** The laws recognize that parents and families have an important role in the decision-making process regarding the assessments and educational program of the child. Teachers and administrators must also remember that they rely on community support for the development, funding, and continuation of their educational programs and services and that families—as the "funders" of these services—have a right to know what educational programs are available, who is eligible, how placement decisions are made, and the quality and expected benefits of the programs for the child. Because family involvement is essential, information to parents about the goals and objectives of inclusive classrooms and activities are best communicated in terms of *benefits and outcomes for students and families*.

- **Parent and Family Training for Advocacy.** Parent training and resources should be provided to assist family members to better support the educational goals and related goals of the child. Families need to be educated and empowered to acquire

and to assist in the creation of inclusive services and supports (Nisbit, Covert, & Schuh, 1992). Parents or guardians need information about available school and community support services. They need help from teachers and administrators to understand concepts central to inclusive education such as inclusion, the IEP, self-determination, self-advocacy, service coordination, transition, least restrictive environment, and appropriate placement. Parents need to be informed about the legal and human rights of their children to educational services and supports, including rights under the IDEA, the Americans with Disabilities Act (ADA), the School-to-Work Opportunities Act, and other job training laws. Teachers can provide informal parent education as part of their parent conferencing activities and annual orientation of parents. Inclusion planners and implementors can develop linkages with college and university special education or teacher education programs to help develop parent training courses or seminars.

- **Families As Peer Supports.** Parents and family members can provide basic support to one another in achieving the educational goals of the child. Teachers and administrators can encourage the organization of support groups, in which experienced parents of children with disabilities help newer parents and provide counseling and support as needed.

- **Parents As Transition Team Members.** Parents should be closely involved and supportive of their adolescent child in the process of preparing for and making the transition from school to work or to post–secondary school training. Consulting teachers, special educators, and transition coordinators can be enlisted to provide parent training seminars or to speak at parent orientation sessions and conferences about transition, self-advocacy, and preparation for employment.

- **Parent Resources and Supports.** Parents need additional information and resources to help support successful inclusion of the child with a disability. Some schools have created resource centers by using local, state, or national sources. Others have developed information packets for parents, which are sent home to them before the inclusive placement is made. Some school districts work with their local or state health department, mental health services, mental retardation services, and other agencies to explore how funds from Medicaid waivers might be used to support parent training efforts. These funds can be used to provide information and training to parents about Social Security income (SSI) provisions that provide support services and tax deductions to support employment training for youths, work trials, and post–secondary school education for youth and young adults with disabilities.

- **Parents As Service Coordinators.** Many schools are experimenting with "social work" models of family support. For example, a teacher may be given a caseload of students and their families for whom he or she serves as service coordinator. As service coordinators, teachers take responsibility for contacting and communicating with the families of the students in their classroom. They may be available to visit the homes of students and their families to conduct consultations, or they may help to link the student and family with needed support services. The inclusive classroom relies on the support and close involvement of each student's family.

- **Letting Go: Parents Promoting Independence.** The parental attitude is a key factor in the ability of a student with disabilities to make the transition to responsible adult life. It is important that parents support the student's efforts to become independent and to achieve a quality of life that promotes the ability of the individual to establish and achieve his or her personal goals. It is critical to the transition process that parents learn to release control over the decisions of the young adult's life and transfer the responsibility as appropriate for the level of disability.

Strategies for Facilitating Family Involvement. Many strategies have been used by teachers, principals, and human service professionals to strengthen parent and family involvement in the child's development. The following approaches or strategies offer some exemplary practices in promoting parent and family involvement in provision of services for the child. Family-centered services are based on the following principles and beliefs (Mount & Zwernik, 1988):

- the belief in informed choice among educational service options by the student and his or her family
- the principle that the service system needs to help students and their families to use available school and community resources

- the belief that educational services should be coordinated around the life of the student and family, not around the needs of the school
- recognition of the ability of the ordinary citizen to teach people skills and to help students participate in community life.

Planning for Parent Involvement. A school staff committed to developing a program to improve parental involvement in inclusive classrooms can begin by creating a school committee for this purpose (Jones, 1991). The following sequence of steps can be used to develop such a program (Jones, 1991).

1. Establish a committee of teachers, support staff, parents, and older students.
2. Assess the current status of home-school relationships and parent involvement activities.
3. Conduct parent surveys and interviews to find out about parent needs and interests in inclusion practices and supports.
4. Examine a range of parent involvement programs in other schools, for ideas and activities that have been successful and could be adopted and adapted for use in the school and community.

Creative Strategies To Improve Parent and Family Involvement. School districts use different strategies to engage parents in the active educational process of their child, such as special training sessions, volunteering, parents night, and open house (see Exhibit II–5). Strategies are designed to facilitate family involvement in the inclusion of students with disabilities in the regular classroom.

Parents or Guardians and Self-Determination. The terms self-advocacy and self-determination are becoming widely used. Many children and youths with disabilities have difficulty assuming control of their lives and participating in the educational decisions that are made each year about their educational program. In 1974, a consumer-directed movement called self-advocacy was established in Oregon by a group of individuals with disabilities. Now, most states have self-advocacy groups and organizations, such as those associated with the Association for Retarded Citizens or the Disability Coalition, which are active in starting peer support or self-advocacy groups.

Exhibit II–5 Strategies for Facilitating Family Involvement

Strategy	Description
1. Parent Communication with Teachers	The following strategies are designed to improve the relationship between parents and teachers in inclusive classrooms: • Meet with parents in the preparation and planning for integrating the student into the inclusive classroom. • Make parent involvement a schoolwide effort. • Involve students in encouraging parents to become volunteers in the classroom. • Develop homework assignments that involve the whole family. • Determine the role the family will play in the inclusion process. If time lines are involved, make parents aware of them. • Send notes home frequently, even just to say the student had a good day. • Focus on encouraging parents, and find out why they may be reluctant to get involved. • Consider holding meetings away from the school to engage parents who have traditionally been reluctant to get involved. • Provide child care arrangements for parents when they attend school functions. • Place parents on a "parent resource" list to receive announcements about the class and school activities, exhibitions, and parent activities. • Invite parents to attend demonstration and exhibition sessions during the year to observe the skills gained by the students. • Honor parents publicly for their participation and support of their sons and daughters and the classroom. • Invite parents to participate in the evaluation of classroom activities and projects through interviews and surveys. • Help to establish parent support groups.
2. Parent Training and Supports	The following strategies, which provide information to parents and teach them how to become advocates for their children and how to enter into partnerships with professionals have been very effective for increasing parent involvement: • Providing information to parents about rights and resources, such as those provided under the Social Security Act, and IDEA, as well as the laws providing for school-to-work opportunities and job training • Providing ongoing parent training and seminars throughout the year • Engaging parents in the training of other parents • Using concrete examples and video presentations when talking about service options and planning • Helping parents concretely observe the benefits of having participated in service programs, by arranging visits to the program or to observe their son or daughter once he or she has graduated and made the transition to other levels of service, independent living, or employment. • Conducting parent-professional panel discussions and team training • Developing parent support groups or crisis support teams (Everson, Barcus, Moon, & Horton, 1987)

continues

Exhibit II–5 continued

Strategy	Description
2. Parent Training and Supports (continued)	• Providing services to parents in convenient locations and at convenient times (e.g., basic skills training, language classes, vocational counseling, and employment assistance) Some service systems promote "leadership training" for families interested in improving the service system. A group of family members or individuals with special needs forms a team in partnership with professionals representing agencies with the service system. Together they identify important problems and issues in the system and develop a plan for change that might involve policy changes, changes in the structure of services, or identification of service gaps. Family leadership strategies represent a powerful means of empowering families.
3. Parent Reinforcement of Skill Development in Home and Community	Students can be assisted in social and functional skill development in the home. Parents require some preparation and assistance in identifying which skills the school would like to have addressed and practiced. The IEP team can write the specifics in the IEP or simply request the assistance and cooperation of the parents in the home setting. Parents also have many opportunities to provide direct instruction and to help students practice skill development in natural community environments in which the student will ultimately use the skills. For example, mathematical skills (e.g., estimating, problem solving, and counting change) can easily be practiced in the bank, grocery store, or any other retail store.
4. Use of Student's Natural Support Systems	Use of natural support systems is essential in helping individuals with special needs reach their maximum potential. *Natural support systems* consist of people such as families, friends, neighbors, and peer groups, as well as organizations such as churches, schools, unions, and clubs, which provide support to individuals in need. A social network is essential to help individuals and their families to solve problems in daily life and in periods of crisis. The folk support system has a nourishing and stabilizing effect on the individual during times of change and challenge (Gerhard, Dorgan, & Miles, 1981). The informal support network helps the individual to survive by establishing and maintaining nurturing relationships and by rallying to the individual during moments of need. Members of this network also become essential players in the decision making about needed services and program enrollment. Such networks provide self-esteem, value, and dignity in the individual's life and help to reinforce the motivation and achievement of individuals as they participate in services.
5. Personal Planning	Many personal planning strategies rely on the involvement of families and the informal support network of the individual. Futures planning refers to a long-term planning and problem-solving process that is guided by the desires and needs of the individual and the family. These processes assist a committed group of individuals or families in helping to create and support a desirable future for a person with a disability or special needs.

continues

Exhibit II–5 continued

Strategy	Description
5. Personal Planning (continued)	*"Personal futures planning,"* or *"circles of support"* planning consists of a personal profile, a planning meeting, and a futures plan document. The profile contains a record of the person's life, including important relationships, place, past events, preferences, future dreams, barriers, and opportunities. It emphasizes individual gifts, skills, and capabilities. The planning meeting includes the individual, the family members, and other key persons in his or her life. The meeting follows several steps in developing the plan: • Review the personal profile. • Review the environment, including the events that are likely to affect the individual or family positively and negatively (e.g., graduation, closing of a program or service, death of a family member, or losing a job). • Create a desirable vision of the future. • Identify obstacles and opportunities. • Identify strategies and make commitments to take specific actions to implement the vision. • Start by prioritizing action steps and beginning to work on them. • Identify needs for systems change, constraints of the service system, and obstacles to realizing the vision of the future. Service coordinators can facilitate futures planning for their clients and families. These approaches rely strongly on the personal relationships and promote the connections between the individual with special needs and the community. This process is based on three assumptions: 1. The quality of everyday activities and relationships should be the focus of efforts on behalf of individuals with special needs. 2. Services are not enough; family relationships and friendships offer benefits that cannot be purchased at any price. 3. No single person or service can or should do everything. Persons are more dependent when they must rely on only one or two services to meet their needs (Nisbet, Covert, & Schuh, 1992). These individualized planning strategies can complement the more organized planning procedures such as IEP planning and individualized family service planning.
6. Education and Transition Planning	Special parent conferences are scheduled to discuss any concerns, ideas, plans, or goals that affect the student's education. Schools provide this opportunity on a routine basis, either quarterly or semiannually. In addition, parents are generally invited to school as needed. Longer-range "life planning" typically does not begin until the individual is in adolescence and the parents begin to think about separation from the family and life beyond school. From the earliest identification of a disability, parents or guardians can be helped to begin to think about life planning. Gaining autonomy and self-determination skills should begin in the earliest years. Separations from the parent and family begin in the early years, as

continues

Exhibit II–5 continued

Strategy	Description
6. **Education and Transition Planning** (continued)	children move from home to day care, from day care to preschool, from pre–school to elementary school, and then to middle school, high school, and post–secondary school life. Each transition and adjustment can be difficult, and the individual may need extra support from family members and professionals. Parents can be better advocates if they can view the educational development of the child with the future in mind, rather than simply reacting to present circumstances. Such a view can give parents a more realistic and balanced perspective on the options available and the choices that need to be made as the child matures.
7. **Reduction of Barriers to Generic Community Services**	IEPs should include a plan for how the services provided will integrate individuals into the various forms of the folk support system. Efforts should be made by service coordinators to eliminate barriers that prevent individuals and their families from accessing basic generic community services. **Generic Services**—*A range of services that are available to the general public within the community.* These include health services, recreational services, social services, housing services, and employment and training services. Individual family service plans and IEPs should address barriers to generic services that can support the individual and the family.
8. **Communication of Value of Parent Involvement**	Communication to parents at all points in the developmental continuum should convey the message that they are *needed and valued as contributing members of the educational planning team.* This can be done through written materials that are distributed to parents, special parent support meetings or education seminars, opportunities for parent volunteer activities, and invitations to service planning meetings. As students with disabilities enter service agencies for assistance, parents often feel that their intense and supportive role is no longer needed, and they may begin to feel that their children are now in "other hands." Communication with parents is also critical during the major transition from one service agency to another.

Self-Advocacy—*A social and political movement started by and for people with disabilities to speak for themselves on important issues such as housing, employment, legal rights, and personal relationships* (Smith & Lukasson, 1992). It is related to self-determination in which the individual with a disability is directly involved in informed decision making about his or her education and future.

The term has emerged from the earlier concept of "normalization," which meant enabling people with disabilities to live, work, and play in environments most close to those of "normal," or nondisabled persons in the mainstream of the community. The concept of self-advocacy extends the idea of normalization to include the active participation of the individual in decision making for his or her own future.

The process of building self-determination depends on the *greater shared decision making among the student, the family, and professionals in decisions that affect the future of the individual being served*. Along with building individual capacity to make informed choices and de-cisions comes a greater responsibility and accountabil-ity for the outcomes of those decisions. Students with disabilities and their parents, therefore, become equal partners and share the responsibility for developing IEPs and for the results of those plans.

24. What Inclusion Strategies Can Assist Special Learners in the Transition from School to Work?

Successful Transition Difficult for High School Students. The past few decades of education and job training initiatives have not adequately prepared a large percentage of youths for employment, post–secondary school training, and responsible adulthood. The number of youths exiting the schools who fail to successfully make the transition to post–secondary edu-cation and employment persists. The U.S. Government Accounting Office (GAO) evaluations of education, vo-cational education, job training programs, and youth transition programs claim that there is a lack of coordi-nation among education and training agencies in ef-forts to help youths with transition (GAO, 1989, 1994a, 1994b). A more aggressive effort must be made to pre-pare teachers and related personnel to address the con-tinued poor outcomes for youths.

Inclusion Principles and Strategies for Tran-sition. Several inclusion principles and strategies can be used successfully to assist teachers in the transition planning for students with special needs. The strate-gies are common in most school districts, but the ex-tent to which students with special needs are included in these activities is sometimes limited, for a variety of reasons:

- Students are viewed as unique learners who learn differently and at different rates, and therefore tran-sition services need to be initiated at different times for different students (e.g., in middle school for some and high school for others).

- Individuals have significantly different interests and varying degrees of ability, but all students can gain work skills; career learning experiences are presented in a variety of ways to appeal to the dif-ferent learning styles of students.

- The educational program for each student in the transition phase is based on individual employ-ment and the transition plan, in order (1) to ensure that each student achieves the required standards established for the common core of learning in the occupational area and (2) to motivate youths to achieve their maximum potential.

- A transition curriculum combines development of academic, vocational-technical, and work skills and also emphasizes:
  - **Social responsibility**—The student learns posi-tive attitudes toward peers and learns about the importance of a career and work for adult roles.
  - **Technology**—The curriculum makes effective use of technology, developing in participants both the competence and the confidence they will need in technologically enriched work environments. The curriculum, to the extent possible, exposes stu-dents to the types of technology that they will face in actual work settings.
  - **Problem solving, critical thinking, analysis and synthesis, creativity, and application of knowl-edge**—Students learn how to use academic knowledge to solve real-world problems.
  - **Integration and interrelatedness of knowl-edge**—The student learns that subject matter is not separated in the real world, but is linked closely. For example, knowledge and skills in mathematics and English are linked when the stu-dent has to measure the dimensions of piping and write a report on the specifications needed for replacement of the piping.
  - **Comprehensiveness**—This factor addresses mul-tiple learning styles of students.
  - **Developmental appropriateness**—This factor addresses the developmental level of the students for which the curriculum is designed.
  - **Curriculum relevance**—This factor addresses rel-evance to the community and the skill standards required by business and industry.

−**Flexibility and collaboration**—This factor addresses the ease with which the curriculum can be modified for a variety of learning environments and settings and adapted to promote collaboration among teachers and students.

The Interdisciplinary Team and Transition. The interdisciplinary planning team can include a variety of professionals, including teachers, a job training specialist, staff psychologist, career counselor, transition coordinator, language arts specialist, mathematics instructor, and vocational area instructors. These professionals meet with the students and parents to develop an individual transition plan. The team then meets with the participant and parent as appropriate, to interpret the profile of their interests and preferences and the profile of the student's occupational skill levels and program needs. Career counseling can be conducted individually and in groups throughout the year, with more intensive sessions occurring toward the end of the program and at completion of the program and graduation or on completion of requirements for a general equivalency diploma or for the appropriate certification.

Use of Nontraditional Assessments and Performance Exhibitions. Nontraditional methods of assessing student academic and vocational performance include activities such as individual portfolios of completed work and student exhibitions of products made.

Students may participate in activities such as the following:

- Complete a performance portfolio, and present the portfolio before a panel of peers and industry leaders in special demonstration sessions.
- Participate annually in several exhibitions of products and performance in a specific occupational area, to demonstrate proficiency in one or more skill areas.
- Enter and represent the school in the annual competitions of district vocational clubs or organizations.
- Participate in "team leadership demonstrations," which may include activities such as diagnosing auto repair problems, producing a photographic exhibit of family background, preparing graduation materials for print, or providing on-site child care services for parents attending the exhibitions.
- Complete a job profile before program completion and participate in several job interviews with prospective employers as part of job search activities. The *job profile* is a process that includes participat-

ing in job search activities, writing letters of interest, obtaining letters of reference, completing a job resume and job applications, participating in interviews, and writing a follow-up letter.

The Role of the Teacher and Coordinator for Transition. Many high schools are focusing attention on helping students to think about and plan their lives beyond high school and to prepare for the transition to post–secondary education or work. During the transition phase for special learners, there is a need for teachers who can link the student with other people and for organizations that can help with transition. These organizations may include post–secondary schools, employers, and community service and rehabilitation agencies. The teacher or the transition coordinator, therefore, becomes an important link between the student and the post–high school world.

Schools are experimenting with many new ways to build transition support services into instructional or related service roles in the schools. Strategies used in schools include the following:

- Transition-related responsibilities are added to the teacher's role. In many schools, the transition coordination responsibilities are attached to existing roles, such as the special education teacher, the related services specialist, the vocational education specialist, or the guidance counselor.
- Transition responsibilities are assigned to teams of teachers (subject matter teachers and consulting special education teachers).
- Transition coordinator roles focus entirely on transition supports for students.*

The roles that these individuals play in linking the student and the community may vary greatly, but the functions usually have common elements. Transition coordinator roles may differ in:

- the types of transition coordination and support functions that are performed
- the kind and amount of student and family contact that the coordinator may have
- the relationship of the coordinator with the student and the family
- primary goals of the transition coordination activities
- the size of the transition caseload (group of students who need transition services)

---

*West, Taymans, Corbey, & Dodge, 1994.

- the scope of school and interagency responsibility and authority in the role
- the degree to which the transition coordination functions are attached to a primary role such as teacher, counselor, administrator, or specialist
- the way that the role is evaluated.

There is also considerable variation in how teacher-coordinators view the scope of their roles. There is no "right way" to craft the role of the transition coordinator. *What is important is that the coordination functions are appropriate for and responsive to the needs of students preparing for graduation and transition from school.*

Essential Skills of a Transition Coordinator. Several competencies (knowledge, skills, and attitudes necessary to do the job) are needed by transition coordinators. The many hats that transition coordinators wear include:

- assessment specialist
- counselor who responds to the needs of individual students
- problem solver who resolves conflicts
- human resource developer who trains others and understands collaborating agencies
- manager who keeps records and arranges the schedules of others
- evaluator who assesses the progress of students and helps to evaluate the effectiveness of transition coordination services to students
- diplomat who must negotiate with sensitivity within political environments
- coordinator who links students with community service agencies and other community sectors
- public relations agent who comes in contact with citizens and community agencies.

What Teachers Need To Know about Transition and the Law. The definition of special education, as re-defined in the 1990 amendments to IDEA, strengthened the expectation that all students would have a right to career-vocational education appropriate to their needs. According to the IDEA (section 300.17), the term special education also includes:

- vocational education at no cost to the parents if it consists of specially designed instruction and meets the individual needs of the student
- vocational courses as an organized educational program offering a sequence of courses that di-

rectly prepare students for paid or unpaid employment

- preparation for employment in current or emerging occupations requiring a level of education other than a baccalaureate or advanced degree
- competency-based learning in which learning objectives and outcomes are specified
- applied learning strategies in which instruction is delivered in real-world settings or applied to real-world problems
- competency-based and applied learning strategies that contribute to a student's development of (1) academic knowledge, higher order reasoning, and problem-solving skills and (2) work attitudes, general employability skills, and the occupation-specific skills necessary for economic independence as a productive and contributing member of society
- education in applied technology.

Definition of Transition Services. Transition services are defined as:

- a coordinated set of activities aimed at a specific student outcome (e.g., employment, referral to rehabilitation services, or enrollment in college) that must
  – be based on the individual student's needs
  – take into account the student's preferences and interests
  – include *needed activities* in the areas of instruction, community experiences, and development of employment and other postschool adult living objectives, and, if appropriate, daily living skills and functional vocational evaluation
- activities that promote the movement of a student from school to postschool activities, which may include post–secondary education, vocational training, integrated employment (including supported employment), continuing and adult education, adult services, independent living, or community participation.

This list is not intended to be exhaustive; other activities designed by teachers may be included in transition services.

Transition services for students with disabilities may be considered to be special education services if they are provided as specially designed instruction or related services and if they are required in order to assist a student with a disability to benefit from special education (IDEA, section 300.18).

Transition Component of the IEP. IDEA regulations state that beginning no later than age 16, or younger if determined appropriate (the sooner the better) by teachers and the interdisciplinary team, the IEP of each student with a disability must include:

- a statement of the needed transition services as defined in section 300.18
- a statement of each public agency's and each participating agency's responsibilities for supporting that student in transition
- linkages with community-based agencies or services both before and after the student leaves the school setting.

If the interdisciplinary team determines that the student does not need transition services in one or more of these specified areas, then the IEP must include a statement to that effect and the reason for making the determination.

Transition Support Needed by All Students. All students with disabilities need some kind of transition support or services. The intent of Congress was to ensure that all students do receive some kind of transition support or service.

> Section 602(a)(20) of the act provides that IEPs must include a statement of needed transition services for students beginning no later than age 16, but permits transition services to students below age 16 (". . . and, when determined appropriate for the individual, beginning at age 14 or younger.") Although the statute does not mandate transition services for all students beginning at age 14 or younger, the provision of these services could have a significantly positive effect on the employment and independent living outcomes for many of these students in the future, especially for students who are likely to drop out before age 16.

With respect to the provision of transition services to students below age 16, the report of the House Committee on Education and Labor on P.L. 101-476 includes the following statements:

> Although this language leaves the final determination of when to initiate transition services for students under age 16 to the IEP process, it nevertheless makes it clear that *Congress expects much consideration to be given to the need for transition services* for students by age 14 or younger. The Committee encourages that approach because of their concern that age 16 may be too late for many students, particularly those at risk of dropping out of school and those with the most severe disabilities. Even for those students who stay in school until age 18, many will need more than two years of transitional services. Students with disabilities are now dropping out of school before age 16, feeling that the education system has little to offer them. Initiating services at a younger age will be critical. (Report of the House Committee on Education and Labor, 10 [1990])

Responsibility of Other Agencies. The IDEA regulations also address the role of other agencies in supporting transition of youths from school to employment and post–secondary education. The regulations state that

> If a participating agency fails to provide agreed-upon transition services contained in the IEP of a student with a disability, the public agency responsible for the student's education shall, as soon as possible, initiate a meeting for the purpose of identifying the alternative strategies to meet the transition objectives and, if necessary, *revising the student's IEP*. Nothing in this part relieves any participating agency, including a State vocational rehabilitation agency, of the responsibility to provide or pay for any transition service that the agency would otherwise provide to students with disabilities who meet the eligibility criteria of that agency. (Section 300.18, USC 1401.16)

Consequently, school-linked agencies are required to share the responsibility for transition support services.

Congress believes that teachers, administrators, and schools have a responsibility to ensure that the transition process is a *shared responsibility that does not end until an initial post–secondary placement goal has been achieved.*

Common Concerns about Youth Readiness for Work

The Commission on the Skills of the American Workplace report, *America's Choice: High Skills or Low Wages* (1990), summarized the concerns of a variety of federal government, academic, and community organizations and outlined six broad problems associated with poor worker performance and youth preparation for employment:

1. lack of clear standards of achievement and motivation to work hard in school

2. the high percentage of dropouts

3. the small segment of non-college-bound students prepared for work

4. the lack of employer investment in high-performance work organizations

5. a passive public policy on high school preparation and worker training

6. an inefficient job training system

Literacy Key to Employment. In 1992, the Educational Testing Service produced a report called *Beyond the School Doors: The Literacy Needs of Job Seekers Served by the U.S. Department of Labor.* This report summarizes the results obtained from an individually administered literacy assessment of nearly 6,000 adults representing 20 million persons participating in the Job Training Partnership Act and Employment Service programs. Major findings include the following:

- Individuals with high literacy skill levels have shorter unemployment periods, earn higher wages, and work in higher-level occupations.
- Sixty percent to 65 percent of student or client groups believe they could get a job or a better job if their reading or writing skills were improved through additional education.

- Seventy percent to 80 percent of student or client groups believed their job opportunities would improve with increased mathematical skills.
- Minority students are disproportionately represented at literacy scale levels, with black and Hispanic groups generally scoring lower literacy levels than whites.

In a U.S. Department of Labor 1993 study, *Finding One's Way: Career Guidance for Disadvantaged Youth*, research findings show that most career guidance activities for youths today, particularly for disadvantaged youths, are remarkably limited. Carnine and Kameenui (1990) in *America and the New Economy*, includes a list of basic skills that workers in the "new economy" will need. These skills include:

- academic skills of reading, writing at work, and computation
- communications skills of speaking and listening
- adaptability skills of problem solving and creativity
- developmental skills of cultivating self-esteem, motivation, and goal setting and personal and career development
- group effectiveness skills in interpersonal relationships, negotiation, and teamwork
- influencing skills of organizational effectiveness and leadership.

Vocational-Technical Education and Transition. For the past two decades, the Carl D. Perkins Vocational and Applied Technology Education Act has emphasized full participation of special needs populations in the range of vocational-technical education programs and services. The legislation provides a set of assurances that students with special needs are guaranteed full access in recruitment and enrollment, support services, transition planning, and placement into employment. As a result of this legislation, most school districts included students with special needs in regular vocational-technical classes. Many developed specialized support teams to increase the change of success and completion for students with special challenges. Consequently, there was documented success of student achievement in vocational-technical programs (National Assessment of Vocational Education, Interim Report, 1994; Wagner, 1993).

The study of the U.S. Department of Education, Office of Vocational and Adult Education (1991), entitled *Combining School and Work: Options in High Schools and*

Two-Year Colleges, centers on the role of vocational-technical education in the transition from school to work and how it can contribute to a competent, highly skilled work force. The traditional approaches, including apprenticeship, cooperative education, and school-based enterprise, make deliberate use of work a part of the learning experience. Recent innovations, including vocational academies and technical-preparatory programs, are changing the high school curriculum to unite vocational with academic disciplines. This report from the U.S. Department of Education emphasizes the importance of the role that teachers and employers play in all of the programs through business-school partnerships.

The report of the American Youth Policy Forum (1993), entitled *Improving the Transition from School to Work in the United States*, cites several trends that are responsive to the challenges for youth preparation for employment. These trends include universal access, high academic standards, increased career exposure and counseling, integration of academic and vocational education and of school-to-work experiences, award of a widely recognized credential based on industry-approved standards with a benchmark of international best practice, and clear routes to post–secondary academic advancement.

Need for Change in Secondary Schools. Researchers and teachers have concluded that schools must take the following steps to improve employment outcomes for youths and to reduce the school dropout rate:*

- Develop innovative secondary programs to integrate academic, vocational, and employment skills.
- Provide access for youths who are disadvantaged and for youths who are out of school, both those who completed high school and those who did not, to the range of vocational-technical and community-based employment training options.
- Assess cognitive abilities and learning styles, as teachers carefully consider the learning environments and methods for developing academic and vocational skills in special learners.
- Raise expectations for students with disabilities.
- Provide each learner with an advisor, advocate, or coordinator, with whom the learner plans the transition to employment programs.

- Develop alternatives to traditional assessment of the learner's progress in school-based employment settings.
- Restructure the high schools and offer non-college-bound students a 13th year of technical training.
- Provide remedial education and/or on-the-job training for poor youths.
- Create apprenticeship programs, and increase high schools' ability to prepare students for the workplace.
- Teach all students basic mathematics and English skills by 10th grade.
- Emphasize critical thinking, problem solving, independent learning, and communication skills for all students in the 11th and 12th grade curricula.
- Encourage students who are not planning to attend college to couple their academic courses with a work internship.
- Allow high school students to pursue a 13th year of professional or technical learning in the field of their choice.
- Allow students completing their technical training to take a voluntary national competency test in their chosen area and receive a certificate of competency recognized by employers in the field.*

A systematic approach to transition is needed. Successful transition for youths with disadvantages and special needs, including those with limited English proficiency, call for a systematic approach. Research shows that schools need to include four essential components in their transition planning:

1. **a long-range, coordinated, interagency plan for a system of training and support services in each school,** for students in integrated settings from age 14 through to post–secondary school, as well as transition special supports for the critical "passages" (transitions) between educational settings
2. **systematic professional development** of teachers and related personnel in each school
3. **a cooperative partnership** among public schools, the business community, related and community service agencies, and parents, to achieve common goals for youths and to integrate them into mainstream vocational and employment preparation programs

*Kochhar, 1995; Reich, 1991; Wagner, 1993; West, 1991.

*Clark & Kolstoe, 1995; Rusch, Destafano, Chadsey-Rusch, Phelps, & Szymanski, 1992; Smith-Davis, 1989.

4. **close working relationships with rehabilitation agencies,** which schools are now required to develop, so that eligible youths can obtain additional resources after completing high school.

The IDEA was amended in 1990 to provide extra resources*

- to help schools link with rehabilitation agencies
- to target resources to school settings that provide access to rehabilitation counselors for students with disabilities
- to provide for cooperative arrangements for inter-agency funding of transition services, encouraging investment by the public and private sectors in transition services for all youths
- to provide for early, ongoing information and training for individuals who are involved with or who would be involved with transition services, such as professionals, parents, and youths with disabilities, including self-advocacy training for such youths.

Assessing Skill Achievement. Students in career-vocational and technical education need to have their skill achievements assessed to determine how ready they are to actually perform tasks in a given occupational area. Many occupations have published skill criteria that are being used in vocational-technical edu-

---

*Halloran & Simon, 1995; Gartner & Lipsky, 1992.

cation classrooms to develop curricula and design assessments of student achievement. These skill assessments are based on classroom and work-based skill performance attainment, completion of the national standards certifications for specific vocational areas, and course completion requirements. For example, in the graphics arts industry, students would be required to complete certification in at least one of the eight certification areas before placement into employment in the field. These certifications would be provided by the Printing Industry of America. Similarly, auto mechanic trainees would be expected to complete certification in one of the major certification areas through an area community college certification program. Students participating in child care and medical assistant training programs would be expected to meet state standards and guidelines for child care workers and national standards for medical assistants.

Use of "Authentic" Training Environments and Training Outcomes. Instructional methods and curriculum innovations that have been found to be particularly effective for adolescent special learners include those that integrate academic and vocational skills development and apply them to real-world work environments.

The following list is a summary of strategies considered to be best practices in transition. These are strategies used in districts throughout the country that have proven their success. The more "Best Practices" that are incorporated into the educational agencies, the more successful are their inclusion and transition services.

Summary of Best Practices for Transition Services for All Students

- Establish transition or career academies that offer technical and pre-apprenticeship training in four high-demand occupational areas.
- Develop a regional consortium of LEAs and community agencies to strengthen regional transition planning to improve the quality and quantity of career-vocational and transitional services; improve at-risk students' inclusion in occupational training with nondisabled peers; and improve the preparation of teachers, counselors, and community support personnel to serve students with disabilities.
- Establish a student-centered approach.

- Develop unique strategies to identify, recruit, train, and place youths with disabilities who have dropped out of school.
- Develop interagency partnerships for the long-range planning for new responses within the school system and community.
- Develop a systemwide change plan for transition support for all youths with disabilities in the LEA who have dropped out or who are at risk for dropping out of school.
- Use a unique partnership among school-community organizations for the outreach, recruitment, assessment, and planning for students who have dropped out of school.

continues

continued

- Incorporate planning for dropout prevention and outreach to youths who have dropped out of school into the school's strategic planning and systemwide change initiative to expand services for students with disabilities.
- Provide intensive support to students who return to school to complete their education, including transportation, peer mentoring teams, teacher-advocates, and monetary incentives for time retained in the program.
- Incorporate recent research in alternative performance assessments (exhibitions and demonstrations) of achievement and outcomes in vocational-technical areas.
- Provide an innovative linkage with the Private Industry Council Regional Consortium/JTPA to provide transition and follow-up support for youths who complete the program and to facilitate planning for replication in surrounding county sites.
- Promote self-determination and self-advocacy for youths with disabilities through peer teams and incentives.
- Provide pre-apprenticeship training and opportunity for skills certification; allow out-of-school students to work toward completion of the general equivalency diploma (GED).
- Provide employer assessment, references, and certification of skills.
- Promote access and inclusion in work-based training opportunities.
- Develop and implement procedures for a regional dropout study to analyze factors that influence the student's decision to drop out; profile significant characteristics and risk factors for youths currently enrolled in school; modify school barriers to the participation of youths who have left school; and use study findings on students with disabilities dropping out of school to inform the three-year project replication plan.
- Provide parents with a broader support network through the parent resource center and include parents in the academy exhibitions and demonstrations of student performance, to make training "concrete" and to focus on the product (outcome).
- Include parents in the transition planning process.
- Develop integrated academic-vocational-technical education that meets industry-based performance standards.
- Develop business-education partnerships.
- Provide teacher orientation and training that includes the context of broad school reform and restructuring activities. (At least 80 teachers, counselors, and administrators will receive training.)
- Build on youths' natural attraction to applied work experiences and use of innovative technology.
- Promote students' goal setting and cooperative learning and encourage students to engage in self-evaluation of performance and progress.
- Stimulate sharing of resources among schools, employment and training agencies, and businesses.
- Enable school-based staff to have a major role in making instructional decisions.
- Place a major emphasis on professional development.
- Ensure that health care and social services are sufficient to reduce significant barriers to participation and learning.
- Expose students to technology and current real-world work environments.

Note: LEA, Local education agency; JTPA, Job Training and Partnership Act.

These practices usually require long-term change strategy to address the needs of at-risk and dropout youths in the community. Learning environments must relate what is taught in school to what is required in the world of work or in post–secondary educational settings. Learning "to know" must not be separated from learning "to do."

Placement and Transition Support. Several strategies are available to the transition teacher to enable him or her to directly place students in jobs or to assist students in applying and enrolling in post–secondary school training. These strategies include providing career counseling and information about employment and post–secondary school training opportunities. For students who desire to enter a two- or four-year college or technical school, the teacher can

- assist the student in selecting a college
- assist the student in applying and negotiating for support services that he or she may need
- assist the student to learn how to access campus resources
- arrange for student sessions with the career counselor to discuss job search strategies

- discuss interviewing techniques
- discuss self-advocacy and how to promote one's strengths
- discuss the advantages and disadvantages of self-disclosure of the disability and how to negotiate for needed job accommodations
- have cooperating business leaders host near-graduates in simulated job interviews before the actual interviews, to gain experience and receive real-world feedback from employers.

Why Transition Services for Youths with Disabilities?

- The Individuals with Disabilities Education Act (IDEA) requires each school to provide transition services for all students with disabilities; the School-to-Work Opportunities Act also requires each school to provide them.

- Most students with disabilities and other special needs do not have the benefit of a systematic transition from school to work.

- Approximately 50% to 75% of all adults with disabilities are unemployed.

- Many students with disabilities and other special needs can and should benefit from appropriate vocational education programs, but their enrollment in vocational education remains very low—close to *4% nationally*.

- There is a high rate of underemployment for these youths, who must work in jobs that do not use their skills.

- Studies show that students with disabilities and other special needs drop out of school more frequently than their nondisabled peers.

- Only 18% of the 58% employed were making more than $135 per week.

- Although many studies report much higher rates, the dropout rates for students with different disabilities in one study were as follows:
  –learning disabilities: 37%
  –emotional disabilities: 42%
  –hearing impairments: 28%
  –speech impairments: 24%
  –non handicap: average, 19%

- Students are more vulnerable at different ages. Dropout rates by age are as follows (U.S. Department of Education, 1993a):

Age (Years)	Percentage Who Dropped Out of School
16	55
17	34
18	18
19	19
20	19
21	17
16 to 21 average	25

In a study conducted in several school districts in the state of Washington, data from follow-up showed that, of 1,292 students with disabilities who were no longer in special education, only 58% were employed.

25. What Is the Future for Inclusion in the 21st Century?

International Covenants on Educational Rights of Children. Several international covenants on educational rights of children as needing special care and attention establish the following principles or values for state responsibility for children:

- Basic education should be provided to all children, on the basis of equal opportunity.
- Education should be free at the elementary and fundamental stages and should be compulsory (United Nations Center for Human Rights, 1988).
- Children should be given an education that will promote their general culture and enable them to develop their individual judgment and their sense of moral and social responsibility and to become useful members of society (United Nations, 1960);
- The child who is physically, mentally, or socially handicapped should be given the special treatment, education, and care required by his or her particular condition (United Nations Center for Human Rights, 1988).
- Children with impairments have the right to enjoy a full and decent life, and the state has an obligation to provide for their special needs (Lynch, 1995).
- An active commitment must be made to removing educational disparities.
- Underserved groups (the poor, street children, working children, and rural and remote populations) should not suffer any discrimination in access to learning opportunities.
- The education of persons with impairments should, as far as possible, take place in the general school system. Responsibility for their education should be placed on the educational authorities, and laws regarding compulsory education should include children with all ranges of disabilities, including the most severely disabled (Lynch, 1995).

In order to achieve the goals outlined in these international documents, there is a need for better understanding of the meaning of "success" or "failure" of inclusion and the need for

- planning and support
- preparation for interdisciplinary and team teaching

- integrated curriculum
- integration of technology into instruction
- individualization of instruction for all students
- increased community-based instruction
- supportive attitudes for diverse classrooms
- staff development
- advanced graduate training
- teacher incentives
- parental involvement
- paraprofessional training
- preparation of students for school-to-work transition

Although inclusion may have begun in many schools as a way to integrate students physically into general education classes, the strategies have helped teachers, students, and parents to develop enduring and creative relationships. As we continue along the path of increased teacher collaboration and interdisciplinary and interagency relationships, the inclusion movement will focus its efforts on ten broad goals.

1. Develop a Unified System for Education.
There is a need to create a new organization for education in order to reduce the fragmented approach to educating students who are not learning effectively and are "falling through the cracks." The dual system of separate administrative arrangements for special programs should be eliminated. In maintaining a separate special education system, education will continue to operate on the assumptions that students with disabilities and nondisabled students require two different sets of services, which need different funding, service delivery systems, and organizations. The inclusive schools of tomorrow will assume that designs integrating both types of students will benefit all students (Reynolds, Wang, & Walberg, 1992; Wang & Birch, 1984). Such a concept requires a fundamental change in the way teachers and others think about differences among people and how they view the purpose of education (Gartner & Lipsky, 1992). The results of school reform must benefit all students. In order to better integrate diverse students into general education classes, a greater emphasis will be placed on collaborative team learning and student team projects. Instructional meth-

ods such as these enhance the support of teachers and structure the social relationships for inclusion.

2. Preserve the Rights of Full Participation in Restructured Schools. As the pace of educational restructuring quickens and budget reductions begin to have a greater impact on students and their families, the inclusion rights movement will intensify. Advocates for the students with mild to moderate needs for specialized educational services will advocate more vigorously for inclusion into general education classes and a wider range of school activities. Such a movement will be characterized by a growing public expectation (1) that all youths need a greater role in decision making and self-determination in their careers and futures and (2) that all youths can benefit from participation in mainstream work preparation in school-based and community-based training. In the future, students with disabilities will tutor other students with disabilities and nondisabled students.

On the other hand, as needed special education services and options in the home schools are generally reduced, advocates for the students with severe needs for special education services will more vigorously advocate segregated settings. They will advance the same arguments used in the 1960s and 1970s that led to the evolution of a separate special education system. The same arguments will be heard again if parents believe that they cannot obtain the services they need in "inclusive schools."

The philosophical principles behind these arguments are reflected in many of the laws and policies that govern the education of students with disabilities, even though these laws and regulations may undergo change as educational funds are consolidated and transferred to the states. However, state and local guidelines on inclusion have been written to interpret federal special education law and to provide guidance to schools in the implementation of inclusion at the school level. Since 1975, national, state, and local regulations and guidelines have had the same goals:

- improving the quality of services
- increasing the participation of special populations in the full range of programs and services available, while preserving intensive services for those with the greatest need
- ensuring coordination and collaboration among service sectors to improve access to and efficient delivery of services

3. Create a Revolution of Expectations. Social attitudes about children with disabilities adversely af-

fect expectations about what they can achieve academically. These attitudes cause them to be*

- exempt from standards and tests routinely applied to other students
- allowed grades that they have not earned
- excused from social and behavioral expectations set for other students
- exempt from making personal choices and decisions
- permitted to have special diplomas

These watered-down expectations are thought to be in the best interests of the child (Gartner & Lipsky, 1992). In the future, students with disabilities included in general education classrooms will be expected to be held to the same standards and assessment measures as their nondisabled peers. They will also be expected to acquire the required Carnegie units needed for regular high school diplomas. The expectations expressed in early interpretations of P.L. 94-142 that the IEP should merely enable the child to achieve passing marks and advance from grade to grade, will not be appropriate or acceptable for most students with mild to moderate disabilities.

4. Achieve Rights without Labels. The stigmatization of students and continuation of low expectations of success for students with disabilities should be reduced. This means providing the needed services for students without the damaging effects of classification and labeling (Gartner & Lipsky, 1992).

5. Improve the Placement Process. The placement process needs to be improved, and the adversarial nature of placement decisions needs to be changed. Inclusive schools will increase their focus on how students are identified and placed into classrooms. Policy makers are already proposing alternative methods of funding special education services for students, and such proposals include capping of the number of students who can be provided special education (Council for Exceptional Children, 1994). There will be increased questions about the validity of the learning disability category (percentages of special education students labeled learning disabled vary widely among the 50 states and among 30 large cities; Gartner & Lipsky, 1992). Over the balance of this decade, students with learning disabilities are likely to be fully included in general education classrooms.

6. Improve Family Partnerships. Schools and related support service agencies need help in engag-

---

*Halloran & Simon, 1995; Gartner & Lipsky, 1992.

ing the families of children, youths, and adults as partners in the education, development, and progress of their sons and daughters.

7. Improve School-Community Coordination and Transition to Adulthood.

Schools and related support service agencies need help in coordinating their services to improve early intervention and early childhood development services to ensure that children have a beginning in life that is physically, cognitively, and emotionally healthy. Schools and community agency personnel need to work together to ensure that the gains made by children and youths in kindergarten through grade 12 are not lost in the transition to employment, post–secondary school training, and independent living.

8. Implement Change through a New Generation of Teachers and Support Personnel.

With the great transformations that are occurring in the way youths are educated and prepared for careers and advanced education, there is a need to prepare a new generation of creative teachers and support personnel. These new leadership personnel and change agents must be prepared to respond to the changing life roles that youths face as their families and communities change. They must have the knowledge to collaborate and build inclusive services that embrace academic development, social-psychological development, career development, and preparation for work and broader life roles. College and university training must prepare general and special educators for such collaboration and model collaboration, by integration of course work, assignments, and practical experiences through team teaching.

9. New Emphasis on Reducing Youth Violence.

Deteriorating outcomes for many populations of youths are likely to continue to stimulate new approaches to improving developmental conditions for all youths. New employment preparation ad transition support services are emerging under the Violent Crime Control and Law Enforcement Act of 1994, administered by the U.S. Department of Justice and the School-to-Work Opportunities Act. Educators and job training experts realize the need to respond to changing life roles that youths face, along with deteriorating school, home, and community conditions. New community approaches similar to those in the 1960s and 1970s under the community development block grant initiatives seek to address the environmental problems of youths, such as poor supervision in the home, economic deterioration in communities, and lack of work preparation and employment opportunities. These combined conditions are believed to be associated with problematic youth behaviors such as teen pregnancy, violent and aggressive behavior, substance abuse, and lack of responsible citizenship. Such initiatives can be harnessed to promote inclusive services for all youths.

10. New Roles for the Business Community.

The business community has been concerned about academic preparation, but equally concerned about preparation of youths for contemporary work environments. The business community wants competition among schools, increased private investment in education, and involvement in educational policy. They also want a strong focus on outcomes and accountability for education and work preparation programs (Rigden, 1992). While the "privatization" of public education will be debated for some time, businesses are ready for a greater involvement in new initiatives for linking education and work environments. Programs that can demonstrate success in integrating relevant academic skills and functional and social skills into occupational skills training programs will garner the support of the business community (Kochhar & Erickson, 1993). Programs that serve mixed populations of students with special needs and nondisabled students and that involve wider community resources will be of particular interest to policy makers and the business community.

CONCLUSION

This is the decade of experimentation with shared resources and new community partnerships among the many agencies concerned with the educational and social development of children and youths. It is a time for debate, experimentation, and creative collaboration among the many agencies involved. Such experimentation, however, carries both promises and pitfalls. As school- and work-based programs are restructured to expand transition services to all students, we must pay the "price of vigilance" to ensure inclusion for special populations in these reforms.

III

Resources for Implementation of Inclusion

26. What Public Policies Promote Inclusion?

Before 1975, more that half of the children with disabilities in the United States were either institutionalized or did not receive appropriate educational services. Congress recognized that education, health, and employment outcomes for all children with disabilities remain a great concern throughout the country. Consequently, several laws have been passed to expand state and local coordination efforts to ensure equal access to educational programs and services and to develop supports for students integrated into schools and community programs (Exhibit III–1). These laws have required schools to ensure that, to the extent possible, students with the diverse needs created by disabilities are provided with the opportunity to participate in the full range of school programs and activities offered to their nondisabled peers.

Exhibit III–1 Legislation Promoting Inclusion

Legislation	Provisions
Americans with Disabilities Act of 1990 (P.L. 101–336)	Extends civil rights protection similar to that based on race, religion, national origin, and gender to individuals with disabilities in the private sector Mandates that employers provide ready access to employee facilities, as well as job restructuring, part-time or modified work schedules, appropriate acquisition or modification of equipment, and similar reasonable accommodations for individuals with disabilities
Individuals with Disabilities Education Act of 1990 (P.L. 101–476)	Requires placement into "least restrictive environments" in schools, protection of rights to due process, free and appropriate public education, individualized educational programs, and transition services for youths exiting schools
Carl D. Perkins Vocational and Applied Technology Education Act, 1990 Amendments	Requires "full participation" of students with disabilities in general vocational education classes, which must provide "the supplementary . . . services necessary for them to succeed in vocational education"
Rehabilitation Act of 1973, as amended in 1992 (P.L. 102–569)	Provides employment services, including supported work and independent living services, for individuals with severe disabilities Requires state and local agencies to provide rehabilitation and to plan for and assist youths with disabilities to make the transition from schooling to employment or post–secondary training
National Service Trust Act of 1993 (P.L. 103–82)	Provides for community service in exchange for college scholarships
Goals 2000: Educate America Act of 1993 (P.L. 103–227)	Sets eight challenging educational goals that state and local education agencies are expected to attempt to achieve over the balance of this decade
Job Training Reform Act of 1993 (P.L. 102–367)	Establishes Job Corps Centers for disadvantaged youths who need additional education, vocational and skills training, and/or other support services in order to make the transition into meaningful employment
School-to-Work Opportunities Act of 1994 (P.L. 103–239)	Builds on and advances school-to-work transition programs, such as technical preparation education programs, career academies, mentorship programs, supported work programs, career exploration opportunities, school-to-apprenticeship programs, school-sponsored enterprises, and business-education compacts for all youths preparing for employment or post–secondary training

Note: At press time, legislation, public policy, and legal mandates are undergoing major revision. The importance of successful inclusion is imperative.

27. Assessment Tools: Assessment Tool for Implementation of Inclusion in the Classroom and the School

In this section, an assessment tool for implementation of inclusion of students with disabilities in a regular classroom or school (Exhibit III–2) may also be used as a checklist to guide the inclusion process. An inclusion planning team can use this tool in determining whether current inclusion practices regarding personnel, curriculum and instruction, and school "culture" or attitudes are consistent with best practices for inclusion or guide them as they plan. Inclusive classrooms and schools provide opportunities for access and full participation of all students, to the extent possible, in the full range of academic and nonacademic activities. This tool is designed to look at the full range of activities.

Rating Key for Success of Inclusion
5 = Consistent achievement with high quality (high performance)
4 = Good progress, but improvement needed
3 = Progress, but many problems
2 = Initiation, but limited progress
1 = Lack of initiation or initiation with many barriers remaining (low performance)

Exhibit III–2 Assessment Tool for Inclusion Implementation

Assessment	5	4	3	2	1
Student Assessment					
Are students' disabilities diagnosed and their educational needs assessed in advance of inclusive placement?					
Is the assessment comprehensive, and does it address the range of functional domains that may affect the student's ability to benefit from the inclusive classroom?					
Is initial vision, speech/language, and hearing screening available for students who need it?					
Is diagnostic test information interpreted to teachers so that they understand the implications of the disability for learning and for the teaching environment?					
For students with disabilities, are needs assessments conducted on an ongoing basis, and are they current within three years?					
Are there procedures for obtaining record information about the previous placement?					
Are medical evaluations and medication needs communicated to teachers and related personnel who will be working with the student?					
Are initial and annual assessments of functional skills available for students who need them?					
Are assessment findings interpreted to the student and family in understandable terms?					
What percentage of students in the vocational-technical education classes and activities have disabilities?					
Are there more students who could benefit? Are students with disabilities taught with nondisabled students, or are they segregated?					

continues

Exhibit III–2 continued

Assessment	5	4	3	2	1
What percentages of students participating in work-based and transition services and activities have disabilities? Are there more students who could benefit? Are students with disabilities taught with nondisabled students, or are they segregated?					
What percentage of students participating in extracurricular school activities and special programs have disabilities? Are there more students who could benefit? Are students with disabilities taught with nondisabled students, or are they segregated?					

Environment for Inclusion: Educational

Do personnel record and share information about the number of students enrolled in home schools from more restrictive settings, such as hospitals, rehabilitation agencies, institutions, correctional facilities, or residential programs?					
Are IEPs developed and continued for each student placed into an inclusive classroom?					
Are IEP reviews held annually with representation from an interdisciplinary team, including the student, parents, teacher, consultant, and pertinent support service personnel?					
Are training goals that are related to function and social skills addressed in the IEP as needed?					
Does the IEP include short- and long-range goals?					
Are goals and objectives that have priority distinguished by the interdisciplinary team from those to be addressed informally?					
Does the IEP identify service barriers and services needed but not available?					
Does the IEP specify expected dates for achievement of goals and provision of needed services?					
Are needed related services documented in the IEP with specific dates of provision?					
Do teachers and related personnel make accommodations for students with disabilities to allow reasonable participation in extracurricular opportunities generally available to all students, including student clubs, sports as appropriate, drama and theatrical productions, chorus, debate teams, trade-related clubs, student governance organizations, booster clubs, and student fund-raising activities?					
What percentage of students participating in guidance counseling have disabilities? Are there more students who could benefit? Are students with disabilities taught with nondisabled students, or are they segregated?					
Are students with disabilities offered guidance counseling in their high school years?					
When appropriate, are students with disabilities included in college preparation seminars or counseling sessions available to nondisabled students?					
Are students with disabilities who are placed into general education classes included in instructional activities in which technology is used?					

continues

Exhibit III–2 continued

Assessment	5	4	3	2	1
Do teachers and related personnel provide accommodations to enable students with disabilities to participate in technology-related activities generally available to all students, including libraries, computers for on-line activities, information centers, technology laboratories, and school-based weather stations? Do these accommodations include modifications in the physical layout of the center, adaptations to equipment that may be necessary for use of the technology, and participation in student group activities using technology?					
Are students with disabilities given opportunities to participate in school-to-work activities that directly address their needs? Are services explicitly described, and are activities and resources to support participation in these opportunities provided?					
Are teachers informed in advance about the expected success of a student placement into general education classes?					
To the extent reasonable, are students with disabilities included with all students in the same testing and evaluation experiences required of all students (e.g., national or state competency tests and achievement tests)?					
Are teachers provided with technical assistance and support services that are adequate to enable the student to benefit from the inclusive placement and to help other students accept the student and create a positive environment?					
In advance of a student's placement into the general education classroom, do teachers receive the administrative and IDT rationale for a decision to place a student into the classroom?					
When a student is placed into the general education classroom, do teachers receive a statement of the expectations of the IDT for the benefits of the placement and the expected progress of the child in the classroom within the year?					
Are teachers provided with technical assistance and support services necessary to accommodate students with disabilities in their classroom?					
Are teachers knowledgeable about the range of options for inclusion within the school?					
Are teachers provided with technical assistance as needed to facilitate accommodation so that students with disabilities can participate in the full range of nonacademic and extracurricular opportunities generally available to all students, including student clubs, sports (as appropriate), drama and theatrical productions, chorus, debate teams, trade-related clubs, student governance organizations, booster clubs, and student fund-raising activities, as well as the full range of technology-related opportunities generally available?					
Are teachers provided with technical assistance as needed to help students with disabilities access the technologies that are used in instruction, including libraries, information centers and technology laboratories, and school-based weather stations? Do these accommodations include modifications in such centers, adaptations to equipment that may be necessary for use of the technology, and participation in student group activities using technology?					

continues

Exhibit III–2 continued

Assessment	5	4	3	2	1
Are teachers provided with technical assistance as needed to facilitate accommodation so that students with disabilities can participate in the full range of career-vocational programs and services available to all students, including vocational education, career planning activities, job training and placement opportunities, transition services, and assistance in planning and making applications to colleges and other post–high school programs?					
Are teachers provided with constructive problem-solving strategies and a fair and accessible process in which the teacher may raise issues or concerns at any time about placement of a student or the student's progress or behavior and may request a consultation or assistance in problem solving or in seeking additional support?					
Do teachers working as teams have common planning time each week to develop agreed-upon goals for students they share?					
Have teachers examined the system of classroom performance assessment they will use and considered accommodations and nontraditional assessments for students with disabilities? Have they considered assessments for an interim period in order to measure learning and competency gains in academic achievement and in social and behavioral achievement?					

Environment for Inclusion: Physical and Support Services

Assessment	5	4	3	2	1
When students with disabilities are placed into the general education classroom, do they have access to a range of support services that they may need in order to benefit from the educational program, including speech and hearing therapists, assistive technology, special education consultation, health supports, guidance, and counseling?					
Is the placement notice adequate to provide time for the students and parents to be informed in advance about classroom accommodations a student may need and to have an introduction to or training in the use of modified equipment and materials, at least at the time of placement into the classroom?					
Is the placement notice adequate to provide time for the teachers or teaching team to be informed in advance about classroom accommodations a student may need and to have an introduction to or training in the use of modified equipment and materials, at least at the time of placement into the classroom?					
Are students informed about potential emergency situations that may arise from the disability and may require them to receive emergency treatment or procedures in the classroom?					
Is the receiving teacher or teaching team informed about the student's disability and whether the student has a physical, medical, emotional, or behavioral problem that might result in the need to take an emergency action?					
Are students and parents informed about the emergency management policies and procedures of the school that are clearly defined in order to guide the actions of teachers and other personnel in the event of a behavioral, medical, or natural emergency?					
Is there a written school policy about emergency procedures in the classroom?					
Are teachers and related personnel trained and knowledgeable of the emergency procedures or actions that may need to be taken?					

continues

Exhibit III–2 continued

Assessment	5	4	3	2	1
Are students provided with information in advance about the supplemental materials, equipment, or personnel deemed necessary by the IDT to enable the student to benefit from the educational and social program in the classroom, including but not limited to physical assistive devices or equipment, technology adaptations (computer adaptations), physical adaptations to the classroom, personal or classroom aides, instructional materials, interpreters, recording devices, or other equipment?					
Are teachers informed about the extent of the student's disabilities and if a student placed into the classroom has a physical, medical, emotional, or behavioral problem that might result in the need for a teacher to take an emergency action?					
Are teachers informed about and trained in the emergency procedures or actions that may be needed to respond to an emergency in the classroom, including possible medical, behavioral, physical, or other emergency? Are these procedures in writing?					
Are teachers trained in emergency procedures that may be needed in order to safely guide their actions in the event of a behavioral, medical, or natural emergency?					
Are teachers provided with the supplemental materials, equipment, or personnel that are deemed necessary by the IDT for the student to benefit from the educational and social program in the classroom, including but not limited to physical assistive devices or equipment, technology adaptations (computer adaptations), physical adaptations to the classroom, personal or classroom aides, instructional materials, interpreters, recording devices, or other equipment?					
Are teachers informed, in advance of placement, about classroom accommodations, and are they trained in the use of such equipment and materials at least at the time of the student's placement into the classroom?					
Is a directory of support services available and used by teachers and inclusion implementors?					
Is each student included in the regular classroom assigned to a teacher mentor, advocate, or coordinator who can assist and support the student in his or her efforts to succeed in the new classroom?					
Are students provided with comprehensive vocational assessment as part of the transition services required under the IDEA?					
Environment for Inclusion: Attitudinal					
Do teachers and related personnel believe that, to the maximum extent possible, students with disabilities belong in classrooms and other school and community settings with students who are not disabled and that special classes, separate schooling, or other removal of children with disabilities from the regular educational environment occurs only when the nature or severity of the disabilities is such that education in regular classes with the use of supplementary aids and services cannot be achieved satisfactorily?					
Do teachers and related personnel believe that social inclusion is an essential element of successful inclusion and that students must feel that they belong?					
Do teachers and related personnel believe that students with disabilities placed into general education classrooms should be as involved in cooperative learning and peer instruction as are all students?					

continues

Exhibit III–2 continued

Assessment	5	4	3	2	1
Are teachers committed to the development of a caring school community that fosters mutual respect and support among personnel, parents, and students?					
Are teachers committed to the belief that students with disabilities can benefit from friendships with nondisabled students?					
Do teachers actively intervene in students' behaviors (e.g, taunting, teasing, or isolating a student with a disability) that violate the belief that all students belong in the classroom or other school setting?					
Does the administration create a school environment and culture in which they fully support the commitment to inclusion and the development of inclusive practices?					
Are all communications with parents and the community integrated, or are there separate newsletters or PTA notes for parents of students with special needs?					
Do teachers and administrators celebrate the successes of inclusion by teachers? Do they reward excellence in teaching of diverse classrooms, excellence in team teaching or consultations, and excellence in accommodations?					
Do teachers and administrators celebrate the successes of inclusion by students? Do they reward excellence in student achievement in inclusive classrooms, excellence in peer mentoring and support, excellence in student participation in extracurricular activities, and excellence in general participation?					
Do teachers and administrators celebrate the successes of inclusion by parents? Do they reward excellence in parent involvement, excellence in parent-to-parent mentoring, excellence in parent volunteering, and excellence in general involvement?					
Inclusion Planning and Commitment					
Does the school inclusion plan include assurance that the school will promote the inclusion and full participation of all students, including low-achieving students, students with limited English proficiency, students with disabilities, and school dropouts, in the full range of school-to-work transition programs, including outreach, recruitment, assessment, enrollment, and placement activities?					
Does the inclusion plan state that students with disabilities must be educated with students without disabilities?					
Does the inclusion plan state that special classes, separate schooling, or other removal of children with disabilities from the regular educational environment should occur only when the nature or severity of the disability is such that education in the regular classes with the use of supplementary aids, services, and support cannot be achieved satisfactorily (I.D.E.A.)?					
Does the inclusion plan require that an effective delivery system of specialized services in the school and in each inclusive classroom will be established to reduce the need to remove the student from the classroom or home school to obtain special education and related services?					
Does the inclusion plan specify objectives for "mainsteaming," including statements similar to the following:					
• to educate all children with disabilities in regular school settings regardless of the degree or severity of the disability unless the severity of the disability is such that education in regular classes with supplementary aids and services cannot be achieved satisfactorily?					

continues

Exhibit III–2 continued

Assessment	5	4	3	2	1
• to allow special education students to participate in regular education classes with support provided as needed by the special education staff, related services staff, support personnel, and other local school personnel?					
Does the school plan address the needs of all students regarding access to and participation in classroom activities, materials, and technology?					
Does the school plan address coordination of inclusion efforts with other school-linked agencies, such as vocational rehabilitation service agencies, social and human service agencies, health service agencies, and other agencies responsible for coordinating services to children and youths?					
Does the inclusion plan describe the manner in which the school will provide vocational and school-to-work transition activities to youths who wish to enter occupations?					
Are the needs of students with disabilities and supports addressed in a coherent school-based plan for career-vocational services and school-to-work opportunities that explicitly described services, activities, and resources to support student participation in these opportunities?					
Does the inclusion plan address assistance to teachers in adapting curriculum, classroom setting, materials, assessments, and teaching strategies in order to accommodate students in the classroom and enable them to benefit from the educational program?					
Does the inclusion plan describe how the school will provide leadership, supervision, and resources to support inclusive practices throughout the school?					
Does the inclusion plan reference major laws and regulations that provide the authority for inclusive practices, including the Individuals with Disabilities Education Act, the Americans with Disabilities Act, the Rehabilitation Act (section 504), the Carl D. Perkins Vocational and Applied Technology Education Act, the School-to-Work Opportunities Act, the Community Services Act, the Improving America's Schools Act, and other related acts? (These statutes contain several provisions designed to ensure full participation of youths with disabilities in the range of programs.)					
Does the inclusion plan show a relationship to the school's activities and programs under the School-to-Work Opportunities Act, the Goals 2000 plan, and other related school improvement initiatives?					
Does the inclusion plan address the inclusion of students in state or national testing or assessments of academic achievement, performing arts performance, or other competency testing?					
Does the school have a plan for outreach to students with disabilities who have dropped out of school?					
Do teachers and administrators intervene when support services are not provided when needed and specified in the IEP?					
Do teachers and administrators participate in inclusion advocacy and efforts to develop inclusive services, settings, and opportunities?					
Does the school ensure that waivers of statutory and regulatory requirements do not undermine the efforts to promote inclusion and full participation?					

continues

Exhibit III–2 continued

Assessment	5	4	3	2	1
Involvement of the School and Community					
Does the school have a plan to inform parents, students, and consumer organizations, such as the PTA, parent advocacy groups, and student organizations, about the plans for inclusion?					
Does the school inform teachers and key support service personnel who will have primary responsibility for any new programs or initiatives that will affect instruction or student services?					
Does the school have a plan to inform the school-linked agencies and the support service agencies about the inclusion initiative?					
Does the school or do individual teachers conduct information seminars about the inclusion initiative for parents and other community members?					
Does the school have informational brochures and materials that explain the mission and benefits of inclusion initiatives?					
Have collaborating business partners been informed about the inclusion initiatives?					
Has the school staff reached out to the local college or university to request technical assistance?					
Interdisciplinary Planning and Parent Involvement					
Do teachers and related personnel have knowledge of support services, related services, and community resource agencies?					
Do teachers make contact with the families regularly?					
Do teachers make special efforts to involve parents of students with disabilities and other special needs?					
Is each student with a disability assigned a teacher/service coordinator who is identified to the student and family?					
Are teachers trained in how to identify and refer students to needed support services inside and outside the school?					
Are students with disabilities and other special needs who are placed into general education classrooms informed about their disabilities and the special accommodations that will be implemented in order to accommodate them in the classroom?					
Are parents and students informed in advance about the administrative and IDT rationale for a decision to place the student into an inclusive classroom? Are they given a statement of the expectations of the IDT for the benefits of the placement and expected progress in the classroom within a specified period of time?					
Are parents informed about the reasons for placement into the general education classroom? Do they receive information in advance about the administrative and IDT rationale for a decision to place the child into an inclusive classroom and a statement of the expectations of the IDT for the benefits of the placement and the progress expected in the classroom within a specified period of time?					
Are students with disabilities informed in advance about a change in placement?					
Does the advance notice provide adequate time to allow the student to visit the school or classroom and teacher and obtain the needed information about new expectations and curriculum requirements and accommodations needed?					

continues

Exhibit III–2 continued

Assessment	5	4	3	2	1
Is the student with a disability notified of IEP meetings in advance and invited to such meetings?					
Is the student involved in the development of the IEP and the goals and objectives—academic and nonacademic—established for the school year?					
Are students generally present at the IEP meetings, and if not, is there a procedure to determine why students are not present?					
Are students involved in their own transition planning? Are students involved in developing their goals and objectives for the school year?					
Are students and parents provided with access to the student's IEP and ITP at any time after placement into the classroom?					
Are teachers provided adequate time to participate in their students' IEP meetings and in the development of the IEPs? Are they informed of their right to be present and to participate in the IEP placement meeting prior to placement in order to discuss and learn about needs and available accommodations?					
Does the teacher have access to a fair process in which he or she may raise issues or concerns at any time about the student's placement and progress and may request a consultation or assistance in problem solving or in seeking additional support?					
Are teachers informed in advance about a student's placement and about the student's right to participate in an IEP meeting to discuss the change?					
Does the student have access to a fair process in which he or she may raise issues or concerns at any time about the placement and his or her progress and may he or she request a consultation or assistance in problem solving or in seeking additional support?					
Are parents informed about the variety of activities—academic and nonacademic—in which their child is involved?					
Are parents informed about the accommodations that are needed to enable the student to be included in the general education classroom?					
Are parents informed about IEP meetings and invited to attend each IEP meeting?					
Are parents informed of their right to participate in the development of the student's IEP, the expectation that they will do so, and their right to be present and participate in the IEP placement meeting prior to placement in order to discuss and learn about needs and available accommodations?					
Are parents informed when it has been determined that their child has a physical, medical, emotional, or behavioral problem that might result in the need to take an emergency action by teachers or other school personnel?					
Does the student's IEP include goals related to physical status, vision, hearing, or mobility?					
Does the student's IEP include goals related to functional skill and adaptive behavior?					
Are the student's IEP goals monitored to review accomplishment within stated periods?					
Does the student's IEP include a transition component that includes career-vocational education goals and transition goals?					

continues

Exhibit III–2 continued

Assessment	5	4	3	2	1
Are teachers and related personnel provided with and informed about mediation procedures in which parents can raise issues or concerns at any time about their child's placement and progress and may request a consultation or assistance in problem solving or in seeking additional support or suggestions on how the home environment can support the problem-solving process?					
Are teachers and related personnel informed about the rights of parents to due process and about the procedures that are available to parents for requesting a due process hearing?					
Are teachers conveying information and communicating with students and families in their native language or using appropriate accommodations (e.g., sign language)?					
Are parents provided with and informed about procedures for a fair and accessible process or for mediation procedures, in which they may raise issues or concerns at any time about their child's placement and progress and may request a consultation or assistance in problem solving or in seeking additional support or suggestions on how the home environment can support the problem-solving process?					
Are parents informed about their rights to due process and about the procedures that are available to them for requesting a due process hearing?					

Teacher In-Service Training for Inclusion

	5	4	3	2	1
Are there trained special educators providing consultation or team teaching who understand the needs of students with disabilities and the methods and materials needed to provide specialized educational services and who are available within the school to work with general education teachers?					
Does the school provide resources for ongoing in-service training of teachers and related personnel to prepare them for team teaching, special education consultation in the classroom, and general accommodation of students with disabilities in their classroom?					
Does the school provide resources for technical assistance to teachers and related service personnel to support and guide their inclusion efforts?					
Are teachers informed about the range of available student support services in general education classrooms, including guidance and counseling, career counseling, peer support and mediation services, assistance with application to colleges or for post–secondary placement, health services and counseling, and other supportive services?					
Does the school or district center program have personnel trained in career-vocational education? Are there a sufficient number of direct support service and instructional staff to ensure access to the range of educational, career-vocational, technical and technology-related, and transition services, and are they adequately prepared for these tasks?					
Does the school actively recruit individuals with disabilities into roles such as teachers, support personnel, noninstructional personnel, volunteers, and guest speakers?					
Does the school's in-service training for inclusion include school-linked agency personnel for joint training (e.g., regular educators, special educators, career-vocational educators, and related services personnel)?					

continues

Exhibit III–2 continued

Assessment	5	4	3	2	1
Resources and Technical Support Needs					
Does the school have a plan for providing clear leadership, supervision, and adequate resources to support inclusive practices throughout the school?					
Does the school budget reflect adequate resources for addressing the goals in the inclusion plan for developing activities that promote the full participation of all students, including students with disabilities, in the full range of school programs and activities?					
Does the school budget provide adequate resources to develop supplementary and support services that promote the full participation of all students in school activities?					
Does the school ensure that the career-vocational and school-to-work transition programs are preparing students for occupations in which job openings are projected or available within the community, on the basis of a labor market analysis?					
Is adequate technical assistance provided to teachers and specialists when they need it?					
Data Collection and Evaluation and Improvement of Inclusion Practices					
Are decision-making processes for student placement documented and communicated with teachers?					
Is there documentation of the number of students with disabilities placed into inclusive settings and of the change in the number of students transferred to more inclusive settings?					
Is there documentation of referral information and of decisions of the inclusion intake team or the interdisciplinary team?					
Are data recorded on the number of student cases reviewed and the number of students referred for placement?					
Are data recorded on the number of students removed from inclusive classrooms and the reasons for such removal?					
Is follow-up information collected on students who graduate from high school?					
Is information recorded on the referrals to support services and related service providers?					
Is information recorded on the time lag between referral and entry into inclusive classrooms or programs, after students and parents have been notified and have consented?					
Are reasons for rejection of placement documented?					
Are follow-up interviews of students conducted?					
Is enrollment for advanced training and for completion of post–secondary degrees and certifications conducted?					
Are data on job placement and job retention gathered?					
Is the ratio of students with disabilities to students without disabilities in general education classrooms documented?					
Is the stability of student placement recorded?					
Is there relative consistency in the numbers of students with disabilities in regular classrooms?					

continues

Exhibit III–2 continued

Assessment	5	4	3	2	1
Do teachers and administrators conduct questionnaire surveys to assess student and parent satisfaction with student placement?					
Does the school assess teacher and specialist satisfaction with inclusive practices and resources?					
Are students and families involved in evaluating inclusion practices?					
Do teachers and administrators review the problem-solving and mediation strategies to determine if changes are needed?					
Are there annual evaluation reviews by the inclusion planning team regarding the effectiveness of planning, in-service training, and resource development?					
Are incidents of crisis intervention documented?					
Do teachers document parent visits and teacher consultations?		·			
Do teachers evaluate parent involvement in student's overall programming and changes in such involvement?					
Do teachers and administrators "reinvest" the evaluation results or use them for improvement of inclusive practices?					

Note: IEP, Individual Educational Plan
IDT, Interdisciplinary Team
IDEA, Individuals with Disabilities Education Act
PTA, Parent-Teacher Association
ITP, Individualized Transition Plan.

28. Tools for Assessment of School Structure and Inclusion Team and Planners for Potential To Support Inclusion

Assessing the School Structure To Support Inclusion

Issue	Explanation
1. Understand the diversity of the individuals and units involved in inclusion implementation.	Involving teachers and other professionals from different parts of the school and different disciplines makes coordination a challenge. Each team member has his or her own philosophy, educational approaches, knowledge and skills in the classroom, understanding of subject matter areas, classroom procedures and regulations, standards and professional roles, and responsibilities. This diversity enriches the process of setting shared goals and is important in the evaluation of the inclusion effort.
2. Determine what written collaborative agreements and planning processes are already in place.	Many inclusion planning initiatives lack formalized agreements to guide their activities. Such agreements or operating procedures are crucial to the development of coordinated activities, because they define the common goals and objectives and the authority for teacher action.
3. Examine the policies and funding restrictions of the school-related service agencies that may be involved in the inclusion partnership.	Various school units and related agencies have evolved from separate funding streams, public law, or historical initiatives. They therefore have different eligibility requirements and are concerned with different target student groups (e.g., disadvantaged or gifted). It is important to examine and understand these differences in developing agreements and cooperative activities and in defining inclusion outcomes. Also, recent changes in special education, general education, vocational-technical education, and disability laws will affect school priorities and the way programs are expected to operate.
4. Assess the capability of team members for data collection and reporting.	Teachers and related service professionals define and report their activities and performance goals and outcomes differently. Inclusion team members must understand these differences and seek to integrate their performance goals and outcomes. For example, if a consulting resource teacher is teamed with a general education teacher to teach science, they must agree on how they will measure achievement for all students, including those with disabilities; how they will collect assessment information for all students; and how they will report "progress" for the inclusion students in academic, social, functional, and other domains.

continues

Issue	Explanation
5. Consider the economic "health" of the school and related service agencies and its impact on the ability of key professionals to collaborate.	When funds for schools are eroding and local economies are intensifying competition for diminishing funds, the demand for educational accountability tends to increase. These forces can be harnessed to strengthen the collaboration and sharing of resources within and among schools and community agencies.
6. Assess the level of parent involvement and the family supports needed.	Since parent involvement is considered one of the most important factors in the success of students' readiness for inclusion and successful transition to inclusive classrooms and settings, parent involvement must be assessed. Collaborative activities will remain weak if parents are not viewed as, and given the resources to be, essential players in the assessment of needs and in the development of the inclusive initiative. Capacity for parent training, information dissemination to parents, and opportunities for their direct involvement must be assessed.

Assessing Team Member Attitudes

Issue	Explanation
7. Be sensitive to political pressures and pressure groups.	As local economic pressures force schools to economize, inclusion planners must be prepared to show how school inclusion activities and community linkages can contribute to cost-effective programs.
8. Be sensitive to territorial attitudes.	Encroachments of professionals and school units on each other's "territory" can threaten people's comfort with traditional ways of operating and making decisions. A collaborative initiative like inclusion changes the way everyone in a school conducts business, and this should be made clear to all professionals from the beginning of the inclusion initiative.
9. Consider issues involved in staff turnover, and carefully select inclusion team leaders for long-term continuity of the initiatives.	Many inclusion failures can be traced to high turnover rates among key personnel in the schools. Established relationships and the emergence of "champions" (energetic and enthusiastic leaders) contribute to confidence and trust among inclusion planners and can accelerate collaborative efforts. As old links break apart through attrition, the effort can weaken. For example, the loss of a respected champion for an inclusion model, who has fought to preserve the collaboration in a time of economic constraint, can result in the loss of months or years of development progress.

Assessing Knowledge and Training Needs of Inclusion Planners

Issue	Explanation
10. Work to build early understanding of respective goals and missions among inclusion team planners and implementors.	Teachers of general education and special education as well as related service personnel, must understand each other and their distinctly different goals and missions. They must recognize each other's complementary strengths. This factor is essential to early crystallization of team collaboration. Seminars in early readiness for inclusion are worth every hour of time, and continued training can keep the momentum high.
11. Explore and share existing models for inclusion and team collaboration.	There is a need to develop model practices for the development of inclusion and team collaboration to address the needs of students with disabilities in inclusive schools. A variety of models and development practices should be explored, and these ideas should be discussed with inclusion team planners and school leaders.
12. Explore relationships with local universities to assist in development of the inclusion process.	Many colleges and universities have entered relationships with schools, local and state education agencies, and community service organizations to provide resources and technical assistance for new initiatives. Universities can provide the time and expertise of graduate students for in-service training, as well as faculty expertise to design instructional materials, provide technical assistance, and develop grant proposals for additional resources. Universities can help champion local initiatives in communities in which there are political or resource barriers. Frequently, the availability of grant funding for an inclusion initiative can provide the stimulus for action in the event of "foot dragging" from school administrators.

29. Assessment of Effectiveness in Coordination of Inclusion

Inclusion Coordination Function	Measure of Effectiveness
Student information and referral for classroom placement	• Existence of student placement decision-making processes and change in the number of students transferred to more inclusive settings • Availability of parent and community information on inclusion procedures and policies • Documentation of referral data and team placement decisions
Review and screening of student needs	• Number of student cases reviewed and number of students referred for placement • Performance of follow-up on results of referrals • Availability of support service directory and use by teachers and inclusion implementors • Number of referrals to support service and related service providers • Reduction of time lag between referral and entry into inclusive classroom or program, after student and parent have been notified and have consented • Documentation of reasons for rejection of placement
Assessment and diagnosis	• Adequacy of procedures for obtaining past record information • Interpretation of student educational needs on the basis of assessment data • Length of time in assessment status • Comprehensiveness of student assessment information • Identification of student strengths and needs and provision of information to teachers as appropriate for educational interventions needed in the classroom • Communication of medical evaluations and medication needs to teachers and relevant personnel • Performance of initial speech/language screening for students who need it • Performance of initial assessment of functional skills for students who need it • Performance of annual assessment of functional skills for each student who needs it • Interpretation of assessment findings to the student and family in understandable terms

continues

Inclusion Coordination Function	Measure of Effectiveness
Individual education program planning and development	• Number of students enrolled in home schools from more restrictive settings, such as hospitals, rehabilitation agencies, institutions, correctional facilities, or residential programs • Adequacy of IEP development • Adequacy of annual IEP review • Development of IEP goals related to function and social skills as needed • Inclusion of short- and long-range goals in IEP • Distinction of goals and objectives with priority status by the interdisciplinary team • Identification, in the IEP, of service barriers and services needed but not available • Setting, in the IEP, of expected dates for achievement of goals and provision of needed services • Documentation of related services needed, with specific dates of provision
Support service coordination and linking	• Knowledge by teachers and counselors of support services, related services, and community resource agencies • Existence of regular family communications • Assignment of each student to a teacher/service coordinator who is identified to the student and family • Identification and procurement of needed support services inside and outside the school by teachers and coordinators
IEP monitoring and follow-up	• Achievement by student of goals related to physical status, vision, hearing, or mobility, etc. • Gains of student in levels of adaptive behavior or independent functioning • Accomplishment of individual IEP goals within stated periods • Existence of up-to-date student IEP and record information • Stability of student placements and length of time in current placement • Minimum review period of six months for individual service plans (of the service delivery agencies) • Availability of medical or nursing services for each student on medication or who needs medical attention • Documentation of student's progress in vocational programs and employment sites • Documentation of crisis intervention activities and availability of procedures • Documentation of parent visits to school and teacher consultations • Amount of family involvement in student's overall programming • Number of students removed from inclusive classrooms • Advance notice to student and family of discontinuation of support services, changes in placement, or intent to remove child from the classroom

continues

Inclusion Coordination Function	Measure of Effectiveness
Inclusion advocacy and support advocacy	• Intervention by teachers and administrators when support services are not provided when needed and specified in the IEP • Participation by teachers and administrators in inclusion advocacy and efforts to develop inclusive services, settings, and opportunities • Change in the number of students with disabilities served in inclusive settings
Inclusion evaluation and student follow-up	• Evaluation of student functioning after secondary school • Performance of follow-up interviews • Enrollment in advanced training and completion of post–secondary degrees and certifications • Job placement and retention • Job or career changes • Independent living arrangements • Accessing of community services
Factors regarding quality of inclusion	• Ratio of students with disabilities to students without disabilities in general education classrooms • Relative consistency of ratio among classrooms (students equitably placed into classrooms) • Qualifications of teachers and special education consultants and specialists • Student satisfaction with placement • Family satisfaction with placement and with support services provided • Teacher and specialist satisfaction with inclusive practices and resources • Student and family involvement in evaluating inclusion practices • Provision of technical assistance provided to teachers and specialists • Development of problem-solving and mediation strategies to avoid disputes and due process hearings

Note: IEP, Individual Educational Plan.

30. Inclusion Bill of Rights

General education teachers have commonly been left out of site-based decisions about implementing inclusion. There is, therefore, a need to address their concerns about their ability to ensure success of students placed into inclusive classrooms. They need an "inclusion bill of rights" that addresses their concerns as key implementors and balances the rights of children and youths, parents, teachers, and administrators in a way that makes the promise, responsibility, and process of inclusion a rational and effective one.

Reconciling Competing Needs and Rights in Inclusion

Can the processes of inclusion really address and reconcile the competing needs and rights of children, parents, teachers, and administrators, each of whom may have competing concerns and needs? We believe it can and must be done. This inclusion bill of rights forges a relationship among and seeks to reconcile the rights and needs of three groups:

1. consumer-students
2. parents and guardians
3. teachers and support personnel

These sets of rights are complementary and form a coherent and coordinated set of responsibilities for inclusion for each of the key participants. Each of these groups is responsible for the success or failure of inclusion, and therefore this bill of rights views the set of principles as necessary for the success of inclusion. Considering the rights and needs of one group responsible for implementing inclusion at the expense of another's is to jeopardize the inclusion process and its quality. All are essential to the process.

As participants in inclusive classrooms, students, parents, and teachers and support personnel have the rights shown in Exhibits III–3, III–4, and III–5.

Exhibit III–3 Inclusion Bill of Rights for Students

Right	Explanation
1. **Right to participate in the full range of school programs and activities**	The right to accommodation of persons with disabilities in the full range of general and special educational programs available to all students, including academic and vocational education, transition services, job training and placement opportunities, and articulated school-college programs.
2. **Right to needed related services in general education class**	The right to access a range of student support services in general education classrooms, including guidance and counseling, career counseling, peer support and mediation services, assistance with application to colleges or post–secondary placement, health services, and counseling.
3. **Right to participate in school extracurricular activities**	The right to accommodation of persons with disabilities in the full range of extracurricular opportunities generally available, including student clubs, sports as appropriate, drama and theatrical productions, chorus, debate teams, trade-related clubs, student governance organizations, booster clubs, and student fund-raising activities.

continues

Exhibit III–3 continued

Right	Explanation
4. **Right to participate in technology-related opportunities**	The right to accommodation of persons with disabilities in the full range of technology-related opportunities generally available, including access to libraries, information centers, technology laboratories, and school-based weather stations and accommodations in such centers; adaptations to equipment that may be necessary for use of the technology; and participation in student group activities using technology.
5. **Right to participate in development of one's own IEP**	The right to participate in the development of the IEP and ITP, to the extent possible for students with severe cognitive disabilities, and the right to be present and to participate in the IEP/ITP placement meeting prior to placement in order to discuss and learn about needs and available accommodations.
6. **Right to advance notice**	The right to an "informed" placement, that is, the right to know at least several days in advance about a change of placement.
7. **Right to know about the existing disability**	The right to know about the existing disability and if there is a physical, medical, emotional, or behavioral problem that might result in the need for emergency action; the right to know that there is a written school policy on emergency management and that the teacher is trained and knowledgeable of the appropriate emergency procedures or actions; and the right to have all of this information in writing.
8. **Right to know about emergency procedures**	The right to know that emergency management policies and procedures for the school are clearly defined in order to guide the actions of teachers and other personnel in the event of a behavioral, medical, or natural emergency.
9. **Right to know reasons for placement**	The right to advance information about the administrative and IDT rationale for a decision to place the student into an inclusive classroom and the right to a statement of the expectations of the IDT for the benefits of the placement and expected progress in the classroom within a specified period.
10. **Right to supplemental supports in the classroom**	The right to supplemental materials, equipment, or personnel that are deemed necessary by the IDT to ensure that the student benefits from the educational and social program in the classroom, including but not limited to physical assistive devices or equipment, technology adaptations (computer adaptations), physical adaptations to the classroom, personal or classroom aides, instructional materials, interpreters, recording devices, or other equipment.
11. **Right to advance knowledge about classroom accommodations**	The right to be informed in advance about the availability of such supplemental materials and equipment and to have an introduction to or training in the use of such equipment and materials at least at the time of placement into the classroom.

continues

Exhibit III–3 continued

Right	Explanation
12. Right to access to IEP	The right to access and review the IEP and ITP at any time after placement into the classroom.
13. Right to communicate problems	The right to a fair and accessible process in which the student may raise issues or concerns at any time about placement and progress and may request a consultation or assistance in problem solving or in seeking additional support.
14. Right to have trained personnel	The right to have teachers and support personnel adequately trained in the education and support of students with disabilities included in regular classrooms.
15. Right to vocational assessment	The right to receive a comprehensive vocational assessment as part of the transition services required under IDEA.
16. Right to trained personnel in career-vocational education	The right to an adequate number of and adequate preparation of direct support service and instructional staff to ensure access to the range of educational, career-vocational, technical and technology-related, and transition services.
17. Right to participate in school-to-work opportunities	The right to participate in a coherent school-based plan for career-vocational and school-to-work opportunities that directly addresses the special needs of students with disabilities and explicitly describes services and provides for activities and resources to support participation in these opportunities.
18. Right to inclusion in school reform opportunities	The right to participate in Goals 2000 and school reform activities and to have individual special needs addressed in such reforms or restructuring.
19. Right to reasonable inclusion in national standards	The right to have the special needs of students with disabilities addressed and assessed in relation to preparation to meet the national standards for academic achievement, work preparation, and job training.

Note: IEP, individual Educational Plan
ITP, Individualized Transition Plan
IDT, Interdisciplinary Team
IDEA, Individuals with Disabilities Education Act

Exhibit III–4 Inclusion Bill of Rights for Parents

Right	Explanation
1. **Right to participate in the full range of school programs and activities**	The right to accommodation of the child in the full range of general and special educational programs available to all students, including academic and vocational education, transition services, job training and placement opportunities, and articulated school-college programs.
2. **Right to needed related services in general education class**	The right to accommodation of the child in the range of student support services in general education classrooms, including guidance and counseling, career counseling, peer support and mediation services, assistance with application to colleges or post–secondary placement, health services, and counseling.
3. **Right to participate in school extracurricular activities**	The right to accommodation of the child in the full range of extracurricular opportunities generally available, including student clubs, sports as appropriate, drama and theatrical productions, chorus, debate teams, trade-related clubs, student governance organizations, booster clubs, and student fund-raising activities.
4. **Right to participate in technology-related opportunities**	The right to accommodation of the child in the full range of technology-related opportunities generally available, including access to libraries, information centers, technology laboratories, and school-based weather stations and accommodations in such centers; adaptations to equipment that may be necessary for use of the technology; and participation in student group activities using technology.
5. **Right to participate in development of the IEP**	The right to have the child participate in the development of his or her IEP, to the extent possible for students with severe cognitive disabilities, and the right to be present and to participate in the IEP placement meeting prior to placement in order to discuss and learn about needs and available accommodations.
6. **Right to advance notice**	The right to be informed in advance about the child's placement and to participate in an IEP meeting to discuss the change.
7. **Right to know about the existing disability**	The right to know if the child has been determined to have a physical, medical, emotional, or behavioral problem that might result in the need for teachers or other school personnel to take emergency action; the right to know that there is a written school policy on emergency procedures and that the teacher is trained and knowledgeable about the appropriate emergency procedures or actions; and the right to have all of this information in writing.
8. **Right to know about emergency procedures**	The right to know that emergency management policies and procedures for the school are clearly defined in order to guide the actions of teachers and other school personnel in the event of a behavioral, medical, or natural emergency involving the child.

continues

Exhibit III–4 continued

Right	Explanation
9. **Right to know reasons for placement**	The right to advance information about the administrative and IDT rationale for a decision to place the child into an inclusive classroom and the right to a statement of the expectations of the IDT for the benefits of the placement and expected progress in the classroom within a special period.
10. **Right to supplemental supports in the classroom**	The right to supplemental materials, the equipment, or personnel that are deemed necessary by the IDT to ensure that the child benefits from the educational and social program in the classroom, including but not limited to physical assistive devices or equipment, technology adaptations (computer adaptations), physical adaptations to the classroom, personal or classroom aides, instructional materials, interpreters, recording devices, or other equipment.
11. **Right to advance knowledge about classroom accommodations**	The right to be informed in advance about the availability of such supplemental materials and equipment in order to support or augment the child's orientation or training in the use of needed equipment and materials at least at the time of placement into the classroom.
12. **Right to access to IEP**	The right to access and review of the IEP/ITP of the child placed into the classroom and the right to frequent communication with teachers and administrators about the child's progress or changes in the curriculum or program that may be related to the child's adjustment to the inclusive classroom.
13. **Right to communicate problems**	The right to a fair and accessible process in which the parent may raise issues or concerns at any time about the child's placement and progress and may request a consultation or assistance in problem solving or in seeking additional support or suggestions on how the home environment may support the problem-solving process.
14. **Right to have trained personnel**	The right to have the child taught by teachers and support personnel who are adequately trained for educating children in inclusive classrooms.
15. **Right to vocational assessment**	The right to have a comprehensive vocational assessment as part of the transition services required under IDEA and to have an interpretation of the results in terms of the child's future program, services, or home enrichment.
16. **Right to trained personnel in career-vocational education**	The right to an adequate number of and adequate preparation of direct support service and instructional staff to ensure access to the range of educational, career-vocational, technical and technology-related, and transition services.
17. **Right to participate in school-to-work opportunities**	The right to have the needs of the child with a disability addressed in a coherent school-based plan for career-vocational services and school-to-work opportunities that explicitly describes services, activities, and resources to support the child's participation in these opportunities.

continues

Exhibit III–4 continued

Right	Explanation
18. Right to inclusion in school reform opportunities	The right to have the needs of the child with a disability addressed in a coherent school-based Goals 2000 and school reform plan.
19. Right to reasonable inclusion in national standards	The right to have special needs of the child with a disability addressed and assessed in relation to preparation to meet the national standards for academic achievement, work preparation, and job training.
Note: IEP, individual educational plan IDT, Interdisciplinary team ITP, individualized transition plan IDEA, Individuals and Disabilities Education Act	

Exhibit III–5 Inclusion Bill of Rights for Teachers and Support Personnel

Right	Explanation
1. Right to know about expected success	The right to know the expectations for students placed into general education classes from the pool of students with disabilities.
2. Right to technical assistance and support services	The right to technical assistance and support services in accommodating students with disabilities in (a) the full range of general and special educational programs available to all students, including academic and vocational education, transition services, job training and placement opportunities, and articulated school-college programs; (b) the full range of extracurricular opportunities generally available, including student clubs, sports as appropriate, drama and theatrical productions, chorus, debate teams, trade-related clubs, student governance organizations, booster clubs, and student fund-raising activities; and (c) the full range of technology-related opportunities generally available, including access to libraries, information centers, technology laboratories, and school-based weather stations and accommodations in such centers; adaptations to equipment that may be necessary for use of the technology; and participation in student group activities using technology.
3. Right to needed related services in general education class	The right to be informed about and to access the range of available student support services in general education classrooms, including guidance and counseling, career counseling, peer support and mediation services, assistance with application to colleges or post–secondary placement, health services, and counseling.
4. Right to participate in the student's IEP meetings	The right to participate in the development of the student's IEP and the right to be present and participate in the IEP placement meeting prior to placement in order to discuss and learn about needs and available accommodations.

continues

Exhibit III–5 continued

Right	Explanation
5. **Right to advance notice**	The right to be informed in advance about a student's placement and to participate in an IEP meeting to discuss the change.
6. **Right to know about extent of disabilities**	The right to an "informed" placement, that is, the right to know if a student placed into the classroom has a physical, medical, emotional, or behavioral problem that might result in the need to take an emergency action; the right to know what type of emergency procedures or action may be required; and the right to have all of this information in writing. (The IDEA law promotes the inclusion of children with chronic health impairments and those dependent on medical technology into the regular classroom.)
7. **Right to know about and be trained in emergency procedures**	The right to know that emergency management policies and procedures for the school are clearly defined and to be trained in safe performance of such procedures in the event of a behavioral, medical, or natural emergency.
8. **Right to know reasons for placement**	The right to advance information about the administrative and IDT rationale for a decision to place a student into an inclusive classroom and the right to a statement of the expectations of the IDT for the benefits of the placement and expected progress of the child in the classroom within a specified period.
9. **Right to supplemental supports in the classroom**	The right to supplemental materials, equipment, or personnel that are deemed necessary by the IDT for the student to benefit from the educational and social program in the classroom, including but not limited to physical assistive devices or equipment, technology adaptations (computer adaptations), physical adaptations to the classroom, personal or classroom aides, instructional materials, interpreters, recording devices, or other equipment.
10. **Right to advance knowledge about classroom accommodations**	The right to be informed in advance about the availability of such supplemental materials or assistive technology or equipment and to be trained in the use of such equipment and materials at least at the time of the student's placement into the classroom.
11. **Right to access to IEP**	The right to be present and participate in a student's IEP placement meeting prior to placement in order to learn about the child and his or her needs for accommodations and the right to access and review the IEP of the child placed into the classroom.
12. **Right to constructive problem solving**	The right to a fair and accessible process in which the teacher may raise issues or concerns at any time about placement of a student or the student's progress or behavior and may request a consultation or assistance in problem solving or in seeking additional support.
13. **Right to receive needed training on inclusion**	The right to have the needs of regular educators, special educators, career-vocational educators, and related services personnel clearly and coherently addressed in the local and state personnel development and to receive needed training for inclusion.

continues

Exhibit III–5 continued

Right	Explanation
14. **Right to have planning time**	For team teachers, the right to have common planning time each week and time to develop agreed-upon goals for joint students.
15. **Right to inclusion support for school-to-work opportunities**	The right to have the needs of students with disabilities and teacher supports addressed in a coherent school-based plan for career-vocational services and school-to-work opportunities that explicitly describes services, activities, and resources to support student participation in these opportunities.
16. **Right to inclusion support in school reform**	The right to have the needs of students with disabilities and teacher supports addressed in the school's Goals 2000 or school reform plan.
17. **Right to inclusion in national standards**	The right to have the needs of students with disabilities and teacher supports addressed and assessed in relation to preparation to meet the national standards for academic achievement, work preparation, and job training.

Note: IEP, individual educational plan
IDEA, the Individuals with Disabilities Education Act
IDT, Interdisciplinary Team.

31. Resources for Parents—Post–Secondary Education/Training Employment and Living

The first resource in this section is a checklist that will be useful in preparing parents to help their child who has a disability to choose among the reasonable options for post–secondary education/training, employment, and independent living (Exhibit III–6). The second resource is a list of information sources (Exhibit III–7).

Exhibit III–6 Checklist for Parents of Students with Disabilities in Secondary School

Prevocational Preparation

____ What vocational preparation opportunities are available before ninth grade?

____ What vocational preassessment services (for job preferences and aptitudes) are available?

____ Do you know your rights? Are you familiar with legislation on vocational education, special education, and school-to-work opportunities and with the Americans with Disabilities Act?

Career and Vocational Preparation

____ Is there a vocational component in the individual educational plan (IEP)? (The IEP consists of goals and plans for the student with disabilities. Be involved!)

____ Is there a team approach to planning (e.g., for special education, vocational education, rehabilitation, and regular education)?

____ Is there a central listing of the vocational programs that are available?

____ What vocational assessment services are there?

____ What support services are available?

____ Can students explore different vocations?

____ Can students get actual real-world work experiences (community-based training)?

____ What school-based employment opportunities are there?

____ Are there semicompetitive employment options if the student is not ready for competitive employment? What are the rules?

____ What decisions do I have to make? When do I have to make them? What grade level? What career or occupational area? What program? What long-range goals for employment and for independent living?

____ What help for making career choices is available?

____ Are there physical or job accommodations that should be made?

____ Do teachers of regular education, special education, and vocational education work together?

____ Are there summer programs for students? How do we get in?

____ Is there a central contact person (service coordinator or advocate) who has continued contact with the student?

____ What transportation is available for different vocational programs?

____ Do you know your rights? Are you familiar with legislation on vocational education, special education, rehabilitation, and school-to-work opportunities and with the Americans with Disabilities Act?

Transition from School to Work

____ Are there transition goals and plans in the IEP?

____ Is there a team approach to transition planning (teachers of special education and vocational education, rehabilitation therapists, regular educators, and community-based personnel and employers)?

____ Is there a policy that explains what happens if an agency identified on the IEP does not fulfill its responsibility for a transition objective?

____ Is there a central listing of the transition services and support services that are available to students with disabilities?

____ What placement assessment and counseling services are there?

____ Are students helped to prepare for job interviews and placement?

____ Are on-the-job supports available once the student is placed into employment?

____ Are there job coaches for community-based work?

____ What decisions do I have to make about post–high school placement? When do I have to make them?

____ Are there physical job accommodations that should be made?

____ Do teachers of regular education, special education, and vocational education work together for transition?

____ Are there summer programs for students? How do we get in?

____ Is there a central transition contact person (transition coordinator or advocate) who has continued contact with the student? Who is that person?

____ Is there an emphasis on self-advocacy?

____ Do you know your rights? Are you familiar with legislation on special education, rehabilitation, community services, and school-to-work opportunities and with the Americans with Disabilities Act?

continues

Exhibit III–6 continued

Post–Secondary School Training

____ What post–secondary school programs in the area are available to my son or daughter?

____ Are there any programs under the Job Training Partnership Act (JTPA) in the area?

____ Who and where are the counselors who can help make post–secondary school enrollment decisions?

____ Should I think about community college?

____ If community college is a possibility, what colleges have special support services and counselors to help the students?

____ Is my son or daughter prepared for self-advocacy? Can he or she tell the employer how he or she is prepared to overcome the barriers? (Don't wait to be asked.)

____ Know your rights. Become familiar with legislation on rehabilitation, school-to-work opportunities, and higher education and with the Americans with Disabilities Act.

Employment

____ What job opportunities in the area are best for youths with disabilities?

____ What businesses have special programs to hire youths with disabilities?

____ What is the general outlook for employment in the region in the following areas: service industry, computer-related fields and data entry, clerical occupations, health occupations, child care and preschool occupations, horticulture, home-improvement industry, personal services, and telecommunications?

____ What job descriptions are there for entry level jobs? (The Americans with Disabilities Act requires specific descriptions for any jobs advertised.)

____ Is my son or daughter prepared for self-advocacy? Can he or she tell the employer how he or she is prepared to overcome the barriers? (Don't wait to be asked.)

____ Do you know your rights? Are you familiar with the Americans with Disabilities Act, the Fair Labor Standards Act, and legislation on rehabilitation?

Independent Living and Life Enrichment

____ Is my son or daughter preparing for independent living in the near future? What is the short- and long-range goal?

____ Is he or she preparing for social participation in post–secondary school activities?

____ Is he or she prepared for involvement in community activities?

____ Is he or she prepared for involvement in avocations and hobbies?

____ Is he or she prepared for serious relationships and marriage?

Exhibit III–7 Sources of Information for Parents of Students with Disabilities in Secondary School

- Student's special education teacher
- County or district transition coordinators
- School vocational education teachers
- County or district community services agency managers or directors (e.g., mental health and developmental disabilities personnel)
- State or local Department of Rehabilitative Services supervisor
- School unit of the Department of Rehabilitative Services
- School or county job placement coordinators
- District or county Office of Adult and Community Education (apprenticeship programs and external diploma program)
- County or district Office of Business-Industry Relations

- County or district Office of Vocational Education
- County or district Office of Special Education Programs
- County or district Community Services Act coordinator
- County or district school-to-work coordinator
- County or district parent resource center
- County or district Human Services Administration
- County or district Commission for Disabled Persons or human rights organization
- State Department of Motor Vehicles (for special permits for students with disabilities)
- State or local Employment Commission or Department of Manpower Services
- Local job training offices
- Local or state Department of Social Services

32. Case Studies

In this section, five cases are presented that represent a range of situations, perspectives, and issues relating to inclusion. These cases in this section can be used as a vehicle for readers to apply and deepen their understanding of the concepts presented in this book.

A case is a story which describes an event or series of events. Cases represent the complexities of a situation, with the various dimensions of the setting, individuals involved and task at hand. A case must be complex enough to offer the potential for several interpretations, yet it must also represent underlying principles which can be discussed and better understood by grappling with the case.

The cases in this section address a number of issues relevant to inclusion. You are invited to read and discuss these cases as a way to better understand how to apply inclusion principles in the real world of schools.

REFERENCE

Shulman, L.S. (1991). Toward a pedagogy of cases. In J.H. Shulman *Case Methods in Teacher Education* (pp. 1-30). New York: Teachers College Press.

High School—A High School Begins an Inclusion Program

...nds High School was in a ...ne, continual teacher turn-...ds, and directionless school ...ctive school program to the growing multicultural school population. Today Crosswinds is an up-and-coming school. A strong administrative team has engaged the faculty in school restructuring efforts. Discipline is tight. The labyrinth of halls at Crosswinds is quiet and empty while classes are in session. Between classes, bustling groups of students walk quickly to their next classes. Students know they cannot enter class late without a pass and that three occasions of tardiness result in suspension. The rules are clear and consistently enforced.

Teachers like working at Crosswinds, and teamwork is a consistent part of their operation. Departments meet regularly to address curricular needs, and ample time in the summer is given for curriculum development. Teachers also work in interdepartmental teams to begin to integrate the curriculum across academic disciplines. The instructional staff, led by the principal, take the school system's standardized testing program very seriously. Student grades and standardized test scores are a clear and closely scrutinized accountability measure for each teacher and department and for the school as a whole. The school's slowly rising standardized test scores are being used by the school system to gauge whether the reforms at Crosswinds are working.

The largest department in this 2,000-student school is the special education department. The department offers comprehensive special education services from special education classes for the full school day to full inclusion of students with disabilities, with monitoring. This year the department actively participated in restructuring the ninth grade program. Every ninth grader was assigned to one of five teams of teachers. Each teacher team served 130 students and comprised teachers of English, social studies, mathematics, science, technology, special education, and English as a second language. The teams had two goals for the first year: to begin to integrate their curriculum across academic areas and to infuse technology into all academic areas.

In order to integrate all students receiving special education services into the teams, the special education staffing was modified so that only two levels of special education services were available to ninth grade students—inclusion in the ninth grade team or self-contained special education. The option to take one or two academic subjects within special education was no longer available for freshman students with disabilities.

It was a challenging year for the veteran special education teachers who chose to work on the ninth grade teams. They were responsible for team planning and team teaching with the academic teachers. Each teacher also offered a one-period class in study skills each day for all the students on the team who had been identified as needing special education services. As in any school year, there were the fluctuations of frustrations and successes. The integration into a regular classroom was a difficult adjustment for many of the students with learning and emotional disabilities. The special education teachers struggled to determine the most productive way to use the time in the study skills class, and student behavior in that class was also an issue. Students seemed to resent the one period of being in special education, and behavior management was a challenge in these classes all year.

The match between the academic curricular expectations and student skills and comprehension levels was tenuous for about 25 percent of the identified special education students. The first half of the year was stressful for both teachers and students, as the teams struggled to integrate the academic material they were teaching. Grades for the first and second marking periods were generally low for identified students with disabilities. By midyear, 11 students had been moved to one of the two self-contained programs, seven had left the school for various reasons, and 40 remained in the program, with grades averaging from D- to B+. The teams also identified about 15 percent of the general ninth grade student population who were in danger of failing ninth grade at midyear.

The school administration, concerned about grades as well as the overall progress of the program, sent a strong message to the teams that grades for all students were a measure of program success. The message was also sent that, for ninth grade students, grades on standardized tests given in the third marking period were of the utmost importance. Each team experienced various crisis points as the pressure to increase student performance grew. The special education teachers, accustomed to celebrating student's small victories and measuring growth in terms of individual performance, at times felt overwhelmed and defeated by this new system. They could see progress and growth as their students struggled to adjust to this demanding ninth grade curriculum, but grade point averages and standardized test scores were inadequate measures of some student's growth.

By the end of the year, exhausted ninth grade team members took time to reflect. The special education teachers agreed that the weekly meetings of the ninth grade special education teachers with the special education department chairperson had been a crucial support mechanism. There they could share strategies, express concern for specific students, and share their small victories. By working as a special education team, as well as by teaming with their academic counterparts, they had been able to support the success of students with disabilities in their ninth grade year. All students with disabilities passed ninth grade! Some did so with solid grade point averages, some by the skin of their teeth, and some by moving to a more restrictive special education placement.

At the end of the first year of the ninth grade team approach, the following events occurred:

- Because of cuts in the school budget and redistricting, the school lost 20 teaching positions. The number of ninth grade teams was reduced from five to three, with each team serving 150 rather than 130 students. Students identified as needing special education services would be distributed across two teams.
- Thirty percent of the team teachers (in all disciplines) decided not to continue in the ninth grade program.
- Of the five special education teachers who had worked with the ninth grade teams, one left teaching, one was transferred to another school because of decreased school staffing, two chose to continue

with the program, and one took a position with the self-contained program.
- Ninth grade test scores and grades did not show significant improvement from the previous year. The school principal met with all ninth grade team members at the end of the school year and informed them that the program would be in jeopardy if these important indicators did not improve next year.

Discussion Questions

1. What factors were present in the first year to help make the ninth grade inclusion program a success?

2. What factors are working against the program?

3. What are your major concerns for the program as it enters its second year?

4. What additional evaluation indicators should be used to determine if the program is a success?

5. If you were a parent of a student with a reading disability in the program, what questions would you have for the team of teachers working with your child?

6. On the basis of the information presented, would you consider this program a success?

Maria—Searching for a Program

Maria is tall, slender, and full of energy. Adopted by a couple who had met her through the orphanage where she lived, she came to this country from Brazil when she was 5 years old. Maria adapted well to her new life in the suburbs of a large metropolitan area. She arrived in June and started kindergarten in September. She went to an ethnically diverse public school, which offered instruction in English as a second language (ESL) to about 20 percent of the school population, including Maria. Her school reports about her adjustment to her new country were very positive. Maria's joy in physical activity made her a good playmate at school. Her parents delighted in having a daughter and wondered what challenges first grade would hold for Maria. As new parents, they were anxious to learn how they could best support Maria's social and academic progress.

First grade offered a few challenges. The new ESL teacher felt that Maria was struggling to learn English and that with her Portuguese quickly leaving her, she was showing frustration with expressing herself. Maria's first grade teacher was a veteran. She was firm yet gentle. She had definite rules but offered flexible assignments to meet the diverse learning levels in her class. Maria's report card was a mixture of Ss (satisfactory) and Ns (needs improvement); she needed improvement mostly in work habits such as paying attention and completing assignments. By the end of first grade, although Maria had shown much growth, she was identified as below grade level in reading and mathematics.

Maria's parents were concerned. They were trying to understand what part of Maria's uneven development was due to her acclimation to a new life and what part might be due to learning problems.

Second grade proved to be a challenge for Maria. Her attention in class was irregular at best. Friendships were quickly made and lost. Maria's second grade teacher was more than firm. She had strict rules and procedures, a need for a quiet room, and homework that was at times difficult for parents to comprehend. Maria, on the other hand, never complained about school. Maria's teacher and parents tried a number of communication systems, none of which seemed to work for very long. Maria's mother was worried and frustrated. What problems were caused by the teacher and what problems were caused by Maria's still uneven development? Maria's parents felt they did not have a good reference point for Maria's school experiences. How typical or atypical was she as a student? It seemed that these questions were haunting her parents and that the responses given to them by Maria's teachers were difficult to interpret.

Third grade brought a more flexible teacher but a more rigid and rigorous curriculum. Maria was making slow progress in her academics. Socially, she had made a friend with whom she spent most of her time on the playground. Maria's parents again scheduled meetings with Maria's ESL and third grade teachers. They wanted to try to help Maria more at home. They wanted guidance and insights into Maria. They left conferences appreciating the teachers' warmth toward Maria but wondering what Maria needed to make better academic progress. They worried that Maria's teachers were developing low expectations for her and that they were seen as parents who needed to be handled carefully rather than parents who were looking for answers to how best to make Maria successful in school.

Maria's parents, after much deliberation, employed the services of a private diagnostician to determine if Maria had learning disabilities. At this point, her parents did not trust the school enough to go through the regular school channels of requesting consideration for special education services. The possibility that Maria had significant learning disabilities had never been introduced to them by school personnel.

Maria's test results revealed significant learning disabilities. Maria's parents, in conjunction with the diagnostician, requested a meeting at school to determine Maria's eligibility for special education services. After four years of Maria being a student in the same school, working with the same ESL teacher, and the parents being active communicators with the school, it took the parents' initiative with the support of the diagnostician to initiate Maria's referral for special education services. At the eligibility meeting, there were no disputes. Yes, Maria certainly had significant learning disabilities. Yes, she would benefit from special education services. Yes, test results did indicate that she had made minimal progress in reading and mathematics during the first three grades. Maria's parents were astonished and chagrined at the readiness of the school personnel to agree with the test results. Why had no one at the school recommended that Maria be tested for learning problems?

The next struggle came with Maria's special education placement. The resource program at the school was taught by a strict and controlling teacher. On observing the class, Maria's parents found the instruction dry and unmotivating, with learning by rote. They could not see how the resource instruction would accelerate Maria's academic progress. Thus, Maria's parents fought for a more intensive special education program, which seemed more likely to offer Maria the environment she needed in order to achieve success. This program, which was offered within the same school system, was in a school ten miles from Maria's house. It took a summer of meetings to obtain the placement, but by September of fourth grade, Maria was in a special education program.

The fourth grade was a whole new school experience for Maria. She was given work that was within her reach. Evening homework battles ceased. Spelling and mathematics papers came home with marks of 90 percent and 100 percent. Maria and her parents could see that she was learning. The structure, level, and pace of the intensive special education placement met Maria's needs. Maria's parents know that they and Maria have won something and lost something with this placement. They are not part of a neighborhood school. School communication is much more difficult, and this program is only minimally part of the school. School newsletters and Parent-Teacher Association meetings are not relevant to Maria's program. Maria misses her good friend from her neighborhood school, and as a fourth grader in a new school, she has found that new friends have been slow in coming. Maria will return to the same program for fifth grade, but then elementary school ends. It will be time to determine her middle school program. Maria's parents wonder what decisions await them and how satisfactory communications with school personnel will be. They know that they are known as vocal parents. Is that an advantage? How do they continue to obtain guidance on the mix of services that will best meet Maria's needs? What type of placement should they want for Maria?

Discussion Questions

1. Why do you think that school personnel did not refer Maria for consideration for special education?

2. What should be the major considerations given to Maria's middle school placement?

3. What assistance do the parents need to best fulfill their role in Maria's placement decisions?

4. What inclusion principles and issues directly relate to this case?

Mattie Sullivan—An Experienced Teacher Finds the Secrets to Co-Teaching

I have been a special education teacher for seven years in middle school. I began teaching in a seventh grade self-contained program. I had ten students with learning and emotional disabilities whom I taught all day. It was demanding and emotionally draining work, but I loved it. I enjoyed finding ways to motivate students to learn. I worked hard to forge relationships with their families, and at the end of each school year, I could see the progress the students had made in growing up. I was successful in integrating some of these students into general education classes, but for the most part, they worked with me for all their academic subjects. Most of these students were subsequently placed in the eighth grade self-contained program. That program represented a step in maturity for them; rather than just having one teacher all day, they circulated among four special education teachers who were responsible for teaching different academic and functional curricula.

I am now a resource teacher; I co-teach with four general education teachers and provide direct resource instruction to students for one or two periods a day. I am responsible for 20 students, 14 boys and 6 girls who range in academic achievement from second to sixth grade levels. I had a rough transition to co-teaching, but I am now effective as a co-teacher.

When the central school system administration decided that special education would take a more inclusionary approach, we were given little time to prepare for this new type of program. There was a three-day summer workshop for all special education teachers who would be co-teaching the next year. I left the workshop with good information and with the knowledge that the new school year would be dramatically different for me from previous years.

Three experienced teachers, none of whom I knew well, and one first year teacher were to be my new partners. I tracked down these teachers and discussed the co-teaching with them. I made my first tactical error the first week of school. My co-teachers and I decided that, during the first week, I would observe their teaching styles and classroom procedures. This approach would also allow me to observe the students with disabilities to determine their ability to handle basic classroom demands, such as listening, taking notes, getting along with classmates, and participating in discussions. I also devised some informal reading inventories that would help us to assess all students' ability to handle course reading demands.

I now realize my basic mistake: I never considered the co-teachers' classrooms as also my own. Because I saw myself and my students as experimental visitors, I was not an equal instructor in the class. By starting out as an observer, I also confused the students. They didn't see me as a real teacher, but as an aide.

Another complication was that I never was able to establish a schedule of regular planning time with these co-teachers. When we were able to plan, I was able to assume a viable teaching role in the classroom and to suggest useful modifications. When our planning meetings were disrupted, I was forced into the position of behavior management aide. Without advance planning I would enter the classroom with only a vague idea of the lesson content and no advance notice of the methods the teacher planned to use. On some days, class sessions did not go well because of student frustration, confusion, or lack of motivation. When students needed to be removed from class, I was always the person who left the class with the student. If student groups were off task in class, I took responsibility for getting them back on track. In the long run, this role did not help my relationship with the students, and it certainly threatened my sense of being a competent teacher.

I was successful in working with my co-teachers in determining grades and in structuring some assignments so that the students with disabilities had oppor-

Source: Adapted from Fried, M., A Winding Path to Co-Teaching in *Cases in Urban Teaching*, J.M. Taymans, Ed., pp. 3–7, George Washington University, Department of Teacher Preparation and Special Education, 1995.

tunities to express what they were learning in ways that would help them achieve passing grades. I also developed good communication with most of the families. As I ended the year, and assessed the gains and losses in my new position, I felt that my sense of satisfaction and competence as a teacher had suffered most. Thus, with a year of experience under my belt, I made strategic changes in the way I began my second year of co-teaching.

I met with the principal and the department chairperson to get approval and support for my plan for year two. Their understanding and support were crucial to the success of that year. With their help I made the following changes. I assisted in choosing a new group of co-teachers so I could have a fresh start. The principal gave us planning time over the summer so that I could learn about their curricula and teaching methods prior to the opening of the school year. The summer work time also helped us do some long-term planning and to clearly identify an equal planning and teaching role for me. We also determined how we wanted to handle behavior management and again planned equal roles in how we would handle disruptive situations. By the beginning of the school year, I had developed a professional and cordial relationship with these teachers, and we all expected that I would function as a teaching professional in our team-taught classes. During the first week of school, I was an active presenter in all the classes, which made my role clear to all students. By the end of the first week, I was learning directly about my co-teachers' style, and they in

turn were learning about mine. I also regularly informed the principal, my co-teachers, department chairpersons, and my department chairperson of our scheduled planning times, with the expectation that these planning times would be honored and supported by the administration. My second year was a success.

Discussion Questions

1. Of the mistakes Mattie Sullivan made the first year, which ones do you think were the most costly to her effectiveness as a special education teacher?

2. What systemwide administration procedures would you recommend to make this inclusionary effort more effective for all teachers in Mattie Sullivan's position?

3. Mattie spends much more time describing her efforts at working with her co-teachers than describing efforts to meet her students' needs. Why? Does this concern you?

4. Develop a list of do's and don'ts based on this case. Who should take responsibility for each item (e.g., school principal, central administration, school staff, special education teacher, families, students, or teacher education programs)?

Lucas Thompson—A New Teacher Faces Multiple Barriers to Inclusion

"You have a job because of eleven eighth grade students. Your job is to make them successful." These are the words I heard from the principal of Walker Middle School, where I had just been hired for my first teaching position. With heightened anticipation, I contemplated getting to know this group of students during their crucial year before entering high school. I was anxious to implement all that I had learned in my special education master's degree program.

Walker Middle School, which serves seventh and eighth grade students, had been engaged in inclu-

Source: Adapted from Kinkaid, L.R., The Trials and Tribulations of a First-Year Team Teacher (Weathering Structural Flaws: Experiences of a First-Year Multilevel Teacher) in *Cases in Urban Teaching*, J.M. Taymans, Ed., pp. 12–17, George Washington University, Department of Teacher Preparation and Special Education, 1995.

sionary programming for five years. The administration had decided to make some scheduling changes so that the special education students placed in general education classes would be better dispersed throughout the school. The mainstreaming model had resulted in some unsatisfactory results. As the special education case load rose, one special education teacher with his group of 15 to 25 students would be assigned to one general education teacher's subject area class each period. These classes were seen as special education classes of low-achieving students, which many of the general education teachers found undesirable. These classes with their large number of students (averaging 30) and the concentration of students with identified learning needs were difficult to manage, even with two teachers. In the new scheduling system, no more than five students with a need for special education services were assigned to a general education class. This improved integration approach proved to be a logistic nightmare for me.

I was one of three special education teachers in the school. My two colleagues, both in their second decade of teaching, were responsible for the seventh grade students. I was responsible for all of the eighth grade students. The 11 special education students in the seventh grade had two special education teachers working with them and their two general education teachers. The eighth grade students had me. Thus, the seventh grade students received twice the support as the eighth grade students. My students were distributed across eight general education teachers, four of whom were first year teachers like myself. The final part of the equation was that I averaged three special education students per general education class, while the seventh grade special education teachers averaged five per class.

I was constantly faced with impossible scheduling decisions. While I was helping three students in English, the other eight were dispersed throughout various academic and elective subjects with no support available to them. I spent the first marking period in frantic activity, with the constant feeling that I was still trying to figure out how to do this increasingly impossible job. The end of the first marking period confirmed my doubts. Over half of my students were failing or close to failing one or more subjects. On reviewing their individual educational plans (IEPs), I determined that most of the students for whom I was responsible were receiving less than the level of services indicated on their IEPs. I went to my department chairperson with a list of questions.

1. Why am I the only special education teacher working with the eighth grade?
2. Why are there so few students with identified learning needs per class in eighth grade compared with seventh grade?
3. How can I offer students the level of services indicated on their IEPs when I barely see some students at all?

My questions and concerns were not welcome. My department chairperson suggested that I schedule direct service "pull out" time with some students. After considering this option, I could not see how having them miss class time would help them or how I could manage co-teaching with such a schedule.

I then addressed my concerns to my principal, who was displeased with my criticisms of the schedule. She had personally developed the eighth grade schedule in consultation with the special education chairperson. Ultimately, we were able to make some schedule changes, but the result still left me with too many teachers to collaborate with and too little time to deliver the level of service indicated in some IEPs.

I spent much time and energy in developing study guides and practice tests for students and in keeping parents informed of upcoming tests and major assignments, to garner support at home. I put weekly monitoring sheets in co-teachers' mailboxes in an effort to track student progress. Some teachers responded quickly; others did not.

I ended the school year exhausted and defeated. I was able to use very little of what I had learned during my teacher education program. I felt that I had rocked the boat at my school and was seen as a malcontent. I resigned my position. I know I want to teach, but not in a school or a school system that offers so little support. As I revisit the principal's first words to me, they sound like a tease: "You have a job because of eleven eighth grade students. Your job is to make them successful."

Discussion Questions

1. Describe the philosophy that is implied in the new integration schedule.

2. What administrative supports would you suggest to make the program a success schoolwide and within the special education department?

3. What skills did Lucas Thompson need to be effective in his position? Is this a position appropriate for a first year teacher?

4. If you were a parent of a student on Mr. Thompson's case load, what would you want to have happen?

5. What implications does the eighth grade program have for students' success in high school?

6. On the basis of the issues presented in this case, develop five principles of effective inclusionary programs at the middle school level.

Chris—A Family's Quest for Neighborhood Schooling

Chris Della, 7 years old, is the youngest of three boys. He lives at home with me (his mother), his father, and his two brothers—Tom, who is 12, and Joe, who is 9. Chris has mental and physical challenges. His cerebral palsy necessitates the use of a wheelchair. His speech is limited and difficult to understand. Intellectually, he is more like a 4-year-old than a 7-year-old.

Chris has received special education services since infancy. We have continually worked with a group of professionals who have helped us set and meet goals for our special son's development. Chris is an integral part of our family. Like our other sons, he is comfortable in our community, attending church and local events and participating in recreation programs and scouting. Our goal for Chris is that he lead a happy and productive adult life, with as little assistance from others as possible. We know that, at age 7 it is impossible to project the possible and it is desirable to shoot for the stars.

Fortunately, we have formed strong bonds with other parents who have children with multiple challenges. Through a parent-support group we belong to we have developed our vision of the school program we want for Chris. We want Chris included in our neighborhood school, which will help him to remain part of our community. Our focus on inclusion has put us at odds with many of the professionals who are part of our lives. This desire for inclusion and the resulting conflict with professionals is a common bond within our parent support group.

The school system wants Chris in "special programs," which are either wholly or partially separated from mainstream education. As we look back, we think we made a mistake by placing Chris in a therapeutic preschool program. The teachers and staff were wonderful, but once we had placed him in a restrictive program, we found that it was impossible to remove him from it. This was an unexpected disappointment. We did not like being in conflict with professionals who truly cared about Chris.

Professionals who work with students who have disabilities seem to be an overworked group of individuals. Formally scheduled meetings with parents have a tight time frame. Many meetings are structured so that parent questions come at the end of a presentation of what the professional team has already planned. We know that we are seen as troublemakers, as parents who are in denial of our son's problems. This label does not help us, Chris, or the professionals who work with him. We expect that Chris will develop slowly, but we also know that spending the school day in a separate school with other students with limited mobility and language will only slow his development and marginalize Chris in our community. We have been able to integrate Chris into community activities. Why can't he be a part of our neighborhood school?

We are involved in due process hearings to obtain a determination on our request that Chris be "released" from the special center and be placed with an aide in our neighborhood school. Yes, this may mean complications for the school's transportation systems, and it may require the school to hire a paraprofessional who can be supervised by a professional special educator to meet Chris' wide-ranging needs during the day.

We want to give it a try for a year and see if Chris' development is slowed or harmed in any way. Our best guess is that it will not slow his development. Other parents' experiences tell us that he will be more motivated and stimulated in his neighborhood school and thus make greater progress. Isn't this what federal legislation guarantees—that all students be allowed the most appropriate placement to meet their long-term needs? We know Chris will receive less intensive special education and related services, that it will be an adjustment for all individuals involved with Chris' inclusion into his neighborhood school, and that it will take valuable professional time to make this all work. But we also know that inclusion is the intent of federal legislation—to meet individual needs, not to impose a service delivery template based on disability categories. Our best guess is that Chris and his classmates will make the adjustment most easily and that the professionals will have the greatest adjustment because they are stymied by their professional ideas of what makes sense to them.

Chris is successful and appreciated at home and within the community. Why does the school system have to be different? What do all those degrees and salaries mean in relation to what is best for my son? We are at a stage in our relationship with the school system where it is us versus them; yet I sincerely believe that we all want what is best for Chris. Our problem is in what the school system will allow themselves to consider as possible for Chris. My only choice is to remain steadfast in my role as Chris' mother to be his advocate. Unfortunately, the school system sees its only role as cost containment and defense of convenient service delivery structures. I wonder after all these years what federal legislation has accomplished.

Discussion Questions

1. How would you describe this parent's definition of inclusion?

2. What are her reasons for wanting her son included in his neighborhood school? Is she being reasonable?

3. What barriers is she facing?

4. What legislation supports including Chris in his neighborhood school?

5. What steps could the school system have taken to prevent an adversarial relationship from developing?

6. What advice would you give the parents as they continue to advocate for full inclusion?

IV

Trainer's Resource

33. Development and Implementation of Inclusion

This handbook provides several tools for development and implementation of inclusion. It is also useful for designing staff orientation and training programs. There are ten steps that provide the framework for orientation and training of the team that plans the development and implementation of inclusion practices in the classroom and the school. These steps

- can be initiated by a single teacher or jointly by several teachers
- are relevant for schools that have not initiated inclusive practices and have collaborative practices or relationships that are underdeveloped

- are relevant for schools that have begun to implement inclusive practices and have developed more advanced collaborative relationships
- can form the basis for the design of evaluation of inclusion initiatives, relationships, and outcomes

These steps are designed to assess readiness for implementation of inclusion and to provide a "path" of activities and strategies for those who are beginning the process of developing inclusive practices. They can help inclusion planning teams to develop relationships and processes that are uniquely suited to the local school, service system, or community.

Ten Steps in Assessing Readiness for Implementation of Inclusion

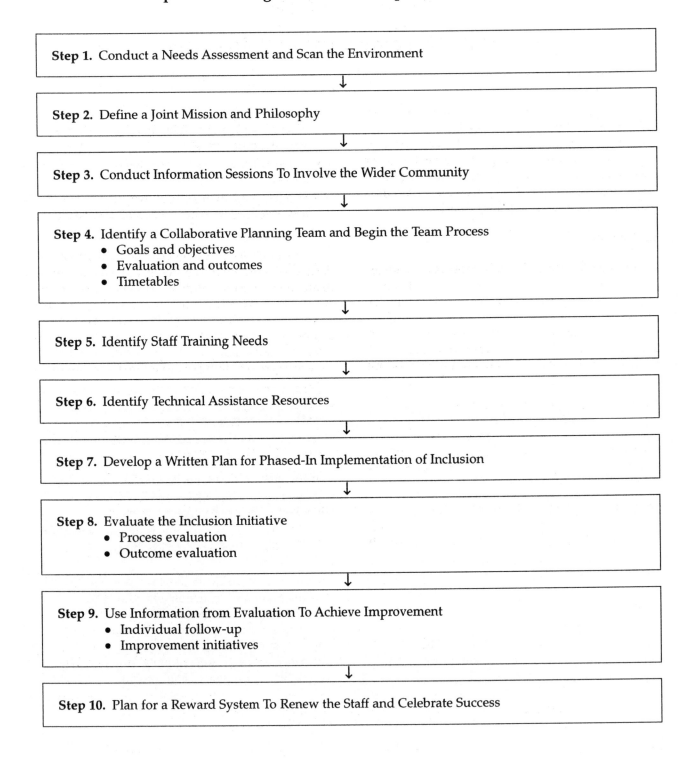

Step 1. Conduct a Needs Assessment and Scan the Environment

Step 2. Define a Joint Mission and Philosophy

Step 3. Conduct Information Sessions To Involve the Wider Community

Step 4. Identify a Collaborative Planning Team and Begin the Team Process
- Goals and objectives
- Evaluation and outcomes
- Timetables

Step 5. Identify Staff Training Needs

Step 6. Identify Technical Assistance Resources

Step 7. Develop a Written Plan for Phased-In Implementation of Inclusion

Step 8. Evaluate the Inclusion Initiative
- Process evaluation
- Outcome evaluation

Step 9. Use Information from Evaluation To Achieve Improvement
- Individual follow-up
- Improvement initiatives

Step 10. Plan for a Reward System To Renew the Staff and Celebrate Success

34. Staff Development and Training

Inclusion planning and implementation can be accomplished in the Ten Steps in Assessing Readiness for Implementation of Inclusion. Each of the steps includes four basic components that are useful to the trainer or staff development coordinator. These include suggested readings, discussion questions, strategies for action, and templates for overhead transparencies.

Components

Suggested Sections from Handbook. Readings in the handbook that are related to each inclusion implementation step are provided to help the staff development coordinator prepare participants for training sessions. For example, in step 1, staff development participants could read the sections related to questions 1 through 4 of the handbook in order to prepare for this section of the training.

Discussion Questions. For each implementation step, several discussion questions are provided. These questions can be used by the trainer or staff development coordinator to stimulate discussion about inclusion planning and implementation. The trainer may use these questions in several ways:

- to promote full group discussion

- to assign the participants to groups and have them discuss separately, then share their discussions with the other groups
- to have participants pose related questions for discussion
- to have participants brainstorm actual situations or experiences that are related to the questions.

These questions are designed to help the trainees and participants review the concepts in the handbook and relate them to actual students, situations, and experiences in their school and community settings. Such discussion and consideration of the questions in real life contexts accelerate the learning of participants and increase the likelihood that they will transfer what they have learned in training sessions into their classrooms.

Strategies for Developing Action Plans. For each of the implementation steps, action strategies and work sheets for developing action strategies are provided. The work sheets can be used together with the discussion questions for group work.

Templates for Transparencies. For each implementation step, templates for transparencies are provided to aid the trainer.

35. Step 1—Conduct a Needs Assessment and Scan the Environment

Suggested Sections from the Handbook

The following sections from Part I of the handbook should be reviewed by staff development participants in preparation for step 1 of the planning and training for inclusion:

- Why inclusion?
- What is inclusion?
- What forces shaped inclusion?

Discussion Questions

The following questions can be used by the trainer or staff development coordinator to stimulate discussion about inclusion planning and implementation:

- What current services provided by the district are the most beneficial to all students? To students with special needs?
- What services that do not now exist are most needed by students in the district?
- Which individuals are needed to provide input into the design of the inclusion process?

- What other important and critical information is needed in order to begin the inclusion process?
- After collection of a variety of data from a variety of sources, which issues need immediate attention?

Strategies for Developing Action Plans

The templates for transparencies offer strategies for assessing the strengths and weaknesses of potential members of the team working to achieve inclusion and of the units they represent. The activities in the action work sheet in Exhibit IV–1 can be used by a teacher in a classroom to assess readiness for inclusion. For work in small groups, they can be used together with the discussion questions for consideration of planning issues and for development of an action plan for a school.

Templates for Transparencies

Templates for transparencies that are relevant to Step 1 follow.

Conduct a Needs Assessment and Scan the Environment

- Review the "current" services for special populations available in the school district and community

- Identify needed services not available, but needed

- Survey and/or interview parents, teachers, and consumers to determine the current effectiveness of special education and related services

- Determine key players/individuals responsible for providing special education and related services

- Collect data and analyze the data into manageable, usable pieces of information

Exhibit IV–1 Action Work Sheet: Assessment of Readiness for Inclusion

Activity	How will you do this, and who is responsible?	Target Date of Completion
1. Identify the range of local services available in the existing school and service system, in order to identify services that can be coordinated to support a student in inclusive classrooms.		
2. Identify gaps in services and service needs that are not being met within the school and larger system.		
3. Determine the level of "readiness" of teachers from all subject areas and of related service professionals in cooperating agencies to form a collaboration for inclusion support in the school. (Who is ready and willing to collaborate and what training will they need?)		
4. Determine the expertise and resources that each subject discipline and related services bring to the partnership to support inclusion.		
5. Determine the needs of cooperating community agencies (e.g., health profession, speech and hearing, social services, and rehabilitation).		
6. How should teachers and support personnel be prepared for inclusion?		
7. How should the physical environment be changed for inclusion?		
8. What modifications in curriculum and instruction should be made?		
9. How should the IEP and interdisciplinary team process be used?		
10. What classroom supports are needed?		
11. How can students access available technology?		

continues

HANDBOOK FOR SUCCESSFUL INCLUSION
© Aspen Publishers, Inc., 1996.

Exhibit IV–1 continued

Activity	How will you do this, and who is responsible?	Target Date of Completion
12. How can students be helped to access and participate in vocational, occupational, and technical education?		
13. How can students participate in extracurricular school activities?		
14. How can students participate in community-based and community service experiences?		
Note: IEP, Individual Education Plan		

> ***Preplanning assessment***—*involves (1) defining the local "picture" or landscape of the school organization and services already in place for students with special needs in order to identify an existing foundation for an inclusion initiative and (2) determining the level of "readiness" of personnel and related services professionals to cooperate (Kochhar & Erickson, 1993).*

Preplanning assessment strategies involve:

- Achieving benefit for agencies developing new interagency partnerships and for those seeking to improve existing relationships

- Developing methods for collecting important data needed for planning inclusion activities

- Planning focus groups to determine if parents, teachers, and support personnel can identify strengths and weaknesses of the services available for students with disabilities

- Asking an independent, objective, external professional to conduct the focus group and report to the administration

Issues Related to Readiness of Inclusion Team for Collaboration

Inclusion planners need to know what each team member brings to the relationship—in terms of resources, knowledge, and philosophy about inclusion. Consider some basic questions:

- The *structure of school and community agencies* that are collaborating

- The *attitudes* of the inclusion team members toward inclusion and toward the population of students to be served

- The *knowledge* of each team member about the population of students to be served and about the collaborative team process

HANDBOOK FOR SUCCESSFUL INCLUSION
© Aspen Publishers, Inc., 1996.

Assessing Readiness for Team Collaboration and Coordination

In an inclusion initiative, it is important to first *assess the needs of professionals who will form the inclusion implementation team*.

> *Needs assessment by the inclusion team* is the process of gathering and interpreting information about (1) the student needs for education and support services, (2) the "goal posts," or progress measures toward which the cooperating personnel are working, and (3) the operational needs of the inclusion implementation team members as they invest in real change in the teaching and learning environments (Kochhar, 1995).

Because needs change over time

- Needs assessments should be conducted periodically to adjust inclusion goals and procedures.

- Initial goals and activities defined by the planning team provide a blueprint or map for defining educational needs, and may need to be adjusted.

Levels of Assessment in Inclusion

Assessment of needs for inclusion means knowing the needs of students and their families, the school, and cooperating agencies. It is also an essential step in the process of defining the goals the cooperating team will work toward.

1. **Needs assessment at the individual/student level** is the process of gathering and interpreting information about the educational and support service needs of individuals and groups of consumers being served in different agencies. Assessment of individual needs means identifying the range of developmental, health, academic, vocational, social, and support needs of individuals and families. In the basis of an assessment of individual needs, the cooperating agencies can establish goals and priorities for services.

2. **Needs assessment to define "goal posts"** means assessing the performance of consumers today (baseline performance), establishing performance goals for tomorrow, measuring the "gap" between the two, and finally, setting priorities for services and activities to move individuals and families toward new levels of functioning, progress, or achievement. Individual needs are interpreted in relation to future performance goals. It is a marriage of needs, with goals and directions.

3. **Needs assessment at the interagency level** involves determining

   a. the level of "readiness" of cooperating agencies to form a partnership that creates real change in the school/community environment

   b. the relative strengths and weaknesses that each agency brings to the inclusion partnership

HANDBOOK FOR SUCCESSFUL INCLUSION
© Aspen Publishers, Inc., 1996.

The Resource Environment:
A Circle of Commitment

The term "circle of commitment" is defined as the range of resources in the environment, both human and material, that must be invested in an inclusion effort to improve supportive services and outcomes for students with disabilities and to improve the overall learning environment.

Six Elements in Circle of Commitment to Inclusion

1. **Human commitment:** the key stakeholders, key staff, and advisors in the inclusion planning and implementation team

2. **Resource commitment:** the financial and material resources that are committed to the planning and implementation

3. **Values commitment:** a shared set of values and a belief in the "shared responsibility" for the development and education of individuals and their families in the school and community

4. **Action commitment:** a shared mission, written procedures, and a common set of goals for the inclusion initiative

5. **Outcome commitment:** a shared set of expectations or outcomes for those who will be served or affected by the inclusion initiative—students, teachers, families, and others

6. **Renewal commitment:** a shared long-term plan (a) to continue to review the course of the inclusion initiative, (b) to recognize and celebrate the unique contributions that each group makes to the initiatives, and (c) to continue to renew those commitments (Kochhar & Erickson, 1993; Kochhar, 1995).

---

36. Step 2—Define a Joint Mission and Philosophy

Suggested Sections from the Handbook

The following sections from Part I of the handbook should be reviewed by staff development participants in preparation for step 2 of the planning and training for inclusion:

- What are the major components of inclusion?
- What is the shared responsibility for inclusion?
- What are the major controversies surrounding inclusion?
- What is the conclusion about inclusion?
- How do we develop a rational approach to inclusion?
- What are the benefits and outcomes of inclusion?

Discussion Questions

The following questions can be used by the trainer or staff development coordinator to stimulate discussion about inclusion planning and implementation:

- What are the primary goals for inclusion that the district should address?
- What are current *best practices* in other schools and districts that can be duplicated or modified for this district?
- What do we believe is the purpose of an inclusive classroom?
- How should we proceed to plan for inclusion?

Strategies for Developing Action Plans

The work sheet in Exhibit IV–2 can be used in small groups for training or for action planning. The group can work together to define an inclusion mission statement. The mission statement should describe the *broad purpose* of the initiative and collaborating units and the special areas of joint responsibility. It should include the four elements shown in Exhibit IV–2.

Templates for Transparency

Templates for transparencies that are relevant to Step 2 follow.

HANDBOOK FOR SUCCESSFUL INCLUSION
© Aspen Publishers, Inc., 1996.

Define the Joint Mission/Philosophy

- Identify goals that need to be addressed by the district

- Review BEST PRACTICES in professional literature

- Draft an initial statement that states the direction, mission, and philosophy of the special education program in the district (to be refined later)

- Ask various individuals for input and feedback

- Provide the feedback to the planning team for eventual revisions and further development

Exhibit IV–2 Action Work Sheet: Defining a Joint Mission and Philosophy

Activity	Discuss and write a draft outline for what this section will include.	Target Date for Completion
1. **A statement of context**—A brief introductory paragraph that broadly describes the initiative, how it was initiated, how it addresses current educational needs of students, how it differs from or expands or improves on current methods of promoting inclusion		
2. **A statement of authority for the initiative**—An introductory section that refers to the legal basis for the initiative (e.g., IDEA, section 504, and ADA) and lists the local, state, or federal laws or statutes, regulations, or policies that give authority to this agreement		
3. **General statement of philosophy, purpose of the initiative or agreement, and expected benefits and outcomes**—Includes a broad statement of the goals of the initiative and inclusion planning team and the results anticipated for students.		
4. **Broad goals, roles, and responsibilities**—Defines the goals of the initiative and the roles of key planners, implementors, and the cooperating agencies or community agency personnel		

Note: IDEA, Individuals with Disabilities Education Act of 1990; ADA, American with Disabilities Act. Section 504 of the Rehabilitation Act of 1973, which states: Cooperating agencies refer to any community-based agency which provides support services to assist students with disabilities successfully participate. In general education classrooms (e.g., social services, psychological services, occupational and physical therapy, public health services, mental health services, etc.).

Developing a Mission Statement for Inclusion

A mission statement may include one or all of the following four parts:

1. **A statement of context:** a brief introduction that broadly describes the initiative, how it was initiated, how it addresses current educational needs of students, and how it differs from or expands or improves on the current approach to promoting inclusion

2. **A statement of the authority for the initiative:** an introductory section referring to the legal basis for the initiative (e.g., IDEA, section 504, and ADA) and lists the local, state, or federal laws, statutes, regulations, or policies that give authority to this agreement

3. **General statement of philosophy, purpose of the initiative or agreement, and expected benefits and outcomes:** includes a broad statement of (1) the goals of the planning team for the initiative and inclusion and (2) the results anticipated for the students

4. **Broad goals, roles, and responsibilities:** defines the goals of the initiative, the roles of key planners and implementors, and the cooperating agencies or community agency personnel

Defining a Joint Mission and Philosophy

- Arrange a meeting of key inclusion planners to discuss a joint vision of inclusion implementation and to hammer out broad goals and strategies for achieving that shared vision.

- Design a written *mission and philosophy statement* for the inclusion initiative and develop formal agreements with collaborating nonschool agencies.

- Use two kinds of strategies:

  1. **A classroom-level strategy** or intervention that is designed to improve the availability of and access to supportive services in the classroom and to help solve specific problems and overcome barriers to inclusion identified by teachers in the individual classroom.

  2. **A schoolwide inclusion strategy** designed to assist all personnel in the school, both instructional and non-instructional, to understand the inclusion goals and strategies and to be a part of changing the school's "culture."

37. Step 3—Conduct Information Sessions To Involve the Wider Community

Suggested Sections from the Handbook

All of Part I should be reviewed in relation to step 3 of the planning and training for inclusion.

Discussion Questions

The following questions can be used by the trainer or staff development coordinator to stimulate discussion about inclusion planning and implementation:

- Why does the community need to be involved in an inclusion initiative?
- What sectors of the community should be included?
- Who needs to involved in the inclusion process?
- When and where should the first meeting be held, and what should the agenda be?
- What data should be collected prior to the first meeting, and how can it be used effectively?

Strategies for Developing Action Plans

Involving the community is the first step in implementing a collaborative planning process to develop inclusive practices. The success of any inclusion initiative depends on the ability of the planning team to create a supportive environment for the development of professional collaboration. This process of collaboration begins by *informing key populations within the school and wider community—particularly parents—about intentions to develop or expand inclusive practices.* The work sheet in Exhibit IV–3 can be used for training or action planning. The group can work together to develop an action plan for involving the community.

Template for Transparency

The following template for a transparency is relevant to Step 3.

Conduct Information Sessions To Involve the Wider Community

- Notify the constituents that a new initiative is about to begin

- Set a meeting date and invite all interested parties to attend

- Provide an overview of the data collected, broad goals, and initial steps to be taken

- Invite interested parties to submit their names for participation in the planning process

Exhibit IV–3   Action Work Sheet: Strategies for Informing the School Community about a New Inclusion Initiative

Strategy	How can this be accomplished in your school and community, and who will be responsible?
1. **Inform parent, student, and consumer organizations,** such as the PTA, parent advocacy groups, and student organizations, about the plans for service coordination. Distribute information and solicit input into the plans and roles of these groups in the development of the collaboration.	
2. **Inform educational leaders and school principals,** who have primary responsibility for any new programs or initiatives that will affect instruction or student services. Most school districts and schools establish their educational priorities well in advance (e.g., expansion of special education programs, addition of bilingual program, and improvement of basic skills). *Principals should be among the earliest to be informed of the effort and helped to see how the initiative will aid them in achieving their educational goals and objectives for students.*	
3. **Inform staff and directors of community and adult services agencies,** because their support is vital to an interagency services coordination initiative (new or renewed). Each cooperating (or potential) partner needs to know about an intent to collaborate and the process for forming the collaborative arrangement.	
4. **Develop concept papers and rationale statements,** to help each potential cooperating agency understand the relationship between the collaborative endeavor and their own individual agency mission, goals, and objectives. Each must understand how the new collaboration will help them to achieve their individual agency goals, improve their services and resources, or evaluate their efforts. The mutual benefits to all cooperating agencies must be defined and stressed early in the process.	

continues

© Aspen Publishers, Inc., 1996.

Exhibit IV–3 continued

Strategy	How can this be accomplished in your school and community, and who will be responsible?
5. **Inform relevant teacher unions and educational associations** about new initiatives that involve teaching staff, and help them to understand the potential benefits of collaboration for students and professionals. It might also be helpful to have the county or district educational associations go on record supporting the initiative.	
6. **Conduct local education reform seminars,** including information about or discussion of the interagency initiative.	
7. **Conduct special seminars** on interagency service coordination and co-training with members from a variety of agencies and organizations.	
8. **Plan teacher, principal, and parent coffees** to discuss the initiative.	
9. **Conduct highly visible brainstorming meetings** with heads of agency personnel at all levels to discuss interagency service coordination.	
10. **Develop informational brochures and materials.**	
11. **Conduct business-education seminars.** Include information about the initiative in these seminars, in Chamber of Commerce meetings, or in Private Industry Council meetings (Job Training Partnership Act).	
12. **Solicit editorials and feature articles** in local newsletters and newspapers.	
13. **Conduct meetings with community leaders** to assist in "championing" an initiative in interagency service coordination.	
14. **Develop links with local colleges or universities** to develop meetings or seminars related to new initiatives or to develop grant proposals.	
15. **Use annual reports of cooperating agencies** including descriptions of interagency initiatives and plans.	

Involving the Community

> ***Informing and involving the school community***—In an environment that supports inclusion, *key stakeholders (persons who care about and are invested in seeing inclusion successfully implemented)* become knowledgeable and informed about the need for improved collaboration and the benefits of inclusion for the student, school, and community.

Under current laws, state and local educational agencies are required to increase opportunities for inclusion into mainstream classes and activities and to improve the working relationships of students, families, teachers, and related services personnel concerned with the development of children and youth.

38. Step 4—Identify a Collaborative Planning Team and Begin the Team Process

Suggested Sections from the Handbook

The following sections from Parts I and II of the handbook should be reviewed in relation to step 4 of the planning and training for inclusion:

- What are the major components of inclusion?
- What are the major controversies surrounding inclusion?
- What is the conclusion about inclusion?
- How do we develop a rational approach to inclusion?
- What are the benefits and outcomes of inclusion?
- What are the major strategies for overcoming barriers to inclusion?
- What is the continuum of placement options?
- How are student needs for instruction on inclusion assessed?
- What does inclusion mean for teaching and learning?
- How can readiness for inclusion be assessed?

Discussion Questions

The questions in Exhibit IV–4 can be used by the trainer or staff development coordinator to stimulate discussion about inclusion planning and implementation.

Strategies for Developing Action Plans

As with many educational innovations, inclusion planning and development have been primarily viewed as responsibilities of administrators. However, the inclusion planning process must be viewed as much more than an extension of administrative activities. *Inclusion planning activities should be student centered and teacher centered, rather than "procedural."* Rather than benefiting or being convenient for administrative functions, the inclusion processes and procedures should primarily benefit students and the teaching and learning environment as a whole. The work sheet in Exhibit IV–4, can be used for training or action planning. The group can work together to develop an action plan.

Templates for Transparencies

Templates for transparencies that are relevant to Step 4 follow.

HANDBOOK FOR SUCCESSFUL INCLUSION
© Aspen Publishers, Inc., 1996.

Identify a Collaborative Planning Team and Begin the Process

- Determine who the key players are in developing a strong special education program for the district

- Contact the individuals identified as possible team members and invite them to participate as part of the planning team

- Set up an initial series of planning meetings (dates, times, locations, etc.)

- Meet to review the mission/philosophy statement and finalize that statement (this will direct the planning efforts)

- Develop an action plan that includes action items, timelines, and individuals responsible to conduct activities (this may take several planning sessions)

Exhibit IV–4 Action Work Sheet: Identifying a Collaborative Planning Team

Activity	How can this be accomplished in your school and community, and who will be responsible?
1. Who should be on the inclusion planning team? How will these people be invited to participate?	
2. What incentives should be provided for their time and effort in the planning process?	
3. How should the planning team proceed?	
4. What should be the planning team's purpose?	
5. When and how often should the planning team meet?	
6. What activities should be included in the inclusion process?	
7. When should they take place? Who will be responsible for each activity?	

HANDBOOK FOR SUCCESSFUL INCLUSION
© Aspen Publishers, Inc., 1996.

Planned Change As a Management Practice in the Classroom and the School

- Change and innovation can decay in a short time if school environment factors that support, or fail to support, the change process are not identified early in the inclusion planning process for inclusion.

- Collaborative planning is the process in which teachers and administrators make decisions and plan actions in cooperation with one another.

- Planned change relates to initiation and management of the relationships needed for implementation of inclusion or to actual implementation of the actions agreed on through strategic planning.

- Both collaborative planning and planned change are essential to the change process required for implementation of inclusive classrooms.

Planned Change

- Planned change focuses on the implementation and management of the change process for inclusion and helps teachers to use and modify these forces to achieve a *shared mission*.

- The inclusion planning process must be viewed as a dynamic process that may be imperfect and sometimes not orderly.

- The planning process must support flexibility in student placement so that schools can respond to changing needs of students and learning environments.

- The concepts of strategic planning provide a foundation for understanding, creating, and implementing inclusive practices that are responsive to the needs of students and their families.

Student-Centered Planning

- Inclusion planning activities should be *student-centered*, benefiting students and the teaching and learning environment, rather than benefiting administration.

- Benefits to and effects on students should drive the development of inclusion planning and implementation, from initial definition of the mission and goals to annual evaluation.

- Inclusion planning should be viewed as an intervention or as a planned effort designed to produce intended changes or specific outcomes in the target population.

- The "intended changes in the target population" (students with disabilities) must be clearly specified and agreed on by the collaborating team, and school and community resources must be focused to pursue those outcomes.

- In student-centered planning, the effects on the total learning environment become central to evaluating inclusive classrooms and schools.

Strategic Planning

Strategic planning has been defined as a *"disciplined effort to produce fundamental decisions and actions that shape and guide what a school or organization is, what it does, and why it does it"* (Bryson, 1988, p. 5). Collaborative planning is a form of strategic planning conducted by a team of teachers, administrators, and others to identify and understand how to implement an initiative within the given school environment. Strategic planning also helps these professionals to understand and identify ways that different parts of the school can interact to improve access to mainstream classrooms and activities for all students. This "environment" includes the political, economic, professional, and social influences that characterize and influence the school.

39. Step 5—Identify Staff Training Needs

Suggested Sections from the Handbook

The following sections from Part II of the handbook should be reviewed in relation to step 5 of the planning and training for inclusion:

- What should be included in a staff development plan?
- What factors are most important when planning for inclusion?
- What is an appropriate class size for inclusion?
- What curriculum modifications and instructional strategies are considered best practices for inclusion classrooms?
- What external support services are needed for inclusive classrooms?

Discussion Questions

The questions in Exhibit IV–5 can be used by the trainer or staff development coordinator to stimulate discussion about inclusion planning and implementation.

Strategies for Developing Action Plans

Inclusion requires increased awareness, thoughtful consideration, and meaningful dialogue. Teachers and parents need the opportunity to discuss the complexity and importance of diversity in the classroom and to air their concerns. Well-planned training and professional development opportunities can help the teacher learn how to implement inclusion effectively. On the other hand, change can create resistance among the very people who are needed to implement the inclusion initiative. When teachers sense that the traditional ways of doing things are being abandoned, some may resist or become negative about the future. The inclusion pioneer needs special knowledge and know-how to help champion change and transfer the spirit of opportunity to others who will be involved in the inclusion process. The work sheets in Exhibits IV–5 and IV–6 can be used for training or action planning. The group can work together to develop a training plan.

Templates for Transparencies

Templates for transparencies that are relevant to Step 5 follow.

Identify Staff Training Needs

- Identify participants and topics needing in-service

- Set the dates for in-service early and notify all participants

- Identify potential presenters and resources materials needed for training sessions

- Develop a budget for training (professional service fees, expenses, refreshments, training materials, duplication, postage, notebooks, other related expenses)

- Send out notices to presenters, participants, and other guests

Exhibit IV–5 Action Work Sheet: Identifying Staff Training Needs

Activity	How can this be accomplished in your school and community, and who will be responsible?
1. How can inclusion implementors foster a sense of investment or "ownership" in the initiative?	
2. How should teachers be oriented to the changes that the new collaboration may bring?	
3. What are the overall major training needs of the school, and who should receive such training?	
4. Who are possible presenters and/or trainers for specific topics?	
5. What is the staff training budget, and who is responsible for the expenditures?	
6. Who will be responsible for notifying presenters, participants, and other guests?	
7. How can the teachers share and "celebrate" their successes and honor those who have made important contributions?	

Exhibit IV–6 Action Work Sheet: Developing an Inclusion "Adoption Plan"

Activity	How can this be accomplished in your school and community, and who will be responsible?
1. **Establish link with local and state educational agency training**—Each local and state educational agency organizes in-service training days for teachers, administrators, and support personnel. Interagency planners should use these existing training activities as a vehicle for providing an introduction and orientation to the new inclusion initiative and teacher roles.	
2. **Ensure participation of all cooperating agencies**—Include teachers from all subject disciplines and professionals from all cooperating agencies in the training. This approach increases the likelihood that, over time, action team personnel will come to share a common understanding and vision of the direction of the initiative. The mission statement and inclusion plan should include the schedule for training and staff development.	

continues

Exhibit IV–6 continued

Activity	How can this be accomplished in your school and community, and who will be responsible?
3. Develop inclusion planning materials for training and distribution—Materials must be developed for use in in-service training for teachers and collaborating personnel. These materials should include specific information about the inclusion goals; strategies; teacher and students; key roles and contact persons; the mission and goals as they relate to inclusion; and new support services that will be offered through the initiative.	
4. Adopt new educational and human service practices—Inclusion planners must help key teaching personnel to reassess their teaching practices and adopt new ones. Once the program has been in operation for one or two years, advanced training will be needed. Such training also means using the results of the past year of inclusion implementation to renew and strengthen the initiative, identify barriers and weaknesses, and further define and improve its outcomes.	
5. Evaluate the adoption plan—Inclusion planners must ensure that adoption plans are evaluated. They must ask if the training is having the desired effect on teachers and the classrooms. Is the training reaching all key school personnel? Is interdisciplinary training occurring? Are the teachers involved in evaluating the adoption plan and the training effort? Are teachers satisfied with the training, and what are their recommendations for improvement? Ongoing evaluation should be included in the inclusion mission statement.	

continues

HANDBOOK FOR SUCCESSFUL INCLUSION
© Aspen Publishers, Inc., 1996.

Exhibit IV–6 continued

Activity	How can this be accomplished in your school and community, and who will be responsible?
6. **Provide technical assistance**—Reach out and include experts who can provide help and assistance during the development, implementation, and evaluation phases. Expert consultants such as university personnel, private evaluation firms, and education association personnel can help problem solve for inclusion implementation; develop assessment and monitoring tools; design training material; provide orientation to planners and related personnel; conduct advanced training for staff after the inclusion team has been functioning for one or two years; and help teachers and administrators use evaluation information to make improvements and set new directions.	

Developing an Inclusion Adoption Plan

- The adoption plan is a strategy for fostering the constructive involvement of teachers and related personnel in the development and support of the inclusion initiative, which involves preparing teachers for new practices related to inclusion, enlisting the help of volunteers, and securing the support of students and families.

- The knowledge-sharing process defines the specific areas of new knowledge that teachers and related personnel need to have in order to successfully implement inclusion.

- The knowledge-sharing plan includes a series of professional development, training, and organizational development activities aimed at ensuring that the inclusion initiative is adopted, that is, fully accepted by all who will be involved.

- Change requires teachers to adopt new teaching methods, relationships, procedures, norms, values, and attitudes.

- An inclusion initiative will be **not** be successfully adopted or fully implemented by teachers and related service personnel unless they are **adequately trained in their field, understand the purposes of the collaboration initiative, and are prepared for change**.

- New training and development activities are needed to help key personnel **adopt new practices**.

40. Step 6—Identify Technical Assistance Resources

Suggested Sections from the Handbook

The following sections from Part II of the handbook should be reviewed in relation to step 6 of the planning and training for inclusion:

- What curriculum modifications and instructional strategies are considered best practices for inclusion classrooms?
- What external support services are needed for inclusive classrooms?
- How do interdisciplinary teams coordinate for effective inclusion?
- What are important considerations related to the use of technology?
- How can parent participation be promoted?
- What inclusion strategies can assist special learners in the transition from school to work?

Discussion Questions

The questions in Exhibit IV–7 can be used by the trainer or staff development coordinator to stimulate discussion about inclusion planning and implementation.

Strategies for Developing Action Plans

Many resources are available to schools and districts. Universities, regional resource centers, professional associations, and state educational agencies have professionals who can share information, professional literature, and best practices from exemplary programs. The greater the amount of information, the better will be the decisions at the local level. The work sheet in Exhibit IV–7 can be used for training or action planning. The group can work together to develop an action plan for identifying technical assistance resources.

Template for Transparency

A template for a transparency that is relevant to Step 6 follows.

Identify Technical Assistance Resources

- Determine individuals who would be available to visit classrooms and work one-on-one with teachers

- Consider regional resource centers, state departments of education, universities and colleges, consultants, local district administrators, master teachers, etc.

- Seek out interns, graduate students, volunteers, retired teachers, peer tutors

- Develop a strategy to determine the process to be followed when technical assistance is needed and requested

HANDBOOK FOR SUCCESSFUL INCLUSION
© Aspen Publishers, Inc., 1996.

Exhibit IV–7 Action Work Sheet: Identifying Technical Assistance Resources

Activity	How can this be accomplished in your school and community, and who will be responsible?
1. What types of support will be needed for the inclusion effort?	
2. Who would be available to provide support to classroom teachers involved in the inclusion effort?	
3. What should be the process for providing technical assistance?	
4. Who should classroom teachers contact for technical assistance?	

41. Step 7—Develop a Written Plan for Phased-In Implementation of Inclusion

Suggested Sections from the Handbook

The following sections from Part II of the handbook should be reviewed in relation to step 7 of the planning and training for inclusion:

- What factors are most important in planning for inclusion?
- What is an appropriate class size for inclusion?
- What curriculum modifications and instructional strategies are considered best practices for inclusion classrooms?
- What external support services are needed for inclusive classrooms?
- How do interdisciplinary teams coordinate for effective inclusion?
- What are important considerations related to the use of technology?
- How can parent participation be promoted?
- What inclusion strategies can assist special learners in the transition from school to work?

Discussion Questions

The questions in Exhibit IV–8 can be used by the trainer or staff development coordinator to stimulate discussion about inclusion planning and implementation.

Strategies for Developing Action Plans

Written plans do not have to be long and involved, but they do help teams to remain focused. Written plans provide documentation and set goals for achievement. The written plan has a well-defined set of activities, with accompanying time lines and assigned responsibilities. The work sheet in Exhibit IV–8 can be used for training or for action planning. The group can work together to develop an action plan for developing a written plan for phased-in inclusion.

Template for Transparency

A template for a transparency relevant to Step 7 follows.

HANDBOOK FOR SUCCESSFUL INCLUSION
© Aspen Publishers, Inc., 1996.

Develop a Written Plan for
Phased-In Inclusion

- Secure commitment and support from administration to meet needs and timelines

- Identify potential students for inclusion

- Identify potential teachers/classrooms to match student needs (not convenience directed)

- Set and review timetables, get teacher reaction

- Identify needed resources, including teacher planning time with special education teachers

HANDBOOK FOR SUCCESSFUL INCLUSION
© Aspen Publishers, Inc., 1996.

Exhibit IV–8 Action Work Sheet: Developing a Written Implementation Plan for Inclusion

Activity	How can this be accomplished in your school and community, and who will be responsible?
1. Which students are good prospects for inclusive classrooms?	
2. Which classroom and teachers would best meet their needs?	
3. What is a "reasonable" time line for initial inclusion activities?	
4. What resources will be needed by students and teachers during inclusion?	
5. What schedule will allow teachers (regular and special education) planning time for inclusion?	

42. Step 8—Evaluate the Inclusion Initiative

Suggested Sections from the Handbook

The following sections of Parts I and II of the handbook should be reviewed in relation to step 8 of the planning and training for inclusion:

- What are the benefits and outcomes of inclusion?
- How can readiness for inclusion be assessed?
- What curriculum modifications and instructional strategies are considered best practices for inclusion classrooms?
- What external support services are needed for inclusive classrooms?
- How do interdisciplinary teams coordinate for effective inclusion?
- What are important considerations related to the use of technology?
- How can parent participation be promoted?
- What inclusion strategies can assist special learners in the transition from school to work?

Discussion Questions

The questions in Exhibit IV–9 can be used by the trainer or staff development coordinator to stimulate discussion about inclusion planning and implementation.

Strategies for Developing Action Plans

After inclusion is implemented, an annual evaluation should be conducted to assess success of the initiative and areas that need improvement. Without a formal review of the inclusion process and outcomes, student needs appear to be less significant. Evaluation activities keep the student's individual needs at the focus of decision making and in a position to drive future development or modification of the initiative. The work sheet in Exhibit IV–9 can be used for training or action planning. The group can work together to develop an action plan for evaluating the inclusion initiative.

Template for Transparency

A template for a transparency relevant to Step 8 follows.

Evaluate the Inclusion Initiative

- Conduct formative and summative evaluation activities

- Collect evaluation data (as pertinent)

- Conduct internal review/self-evaluation

- Identify external program consultants and schedule days for visitation

- Synthesize internal and external recommendations

Exhibit IV–9 Action Work Sheet: Developing a Plan To Evaluate the Inclusion Initiative

Activity	How can this be accomplished in your school and community, and who will be responsible?
1. What evaluation activities should be included in the inclusion effort?	
2. What data should be collected and by whom?	
3. Who will be responsible for an internal review of inclusion?	
4. Which external consultants would be able to conduct an independent program evaluation for inclusion?	
5. Who will synthesize the evaluation data, write a final report, and make recommendations?	

43. Step 9—Use Information from Evaluation To Achieve Improvement

Suggested Section from the Handbook

The following sections of Parts I and II of the handbook should be reviewed in relation to step 9 of the planning and training for inclusion:

- What are the benefits and outcomes of inclusion?
- How can readiness for inclusion be assessed?
- What curriculum modifications and instructional strategies are considered best practices for inclusion classrooms?
- What external support services are needed for inclusive classrooms?
- How do interdisciplinary teams coordinate for effective inclusion?
- What are important considerations related to the use of technology?
- How can parent participation be promoted?
- What inclusion strategies can assist special learners in the transition from school to work?

Discussion Questions

The questions in Exhibit IV–10 can be used by the trainer or staff development coordinator to stimulate discussion about inclusion planning and implementation.

Strategies for Developing Action Plans

No program is static. Adjustments are part of the educational process, especially when inclusion efforts are involved. For example, a high school in a suburban area conducted a self-evaluation of the special education program. Six goals that needed to be addressed were identified. Consequently, administrators of the high school contacted a local university for technical assistance and support in restructuring their services. They set in operation a teacher training program, an inclusion initiative, and an evaluation plan. The work sheet in Exhibit IV–10 can be used for training or action planning. The group can work together to develop an action plan for using evaluation information.

Template for Transparency

A template for a transparency relevant to Step 9 follows.

HANDBOOK FOR SUCCESSFUL INCLUSION
© Aspen Publishers, Inc., 1996.

Use Evaluation Information for Improvement

- Conduct individual follow-up visitations with appropriate individuals as indicated by evaluation results

- Decide on revisions, changes, and actions needing improvement based upon evaluation results

- Revise the action plan to include new activities and timelines

- Schedule an event to celebrate successes to date

Exhibit IV–10 Action Work Sheet: Developing a Plan To Use Evaluation Information for Improvement

Activity	How can this be accomplished in your school and community, and who will be responsible?
1. With whom will the evaluation report be shared?	
2. Who will be responsible for revising the inclusion program?	

44. Step 10—Plan for a Reward System To Renew the Staff and Celebrate Success

Suggested Sections from the Handbook

The following sections of Parts I and II of the handbook should be reviewed in relation to step 10 of the planning and training for inclusion:

- What are the benefits and outcomes of inclusion?
- How can readiness for inclusion be assessed?

Discussion Questions

The questions in Exhibit IV–11 can be used by the trainer or staff development coordinator to stimulate discussion about inclusion planning and implementation.

Strategies for Developing Action Plans

Inclusion planners recognize that there is a need for reward and recognition of all collaborating personnel. Celebration of individual and program successes will become important experiences in the lives of those committed to the mission of service coordination. Recognition serves to strengthen commitment and to help in development of camaraderie and a team spirit. Plans for such a "reward system" should be built into the annual plan from the start.

The work sheet in Exhibit IV–11 can be used for training or action planning. The group can work together to develop an action plan for staff renewal and celebration of success.

Templates for Transparencies

Templates for transparencies that are relevant to Step 10 follow.

Staff Renewal and Celebration of Success

- Identify individuals (parents, students, teachers, community representatives, employers, tutors, peer mentors, administrators, etc.) who should receive accolades

- Identify specific events which would be appropriate for celebrating student and program successes

- Determine dates, times, and locations for celebration

- Send out invitations for celebration/events

- Select awards and certificates of appreciation to be presented/distributed at the event

- Send follow-up letters after the event to reinforce the importance and significance of the award

- Publish photos and news releases in local newspapers, newsletters, etc.

HANDBOOK FOR SUCCESSFUL INCLUSION
© Aspen Publishers, Inc., 1996.

Exhibit IV–11 Action Work Sheet: Developing a Plan for Staff Renewal and Celebration of Success

Activity	How can this be accomplished in your school and community, and who will be responsible?
1. What celebration or event should be planned for acknowledging the efforts and successes of inclusion?	
2. Who should be included?	
3. When and where should the event take place?	
4. What kind of awards, certificates, and incentives will be given and to whom?	
5. Who will develop school and district news releases and other communications?	

Staff Reward and Recognition

Staff rewards include activities, gifts, or tokens given to staff to thank them for their effort and participation by

- reminding them that they are valued contributors

- strengthening and ensuring their continued commitment

- recognizing individual student successes

- encouraging the participation of new staff and volunteers

- identifying successes in the community

- soliciting support of parents and community

© Aspen Publishers, Inc., 1996.

Suggested Rewards, Incentives, and Acknowledgments

- Special announcements by local media, including cable television and radio, about new programs or special successes of consumers and families

- Newspaper articles about the inclusion program or individual teacher members

- Articles in educational agency newsletters, business newsletters, annual reports, and community agency newsletters and bulletins

- Breakfasts and "coffees" that give special recognition to teachers, students, or parents

- Reward banquets

- Plaques for individual achievement and service

- Certificates for outstanding contribution and performance by teachers

- A program that offers "volunteer" or "parent of the month (or year)" or "most valuable player" awards

- Pins and buttons with partnership logo

- Dedication of sites or equipment

- Small gifts or mementos

- Photograph displays in schools and community agencies

Concept of Staff Renewal

Staff renewal—activities aimed at "reenergizing" inclusion implementation personnel, reminding them of the mission of the inclusion initiative and the value of their role and renewing their sense of commitment and purpose

- *Renewal* differs from *reward* because it is directed at teachers and related personnel who have been involved in the inclusion team for a substantial period.

- Sometimes, key staff who helped to establish linkages may need to be reenergized or reminded of the mission of the initiative and the value of their role.

- Often, these key individuals include the first "champions" of service coordination who have done more than their fair share in leading and promoting the initiative. They may simply be tired, feeling as though they have reached a "plateau."

- They may feel that their role as initiators and developers has now given way to routine operations, policies, and procedures.

- They need to renew their sense of commitment, spirit, and purpose with the initiative.

- Frequently, those who resist change in the beginning are the most likely to call themselves "pioneers" as the initiative expands!

Renewal Strategies

- Using rewards

- Conducting special "retreats" in which key personnel review the mission, goals, successes, and contributions of teachers over the past years in the partnership and plan new directions for the inclusion initiative

- Developing a video or television production that chronicles the development of the initiative, its accomplishments, and the contributions of its key players (Such a production should focus on impacts and benefits for consumers and families and improvements in the effectiveness of service coordination.)

- Planning changes in previous roles and opportunities for new experiences or responsibilities

- Offering an individual a more prestigious role in the interagency team, such as a role in evaluation or public relations or allowing staff to help other classrooms or schools to initiate inclusion practices

45. Sample Plan for Staff Development

Teachers need specialized training to prepare them for the challenge of planning for and implementing inclusion. Key personnel in the school and in collaborating agencies need a common understanding of the goals of the initiative and individual roles that teachers and related professionals will play. *This understanding is also essential to acceptance (adoption) of the new relationships, to fostering a sense of "ownership" of the new initiative and its goals, and to the ultimate success of inclusion.* Exhibit IV–12 provides an overview of the elements essential to the design of a staff development program, and Exhibit IV–13 provides a sample agenda for orientation and training of inclusion implementors.

There are seven important areas of new knowledge and skills needed by all professionals involved in inclusion planning:

1. the philosophy and legal foundations for inclusion, including local, state, and national education and service goals, such as the national education goals

2. the elements of inclusive services and collaborative team planning
3. the concept of collaborative and strategic planning for change and a range of strategies for implementing inclusion
4. strategies for promoting collaboration and communication
5. strategies for problem solving and overcoming resistance to change
6. increased involvement of students and families
7. use of evaluation to renew or strengthen the inclusion initiative, identify its weaknesses, and improve practices and outcomes

These topic areas are suggested as a guide, not a prescription. They are not necessarily inclusive of all of the information or material that should be covered in orientation and training sessions. Each school will need to develop unique training strategies and materials to meet the needs of its students and teachers.

Seven Topics for Professional Development of Inclusion Planners

---

1. The philosophy and legal foundations for inclusion, including local, state, and national education and service goals, such as the national education goals

2. The elements of inclusive services and collaborative team planning

3. The concept of collaborative and strategic planning for change and a range of strategies for implementing inclusion

4. Strategies for promoting collaboration and communication

5. Strategies for problem-solving and overcoming resistance to change

6. Increasing involvement of students and families

7. Using evaluation to "renew" or strengthen the inclusion initiative, identify its weaknesses, and improve practices and its outcomes

Exhibit IV–12 Essential Elements for a Staff Development Program

Knowledge Sharing Need	Strategy Need
Providing teacher training and orientation to the inclusion initiative	Include in teacher training and orientation the following content: • the inclusion philosophy, concept, and strategies • the inclusion development process • the concept of collaborative planning • the process of change and restructuring to develop inclusive practices • the practice of overcoming resistance to change • the elements of collaboration and communication • strategies for problem solving • key roles and responsibilities of personnel for inclusion
Providing personnel training in the inclusion change process	Provide special sessions related to the change process. Ensure that cooperating teachers and related personnel are oriented to the principles and processes of inclusion, collaboration, and strategic planning centered on student needs and outcomes.
Promoting teacher leadership in inclusion planning	In addition to basic staff training and orientation to new roles, it is important to help teachers understand the broader impacts of the inclusion initiative on the students and their families, the agencies, and the community as a whole. Share with them what the inclusion team is expecting from its effort and what changes are sought in the school and classroom environment and in student outcomes.
Promoting professional collaboration	Communicate the goals of the initiative to all personnel in the school, including noninstructional personnel, as well as relevant school-linked service agencies. Within the school, this might include the mathematics department, English department, special education, vocational/technical education, and English as a second language. Make sure they are aware of the inclusion goals and are prepared to work together.
Promoting cooperation among school-linked service agencies	Ensure that the relevant school-linked service agencies are prepared to work together. Plan for joint training and orientation seminars with school staff, rehabilitation agency staff, social services, and others.
Promoting constructive change	Ensure that teachers and related personnel are knowledgeable about the change process and their roles in it and that they endorse the shared mission for the inclusion initiatives.

Exhibit IV–13 Sample Agenda for Inclusion Implementors' Orientation and Training

Area of Knowledge and Skills	Sample Training Objectives
1. Philosophy and legal foundations for inclusion, including local, state, and national goals (e.g., the national education goals)	Inclusion philosophy and principles of student-centered services Legal authority for inclusion in the locality and state The national education goals Assessment of student needs and the classroom environment Definition of priority goals for inclusion for the locality and state
2. Elements of collaborative team planning and school-linked agency cooperation	Introduction to the inclusion team planning process Functions of inclusion coordination Introduction to the key inclusion partners and how the linkages are established Overview of the cooperative agreement of the partnership, its mission, and goals Relationship of the mission of collaboration to improvements in the teaching and learning environment Overview of the inclusion plan and implementation schedule
3. Concept of collaborative planning for inclusion	Overview of the concept of team collaboration Overview of shared and collaborative planning Introduction to the inclusion team approach to planning
4. Elements of collaboration and communication for inclusion	Communication among school units and personnel Strategies for improving communication and sharing information among teachers, related professionals, and administrators Conduct of effective training sessions and planning meetings Understanding of different perspectives on inclusion
5. Strategies for problem solving and overcoming resistance to change	Overview of problem-solving strategies and use of educational approaches Selection of the right strategy to match the problem Identification of staff resistance to inclusive practices Management of conflict and resistance to change
6. Involvement of consumers, families, and volunteers	Overview of the importance of family involvement in inclusion education Roles of consumers and families in evaluating service coordination
7. Evaluation to renew or strengthen the inclusion initiatives and improve practices and outcomes of inclusion	Introduction of the inclusion evaluation plan and the expected outcomes Highlighted outcomes in relation to improving inclusive services Review of results of annual evaluation Discussion of strengths and weaknesses and development of an "inclusion development" or new directions for the coming year

Bibliography

American Youth Policy Forum. (1993). *Improving the transition from school to work in the United States.* New York: Author.

Behrman, R. (Ed.). (1992). School-linked services. *The Future of Children, 2*(1).

Behrmann, M. (1984). *Handbook of microcomputers in special education.* San Diego, CA: College-Hill Press.

Biklen, D. (Ed.). (1985). *Achieving the complete school: Strategies for effective mainstreaming.* New York: Teacher's College Press.

Board of Education of Hendrick Hudson Central School District v. Rowley. (1982). 458 U.S. 176, 102 S. Ct. 3034, 73 L.Ed. 2nd 690, 5 Ed. Law Rep. 34, p. 3.

Bonadonna v. Cooperman, 619 F. Supp. 401, 28 Ed. Law Rep. 430 (D. N.J. 1985).

Braun v. Board of Education. (1954). 347 U.S. 483, 74 S.Ct. 686, 98 L.Ed. 873.

Brown v. Board of Education. (1954). 347 U.S. 483.

Bruno, R., Johnson, C., & Gillilard, J. (1994). A comparison of reform in special education in England and in Kentucky, USA. *Instructional Journal of Special Education, 9*(1), 53–64.

Bryson, J.M. (1988). *Strategic planning for public and nonprofit organizations* (p. 5). San Francisco: Jossey-Bass.

Carnine, D., & Kameenui, E. (1990). The general education initiative and children with special needs: A false dilemma in the face of true problems. *Journal of Learning Disabilities, 23*(3), 141–144.

Center for Policy Options. (1992) *Issues and options in restructuring and special education programs.* College Park, MD: University of Maryland.

Center for the Future of Children. (1992). *The future of children.* Annual Report, 2(1), 6–18.

Center for the Study of Policy. (1991). *Kids count data book: State profiles for child well-being.* Washington, DC and Reston, VA: Authors.

Clark, G., & Kolstoe, O. (1995). *Career development and transition education for adolescents with disabilities* (3rd ed.). Boston: Allyn & Bacon.

Council for Children with Behavior Disorders. (1993). Position statement on inclusion. *Learning Disability Quarterly.*

Cornett, L.M. (1995). Lessons from 10 years of teacher improvement reforms. *Educational Leadership, 52*(5).

Council for Exceptional Children. (1993a). *Federal outcomes for exceptional children.* Reston, VA: Author.

Council for Exceptional Children. (1993b). *Position Statement on Inclusion.* Reston, VA: Author.

Council for Exceptional Children. (11 January 1994). *Issues in the implementation of IDEA.* Reston, VA: Author.

Council for Exceptional Children. (1995). CEC launches drive to protect IDEA, special education funding. *CEC Today, 1*(10).

Council for Learning Disabilities. (1993). Position statement on inclusion. *CCBD Newsletter.*

Council of Administrators of Special Education. (1993). Position statement on inclusion. *CCBD Newsletter*. Reston, VA: The Council for Exceptional Children.

Dalheim, M. (Ed.). (1994). *Toward inclusive classrooms*. Washington, DC: The National Education Association.

Darling-Hammond, L. (1994). Performance-based assessment with education equality. *Harvard Educational Review, 64*(1), 5–30.

Designs for a New Generation of American Schools, Request for Proposals. (1991). Arlington, VA: The New American Schools Development Corporation.

Dover, W. (1994). *The inclusion facilitator*. Manhattan, KS: The Master Teacher, Inc.

Education Goals Panel. (1993). *Summary of the national education summit*. Washington, DC: Author.

Educational Testing Service. (1992). *Beyond the school doors: The literacy needs of job seekers served by the U.S. Department of Labor*. Chicago: Author.

Erickson, M., & Kochhar, C. (1991). *Evaluating business-education partnerships: Simple to complex*. Alexandria, VA: National Association of Partners in Education.

Evans, D. (1993). Restructuring special education services. *Teacher Education and Special Education, 19*(20), 137–145.

Evans, K., & King, J. (1994). Research on outcomes-based education: What we know and don't know. *Educational Leadership, 51*(6), 18–22.

Evans, S. (1995, March 18). Able-bodied students deal with disabilities. *The Washington Post*, p. B1.

Everson, J.M., Barcus, M., Moon, M.S., & Horton, W. (1987). *Achieving outcome: A guide to interagency training in transition and supported employment*. Richmond, VA: Virginia Commonwealth University, Project Transition into Employment.

Fraser, B., Hubbard, S., Chaner, L., & Weinbauer, A. (1993). *School reform and youth transition: Literature review and annotated bibliography*. Washington, DC: Academy for Education Development, National Institute for Work and Learning.

Frazier, K. (1993). The state of American education. *Rethinking Schools, 8*(2), 16–17.

Fuchs, D., & Fuchs, L.S. (1994). Inclusive schools and the radicalization of special education reform. *Exceptional Children, 60*(4), 294–309.

Fuchs, L.S., & Fuchs, D. (1986). Effects of systematic formative evaluation: A meta-analysis. *Exceptional Children, 53*(3), 199–208.

Gardner, H. (1983, 1992). *Frames of mind: The theory of multiple intelligences*. New York: Basic Books.

Gartner, A., & Lipsky, D.K. (1987). Beyond separate education: Toward a quality system for all. *Harvard Educational Review, 57*(4), 367–395.

Gartner, A., & Lipsky, D.K. (1990). Students as instructional agents. In S. Stainback & W. Stainback (Eds.), *Support systems for educating all students in the mainstream* (pp. 81–94). Baltimore: Paul H. Brookes Publishing.

Gartner, A., & Lipsky, D.K. (1992). Beyond special education: Toward a quality system for all students. *Harvard Educational Review*, reprint series no. 23, 123–157.

Gerhard, R.J., Dorgan, R.E., & Miles, R.G. (1981). *The balanced service system: A model of personal and social integration*. Clinton, OK: Responsive Systems Associates.

Gerry, M.H., & McWhorter, C.M. (1990). A comprehensive analysis of federal statutes and programs for persons with severe disabilities. In L.H., Meyer, C.A. Pack, & L. Brown (Eds.), *Critical issues in the lives of people with severe disabilities* (pp. 495–527). Baltimore: Paul H. Brookes.

Goodlad, J.I. (1991). Better teachers for our nation's schools. *Educational Leadership, 48*(8).

Hallahan, D.P., & Kauffman, J.M. (1994). *Exceptional children: Introduction to special education* (6th ed.). Needham Heights, MA: Allyn & Bacon.

Halloran, W., & Simon, M. (1995). The transition service requirement. A Federal perspective on issues, implications and challenges. *Journal of Vocational Special Needs Education, 17*(3), 94–98.

Halpern, R. (1990). Community-based interventions. In S.J. Meisels, & J.P. Sharkoff (Eds.), *Handbook for early childhood intervention*. Cambridge, England: Cambridge University Press.

Hehir, T., & Latus, T. (1992). Special education at the century's end: Evolution of theory and practice. *Harvard Educational Review*, reprint series no. 23.

Henderson, A.T. (1987). *The evidence continues to grow: Parent involvement improves student achievement*. Columbia, MD: National Center for Citizens in Education.

Herman, J.L., Aschbacher, P.R., & Winters, L. (1992). *A practical guide to alternative assessment*. Alexandria, VA: Association for Supervision and Curriculum Development.

Hodgkinson, H. (1991). Reform versus reality. *Phi Delta Kappan, 73*(1), 8–16.

Hughes-Booker, A. (1994). A survey of teachers in the District of Columbia public schools on the changing nature of seriously emotionally disturbed youth. Unpublished doctoral dissertation.

Janney, R.E., Snell, M.E., Beers, M.K., & Raynes, M. (1995). Integrating students with moderate and severe disabilities into general education classes. *Exceptional Children, 61*(5), 425–439.

Johnson, A., Johnson, J., & DeMatta, R. (1991). Predictive exploration of the educational-failure paradigm. *Canadian Journal of Special Education, 7*(2),164–180.

Johnson, D., & Johnson, R. (1978). Many teachers wonder . . . will the special-needs child ever really belong? *Instructor, 87*, 152–154.

Joint Task Force for the Management of Children with Special Needs of the AFT, CFC, NASM and MSA. (1990). *Guidelines for the delineation of roles and responsibilities for the safe delivery of specialized health care in educational settings*. Reston, VA: Council for Exceptional Children.

Jones, L.T. (1991). *Strategies for involving parents in their children's education*. Bloomington, IN: Phi Delta Kappa Educational Foundation Press.

Kagan, S.L., et al. (1991). *Collaboration in action: Reshaping services to young children and their families*. Unpublished manuscript, Yale University, The Bush Center in Child Development and Social Policy, New Haven, CT.

Kauffman, J.M. (1993). How we might achieve the radical reform of special education. *Exceptional Children, 60*(1), 6–16.

Kaufman, J.M., & Hallahan, D.P. (1993). Toward a comprehensive service delivery system. In J.J. Goodlad & T.C. Lovitt (Eds.), *Integrating general and special education*. Columbus, OH: Merrill/Macmillan.

Kochhar, C. (1995). *Training for interagency, interdisciplinary service coordination: An instructional modules series*. Des Moines, IA: Iowa State Department of Education and the Mountain Plains Regional Resource Center, Drake University.

Kochhar, C., & Erickson, M. (1993). *Partnerships for the 21st century: Developing business-education partnerships for school improvement*. Gaithersburg, MD: Aspen Publishers.

Kochhar, C., Leconte, P., & Ianacone, R. (1987). *Frontiers in employment training: Relating the job training partnership act to vocational education for persons with handicaps*. Washington, DC: The George Washington University.

Kochhar, C., & West, L. (1995). Future directions for Federal legislation affecting transition services for individuals with special needs. *Journal of Vocational Special Needs Education, 17*(3), 83–93.

Kochhar, C.A. (1987). Development of an evaluation model for case management services to developmentally disabled persons in community-based settings. *Dissertation Abstracts International*. (University Microfilms No. 87–25, 264).

Leconte, P. (1994). Assessment of Individuals with Disabilities. Doctoral Dissertation. University Microfilms.

Levine, E. (1994). *Annotated bibliography: 9 Issues of inclusion*. Washington, DC: National Education Association, p. 16.

Levine, I.S., & Fleming, M. (1985). *Human resource development: Issues in case management*. (Human Resources Development Monograph). College Park, MD: University of Maryland at College Park, Center for Rehabilitation and Manpower Services.

Lieberman, L.M. (1988). *Preserving special education, for those who need it*. Newtonville, MA: GloWorm.

Lieberman, L. (1990). RFI: Reunited . . . again. *Exceptional Children*, 56, 561–562.

Lipsky, D., & Gartner, A. (Eds.). (1989). *Beyond separate education: Quality education for all*. Baltimore: Paul H. Brookes.

Lynch, J. (1995). *Primary education for all, including children with special needs*. Washington, DC: The World Bank.

MacMillan, D. (1991). *Hidden youth: Dropouts from special education*. Reston, VA: Council for Exceptional Children.

Madaus, G. (1994). A technology and historical consideration of equity issues associated with proposal to change the nation's testing policy. *Harvard Educational Review, 64*(1), 26–95.

Marzano, R. (1994). Glances from the field about outcomes-based performance assessments. *Educational Leadership, 51*(6), 44–50.

McCoy, K.M. (1995). *Teaching special learners in the general education classroom: Methods and techniques* (2nd ed., pp. 13–30). Denver, CO: Love Publishing.

McLaughlin, M., & Warren, S. (1992). *Issues and options in restructuring schools in special educational programs*. College Park, MD: University of Maryland at College Park, Center for Policy Options in Special Education.

Mills v. Board of Education. (1972). 348 F. Supp. 866.

Minnow, M., & Weissbourd, R. (Winter 1993). Social movements for children. *Journal of the American Academy of Arts and Sciences*.

Mount, B., & Zwernik, K. (1988). *It's never too early; it's never too late: A booklet about personal futures planning.* Minneapolis, MN: Metropolitan Council.

National Alliance of Business. (1987). *The fourth r: Workforce readiness. A guide to business-education partnerships.* Washington, DC: Author.

National Association of State Boards of Education. (1992). *Winners all: A call for inclusive school.* Alexandria, VA: Author.

National Council on Disability. (1993). *Serving the nation's students with disabilities: Progress and prospects: A report to the President and Congress of the United States.* Washington, DC: Author.

National Education Goals Panel. (1993). *Handbook for local goals reports: Building a community of learners.* Washington, DC: Author.

National Education Goals Panel. (1994). *National education goals report: Building a nation of learners.* Washington, DC: Government Printing Office.

National Information Center for Children and Youth with Disabilities. (1993). Including special education in the school community. *News Digest, 2*(2).

National Joint Committee on Learning Disabilities. (1992). School reform: Opportunities for excellence and equity for individuals with learning disabilities. *Journal of Learning Disabilities, 25,* 276–280.

National State Boards of Education. (1992). *Winners all: A call for inclusive schools.* Alexandria, VA: Author.

Nisbet, J., Covert, S., & Schuh, M. (1992). Family involvement in the transition from school to adult life. In Rusch, et al. (Eds.). *Transition from school to adult life: Models, linkages and policy* (pp. 407–424). Sycamore, IL: Sycamore.

Ortize, A., & Ramirez, B. (1988). *Schools and culturally diverse exceptional students.* Reston, VA: Council for Exceptional Children.

Osborne, A.G. Jr. (1988). *Complete legal guide to special education services.* West Nyack, NY: Baker.

Osborne, A.G. Jr. (1992). Legal standards for appropriate education in the post-Rowley era. *Exceptional Children, 58*(6), 488–494.

Office of Special Education Programs. (1994). *National agenda for achieving better results for children and youth with disabilities.* Washington, DC: Cosmos Corporation.

P.L. 94-142. (1989). Education for All Handicapped Children Act. *Federal Register, 54,* 26331.

P.L. 100-407. (1988). Technology-Related Assistance for Individuals with Disabilities Act, 34 CFR, Part 300, Section 300.6.

P.L. 101-392. (1990). Carl D. Perkins Vocational and Applied Technology Education Act.

P.L. 101-476. (1990). Individual with Disabilities Education Act.

P.L. 103-239. (1993). School-to-Work Opportunities Act.

Pisces full inclusion project: What inclusion is and what it is not. (1994). Baltimore: Maryland State Department of Education.

Planned change for personnel development: Strategic Planning and the CSPD. (1991). Lexington, KY: Mid-South Regional Resource Center, University of Kentucky.

Pullin, D. (1994). Learning to work: The impact of clinic and assessment standards in education opportunity. *Harvard Educational Review, 64*(1), 31–54.

Putnam, J. (1993). *Cooperative learning and strategies for inclusion: Celebrating diversity in the classroom.* Baltimore: Paul H. Brookes.

Racino, J.A. (1992). Living in the community: Independence, support and transition. In F. Rusch, L. Destafano, J. Chadsey-Rusch, L. Phelps, E. Szymansk. (Eds.). *Transition from school to adult life: Models, linkages and policy.* Sycamore, IL: Sycamore.

Raywid, M. (1994). Synthesis of research: Alternative schools: The state of the art. *Educational Leadership, 52*(1).

Reich, R. (1991). *The work of nations: Preparing ourselves for 21st century capitalism.* New York: Alfred A. Knopf.

Report to the House Committee on Education and Labor on P.L. 101-476. (1990). House Report No. 101-544, 10. Washington, DC: U.S. Congress, House of Representatives.

Resnick, L. (1990). Literacy in school and out. *Dedalus, 119*(2), 169–190.

Reynolds, M.C., Wang, M.C., & Walberg, H.J. (1992). The knowledge base for special and general education. *Remedial and Special Education, 13*(5), 6–10.

Rigden, D. (1992). *Business and the schools: Guide to effective programs.* New York: Council for Aid to Education.

Rousseau, J.J. (1911). *Emile.* Boston: Charles E. Tuttle.

Rusch, F., Destafano, L., Chadsey-Rusch, J., Phelps, L., & Szymanski, E. (1992). *Transition from school to adult life: Models, linkages and policy.* Sycamore, IL: Sycamore Publishing.

Sage, D., & Burello, L. (1994). *Leadership in education reform: An administration's guide to changes in special education.* Baltimore: Paul H. Brookes.

Sailor, W. (1991). Special education in the restructured school. *Remedial and Special Education, 12*(6), 8–22.

Sailor, W., Anderson, J., Halvorsen, A., Doering, K., Filler, J., & Goetz, L. (1989). *The comprehensive local school: Regular education for all students with disabilities.* Baltimore, MD: Paul H. Brookes.

Salisbury, C.L., Palombaro, M.M., & Hollowood, T.M. (1993). On the nature and change of an inclusive elementary school. *Journal of the Association for Persons with Severe Handicaps, 18,* 75–84.

Sarason, S., & Doris, J. (1978). Mainstreaming: Dilemmas, opposition, opportunities. In M.C. Reynolds (Ed.). *Future of education for exceptional students: Emerging structures.* Reston, VA: Council for Exceptional Children.

Sawyer, R. J., Mclaughlin, M. J., & Winglee, M. (1992). *Is integration of students with disabilities happening? An analysis of national data trends over time.* Rockville, MD: Westat, Inc.

Schalock, R.L. (1983). *Services for developmentally disabled adults: Development implementation and evaluation.* Baltimore: University Park Press.

School Reform and Youth Transition. (1993). Washington, DC: Academy for Educational Development.

Separate and unequal: How special education programs are cheating our children and costing taxpayers billions each year. (1993, December 13). *U.S. News and World Report.*

Shapiro, H. (1990). Society, ideology and the reform of special education: A study of the limits of educational change. *Educational Theory, 30*(3).

Sherer, M. (1994). On schools where students want to be. *Educational Leadership, 52*(1).

Shriner, J., Ysseldyke, J., Thinlaw, M., & Honetschlager, D. (1994). "All means all"—Including students with disabilities. *Educational Leadership, 51*(6), 38–42.

Simpson, R., & Sasso, G. (1992). Full inclusion of students with autism in general education settings: Values versus science. *Focus on Autistic Behavior, 7*(3), 1–13.

Singer, J. D., & Butler, J. A. (1987). The Education for All Handicapped Children Act: Schools as agents of school reform. *Harvard Educational Review, 57*(2).

Sitlington, P. (1992). *Iowa follow-up study for youth with disabilities.* Des Moines, IA: Department of Education.

Sizer, T. (1992). *Horaces's school.* New York: Houghton-Mifflin, Inc.

Skrtic, T. (1988). An organizational analysis of special education reform. *Counterpoint, 8*(2), 15–19.

Skrtic, T. (1991). *Behind special education: A critical analysis of professional knowledge and school organization.* Denver, CO: Love Publishing.

Smith, D., & Lukasson, R. (1992). *Introduction to special education.* Needham Heights, MA: Allyn & Bacon.

Smith-Davis, J. (1990). Exceptional children in tomorrow's schools. In E. Meyen (Ed.), *Exceptional Children in Today's Schools.* Denver, CO: Love Publishing.

Stainback, S., Stainback, W., & Forest, M. (1989). *Educating all students in the mainstream of regular education.* Baltimore: Paul H. Brookes.

Stainback, W., & Stainback, S. (1992). *Controversial issues confronting special education: Divergent perspectives.* Needham Heights, MA: Allyn & Bacon.

Taylor, J.A., & Vineberg, R. (1978). Evaluation of indirect services to schools. In C.C. Attkisson, W.A. Hargreaves, & M.J. Horowitz (Eds.), *Evaluation of human service programs* (pp. 445–461). New York: Academic Press.

Taylor, S. (1988). Caught in the continuum: A critical analysis of the principle of least restrictive environment. *Journal of the Association for Persons with Severe Handicaps, 13*(1), 41–53.

Taylor, S.J., McCord, W., Giambetti, A., Searl, S., Mlinarcik, S., Atkinson, T., & Lichter, S. (1981). *Title XIX and deinstitutionalization: The issue for the 80's.* Syracuse, NY: Syracuse University, Center on Human Policy.

Thagard, P. (1992). *Conceptual revolutions.* Princeton, NJ: Princeton University Press.

The New American School Development Corporation. (1991). Designs for a New Generation of American Schools. Request for Proposals. Arlington, VA: Author.

Turnbull, A.P., Turnbull, H.R., Shank, M., & Leal, D. (1995). *Exceptional lives: Special education in today's schools.* Englewood Cliffs, NJ: Prentice-Hall.

Turnbull, H.R. (Ed.). (1991). *The least restrictive alternative: Principles and practice.* Washington, DC: The American Association on Mental Deficiency.

Turnbull, H.R. (1994). *Free appropriate public education: The law and children with disabilities* (4th ed.). Denver, CO: Love Publishing Company.

Turnbull, H.R., & Turnbull, A.P. (1989). *Free appropriate public education: Law and implementation.* Denver, CO: Love Publishing Company.

Turnbull, J., Barber, P., & Garlow, J. (1991). A policy analysis of family support for families with members with disabilities. *Kansas Law Review, 39*(3), 739–782.

United Nations Center for Human Rights. (1988). *Human rights: The international bill of human rights* (pp. 23, 21, Fact Sheet No 2). Geneva, Switzerland: United Nations.

United Nations Center for Human Rights. (1990). *Human rights: The rights of the child* (pp. 23, 21, Fact Sheet No. 10). Geneva, Switzerland: United Nations.

United Nations. (1960). Declaration of the rights of the child. In *Yearbook of the United Nations 1959.* New York: United Nations, Office of Public Information.

U.S. Department of Education. (1991). Combining school and work: Options in high school and two-year colleges. Washington, DC: Office of Vocational and Adult Education.

U.S. Department of Education. (1992a). *Learning a living—Part 1.* Washington, DC: The Secretary's Commission on Achieving Necessary Skills. (Order number 029-000-00439-1.)

U.S. Department of Education. (1992b). *What work requires of schools: A SCANS report for AMERICA 2000.* Washington, DC: The Secretary's Commission on Achieving Necessary Skills. (Order number 029-000-00433-1.)

U.S. Department of Education. (1992c). *Report to Congress on implementation of the Individuals with Disabilities Education Act.* Washington, DC: Office of Special Education Programs.

U.S. Department of Education. (1993a). *Fifteenth annual report to Congress on implementation of the Individuals with Disabilities Education Act.* Washington, DC: Office of Special Education Programs.

U.S. Department of Education. (1993b). *National agenda to achieving better results for children with disabilities.* Washington, DC: Consumers Corporation.

U.S. Department of Education. (1994a). *Goals 2000: Getting communities started.* Washington, DC: Office of the Secretary of Education.

U.S. Department of Education. (1994b). *Sixteenth annual report to Congress on implementation of the Individuals with Disabilities Education Act.* Washington, DC: Office of Special Education Programs.

U.S. Department of Education. National Commission on Excellence in Education. (1983). *A nation at risk.* Washington, DC: U.S. Government Printing Office.

U.S. Department of Education. Office of Educational Research and Improvement. (1994). *National Assessment of Educational Progress.* Washington, DC: U.S. Government Printing Office.

U.S. Department of Education. Office of Vocational and Adult Education. (1994 January). *National Assessment of Vocational Education, Interim Report to Congress.*

U.S. Department of Labor. Commission on the Skills of the American Workplace. (1990). *America's choice: high skills and low wages.* Washington, DC: U.S. Government Printing Office.

U.S. Department of Labor. (1993). *Finding one's way: Career guidance for disadvantaged youth.* Washington, DC: U.S. Government Printing Office.

U.S. General Accounting Office. (1989). *Vocational education: Opportunity to prepare for the future* (GAO/HRD-89-55). Washington, DC: U.S. Government Printing Office.

U.S. General Accounting Office. (1993). *System-wide education reform: Federal leadership could facilitate district level efforts* (GAO/HRD-93-97). Washington, DC: U.S. Government Printing Office.

U.S. General Accounting Office. (1994a). *Multiple employment training programs* (GAO/HEHS-94-193). Washington, DC: U.S. Government Printing Office.

U.S. General Accounting Office. (1994b). *Transition from school: Linking education and worksite training* (GAO/HRD-91-105). Washington, DC: U.S. Government Printing Office.

U.S. General Accounting Office. (1994c). *Occupational skills standards: Experience shows industry involvement to be key* (GAO/HEHS-94-193). Washington, DC: U.S. Government Printing Office.

U.S. Office of Vocational and Adult Education. (1994). *National assessment of vocational education, interim report to Congress.* Washington, DC: Author.

Wagner, M. (1989). *The school programs and school performance of secondary school students classified as learning disabled: Findings from the National Longitudinal Transition Study of Special Education Students.* Menlo Park, CA: SRI.

Wagner, M. (1990). *Reporting from the National Longitudinal Transition Study.* San Francisco: SRA International.

Wagner, M. (1993). *Summary Findings of the National Longitudinal Transition Study.* San Francisco: SRA International.

Wagner, M., Newman, L., D'Amico, R., Jay, E.D., Butler-Nalin, P., Marder, C., & Cox, R. (1991). *Youth with disabilities: How are they doing?* Menlo Park, CA: SRI International.

Walls, R.T., & Moriarty, J.B. (1977). The caseload profile, an alternative to weighted closures. *Rehabilitation Literature, 38,* 285–291.

Wang, M., & Birch, J. (1984). Comparison of a full-time mainstreaming program and a resource room approach. *Exceptional Children, 51*(1), 33–40.

Ward, M., & Halloran, W. (1993). Transitions. *OSERS News in Print, 6*(1).

Wehmeyer, M., & Ward, M. (1995). The spirit of the material: Student involvement in transition planning under IDEA. *Journal of Vocational Special Needs Education, 17*(3).

Weil, M., Thomas, C., Callahan, J., & Carolis, G. (1992). *Service integration and coordination at the family/client level: Is case management the answer?* Washington, DC: The Family Impact Seminar, The AAMFT Research and Education Foundation.

West, L., Corbey, S., Boyer-Stephens, A., Jones, B., Miller, B., & Sarkees-Wircenski, M. (1991). *Integrating transition planning in the IEP process.* Reston, VA: The Council for Exceptional Children, Division on Career Development.

West, L., Taymans, J., Corbey, S., & Dodge, L. (1994). National survey of state transition coordinators. *Capital Connection, 2*(2).

West, L.L. (1991). *Dropout prevention strategies for at-risk youth.* Gaithersburg, MD: Aspen Publishers.

Will, M.C. (1986). Educating children with learning problems: A shared responsibility. *Exceptional Children, 52,* 411–415.

Will, M. (1983). Transition: Linking disabled youth to a productive future. *OSERS News in Print, 1*(1), 1, 5.

Wvor v. Zitnay, No. 75-80 (S.D. Maine 1978).

Ysseldyke, J., & Thurlaw, M. (1993). *Self-study guide to the development of education outcomes with educators.* Minneapolis, MN: National Center on Educational Outcomes, University of Minnesota.

Index